AF789187

THE END OF NEGOTIABLE INSTRUMENTS

THE END OF NEGOTIABLE INSTRUMENTS

Bringing Payment Systems Law Out of the Past

James Steven Rogers

OXFORD
UNIVERSITY PRESS

OXFORD
UNIVERSITY PRESS

Oxford University Press, Inc., publishes works that further Oxford University's objective of excellence in research, scholarship, and education.

Oxford New York
Auckland Cape Town Dar es Salaam Hong Kong Karachi Kuala Lumpur Madrid
Melbourne Mexico City Nairobi New Delhi Shanghai Taipei Toronto

With offices in
Argentina Austria Brazil Chile Czech Republic France Greece Guatemala
Hungary Italy Japan Poland Portugal Singapore South Korea Switzerland
Thailand Turkey Ukraine Vietnam

Copyright © 2012 by Oxford University Press, Inc.

Published by Oxford University Press, Inc.
198 Madison Avenue, New York, New York 10016

Oxford is a registered trademark of Oxford University Press
Oxford University Press is a registered trademark of Oxford University Press, Inc.

All rights reserved. No part of this publication may be reproduced, stored in a retrieval system, or transmitted, in any form or by any means, electronic, mechanical, photocopying, recording, or otherwise, without the prior permission of Oxford University Press, Inc.

Library of Congress Cataloging-in-Publication Data

Rogers, James Steven, 1951-
The end of negotiable instruments: bringing payments systems law out of the past / James Steven Rogers.
p. cm.
Includes bibliographical references and index.
ISBN 978-0-19-985622-0
1. Negotiable instruments—Law and legislation—United States.
I. Title.
KF957.R63 2011
346.73'096—dc23 2011021045

Note to Readers
This publication is designed to provide accurate and authoritative information in regard to the subject matter covered. It is based upon sources believed to be accurate and reliable and is intended to be current as of the time it was written. It is sold with the understanding that the publisher is not engaged in rendering legal, accounting, or other professional services. If legal advice or other expert assistance is required, the services of a competent professional person should be sought. Also, to confirm that the information has not been affected or changed by recent developments, traditional legal research techniques should be used, including checking primary sources where appropriate.

(Based on the Declaration of Principles jointly adopted by a Committee of the American Bar Association and a Committee of Publishers and Associations.)

You may order this or any other Oxford University Press publication by visiting the Oxford University Press website at www.oup.com

To

Dorothy and Emma

CONTENTS

Preface *xi*

Introduction *xiii*

1. The Sorry State of Modern Payment Systems Law 1

    I. Payment Systems Law in the Twentieth Century 2

    II. What Is Negotiable Instruments Law? 7

    III. Why Is Payment Systems Law Anachronistic? 12

    IV. What Is the Anachronism: Negotiability or Negotiable Instruments Law? 17

2. The Puzzling Persistence of the Law of Checks and Notes 19

    I. The Traditional Account of Negotiability 21

    II. The Law of Bills and Notes in the Classical Era 24

    III. Transfer of Bills and Notes in the Eighteenth and Nineteenth Centuries 31

    IV. Origins of the Myth of Negotiability 39

3. Paperless Paper 45
I. Reification and Documents of Title 47
II. Reification and Securities 49
III. Reification and Notes 54
IV. Reification and Checks 58
V. Metaphor and Reality 64
4. Reports of the Death of the Holder in Due Course Doctrine Are Greatly Exaggerated 68
I. The Demise of Holder in Due Course Doctrine in Consumer Sales 69
II. What Was Really Wrong With the Holder in Due Course Doctrine? 73
III. Continuing Applications of the Holder in Due Course Doctrine 77
IV. Mortgages and the Holder in Due Course Doctrine 82
V. What to Do about the Remaining Problems Caused by the Holder in Due Course Doctrine 89
5. A Visit to the Museum of Negotiable Instruments Law 94
I. Postdating and Antedating 94
II. Signatures by Agents 96
III. Alteration 102
6. The Bank Always Loses 111
I. Basic Principle of Loss Allocation 112
II. History of Check Collection Law 125
III. The Cost of Confusion 134
7. Are Checks Ever Transferred? 146
I. Check Transfer in Payment Systems Coursebooks 147
II. Check Transfer in Cases 152
III. Consequences of Confusion about Check Transfer 163

8. What Would a Modern Law of Promissory Notes Look Like? 167
I. Actions on Notes: Elements and Defenses 167
II. Presentment, Notice of Dishonor, and Protest 170
III. Renewal Notes 176
IV. The Curious History of the Accommodation Party Provisions 179
V. Accommodation Parties and Guarantors 187
VI. Suretyship Defenses 192
VII. Promissory Notes Are Just Contracts 198
9. What Would a Modern Law of Checks Look Like? 200
I. Indorsement of Checks 202
II. Lost or Stolen Bank Checks 205
III. The Unnecessary Complexity of the Check Collection Rules 209
IV. The Unnecessary Complexity of the Check Fraud Rules 216
V. Impostors and Fictitious Payees 221
VI. Checks as Payment Systems Law Rather than Negotiable Instruments Law 225
10. Overcoming the Past 229
I. Repeal, Revision, or Unification 229
II. The Lessons for Practicing Lawyers and Judges 234
III. The Lessons for Teachers of Payment Systems Law 238
IV. Conclusion 240

Index *243*

PREFACE

This book is the culmination of over twenty-five years of work on the commercial law of payment systems. When I began teaching the subject, I quickly realized that much of the law that underlies the check system was built on concepts of negotiable instruments law that developed in response to economic conditions of a bygone era. I began working on what I thought would be a simple project to examine the nineteenth-century roots of the twentieth-century law of negotiable instruments. Along the way, I became fascinated by the history of negotiable instruments law and practice in its own right. Years later, that work resulted in the publication of my 1995 book, *The Early History of the Law of Bills and Notes*. After detours in modern law and law school administration, I returned to my original plan to examine not history itself, but how modern law has been distorted by a failure to understand its history. That is the subject of the present work.

I owe a great debt of gratitude to all students in my commercial law classes over the years. It was in the course of teaching those classes that I began to work through the ideas that are set out in this book.

I have always believed that teaching and scholarship are different aspects of the same intellectual process. This book is a testament to that belief. The students who struggled through my process of developing the ideas presented here can take a large measure of credit for the success of the project.

Special thanks are also due to my wife Dorothy. She not only endured countless hours of dinner table conversation—more accurately, monologues—on the subject, but also volunteered to read a draft of the entire book. If, as I hope, the book is accessible not only to specialists in the law of negotiable instruments but also to the educated general reader, a major portion of the credit is due to Dorothy's keen eye and steady sense of what did and did not make sense.

Some material in Sections 1 and 2 of Chapter 2 is adapted from *The Myth of Negotiability,* 31 B.C. L. Rev. 265 (1990). Some material in Section 1 of Chapter 6 is adapted from *The Basic Principle of Loss Allocation for Unauthorized Checks,* 39 Wake Forest L. Rev. 453 (2004). Some material in Section 3 of Chapter 9 is adapted from *Unification of Payments Law and the Problem of Insolvency Risk in Payment Systems,* 83 Chi-Kent L. Rev. 689 (2008). Some material in Section 4 of Chapter 9 is adapted from *The Irrelevance of Negotiable Instruments Concepts in the Law of the Check-Based Payment System,* 65 Tex. L. Rev. 929 (1987).

INTRODUCTION

This book deals with the subject that lawyers call "negotiable instruments law." The current version of American negotiable instruments law is set out in Articles 3 and 4 of the Uniform Commercial Code (U.C.C.). Ask any modern lawyer familiar with commercial law what Articles 3 and 4 of the U.C.C. are about, and the answer is likely to be "that's the law of checks and promissory notes." Ask a bit more, and you may learn that this body of law has been with us for quite a long time. For hundreds of years, the law of negotiable instruments has been regarded as an important and distinct body of law in the Anglo-American legal system. A mastery of negotiable instruments law, or, perhaps more realistically, a familiarity with its basic concepts and rules, has been regarded by law faculties and bar examiners as an essential component of the education of lawyers. Generations of law students have regarded the task of learning negotiable instruments law as a necessary evil. The evil is apparent to anyone attempting to wade through the dry, arcane, and technical rules of this body of law; and the necessity is reluctantly admitted on the grounds that, after all, things like promissory notes and checks are terribly important in the business and financial world, so a lawyer would do well to learn the applicable rules.

In the past few decades, terminology and focus have shifted somewhat, so that courses and law books dealing with this subject commonly use a name such as "Payment Systems." As new ways of making payment have developed, the law of payment systems has become more and more complex. In addition to checks, we can now make payment by credit cards, debit cards, and various electronic systems. In most fields of law, developments of that sort would be reflected by changes or additions to the basic structure of the legal rules. Payment systems law has been different. Each new payment system has given rise to a different body of law. Efforts to create a unified body of law for all payment systems have so far been unsuccessful.

Discussions of reform of payment systems law typically assume that the existing law works well for the traditional paper-based system of checks and promissory notes. The usual view is that the problems that confront payment systems law have been created by the evolution of new technologies. This book argues that this assumption is unfounded. The basic idea of the book is that much of the trouble with current law of payment systems comes from the fact that U.C.C. Articles 3 and 4 are anachronistic. The law of negotiable instruments developed centuries ago when instruments issued by private parties circulated as a form of money. While that system has long since passed into history, there has been no significant rethinking of this body of law. Indeed, much of the current law of checks and notes is the product of nothing more than historical fluke. The law could be much simpler if it were written for how checks and notes are actually used today, rather than being based on concepts derived from the past.

The anachronism of payment systems law has serious consequences. As each new payment system develops, lawyers must spend time figuring out which legal box to place it in. Users rarely understand the differences in their legal rights that can result from minor differences in the way that a payment is handled. Doctrines that made sense centuries ago cause serious problems today. Most of us learned at an early age that we should not indorse a check in blank and carry it around, because if we lose the check, we will suffer the loss of the money. People who are relocating have been known to get a bank check representing their life savings, intending to deposit it in a new account in their new hometown. If they lose the check, they face serious problems. As we shall see, there is no reason for the law to be that way. It is just the product of unexamined application of doctrines that should have died out long ago.

The argument proceeds as follows. Chapter 1 surveys the state of the modern law of payment systems. It develops the basic thesis of the book—that the law of checks and notes, as set out in Article 3 of the Uniform Commercial Code, is anachronistic and all but incoherent. Chapter 2 surveys the history of negotiable instruments law. It shows that the transactions that gave rise to the law of bills and notes in the eighteenth century were unlike anything that we encounter in the modern era. Chapter 3 explores a fundamental aspect of negotiable instruments law—the idea that the paper instrument is the indispensible embodiment of the obligations that it represents, so that one who wishes to deal with the underlying rights must get hold of the piece of paper. It shows that while this "reification" approach made sense at the time when negotiable instruments law developed, it makes no sense today. Chapter 4 examines twentieth-century developments concerning the central concept of negotiable instruments law—the holder in due course doctrine. Although it is often assumed that the problems caused by the holder in due course doctrine were solved by developments in the mid-twentieth century, this chapter shows that the holder in due course doctrine continues to lead to unjustifiable results in settings not captured by these reforms.

Chapter 5 examines the actual origins of a variety of rules that are set out in Article 3. It turns out that large parts of Article 3 are nothing more than statutory resolutions of issues that ceased to have any relevance centuries ago, such as arcane disputes about the long-since repealed Stamp Acts. Chapter 6 examines a common assumption about the law concerning unauthorized check transactions—that the bank always wins. It shows that the usual quip has it backwards. The baseline rule is that the bank always loses, that is, the banks, as the providers of the check payment system, bear the risk of loss from unauthorized payment transactions. Chapter 7 considers whether the basic concept of negotiable instruments law—that instruments are routinely transferred from person to person—makes any sense with respect to checks. Law texts routinely present hypotheticals in which a check drawn by one person payable to another is indorsed and transferred by the payee to some other person. In fact, checks are hardly ever transferred outside the banking system. The chapter shows how the confusion over check transfer has distorted the profession's understanding of the basic rules for allocation of losses from check fraud. Chapter 8 considers whether it makes sense to base the law of promissory notes on concepts of negotiable instruments law. It shows how doctrines that made sense in former times operate today as an obstacle to reaching simple, just results. The chapter shows that there is no reason to have a special statute on promissory notes. Rather, the law would be clearer and simpler if issues concerning notes were treated as part of the general law of contracts. Chapter 9 examines whether it makes sense to base the law of checks on the concepts of negotiable instruments law. It shows that if we wrote the law on the basis of how checks are actually used and processed today, rather than how things might have happened a century ago, the law could be far simpler.

The final chapter considers how to develop a sensible modern law on the subjects governed by U.C.C. Articles 3 and 4. The theoretical answer is simple. Articles 3 should be repealed and Article 4 should be completely rewritten. To be realistic, however, repeal is unlikely to be feasible. Thus, for the foreseeable future, lawyers will have to find ways of avoiding the confusion that this statute has produced in recent times. The chapter examines how modern lawyers and law professors can deal with the problems presented by this profoundly anachronistic body of law.

Lawyers and law professors who regularly deal with payment systems problems will probably be familiar with negotiable instruments law in general and U.C.C. Articles 3 and 4 in particular. To other lawyers, however, these subjects may be little more than a vague, and largely unpleasant, recollection from law school or a bar review course. Accordingly, it may be useful to provide a thumbnail sketch of the basic concepts of negotiable instruments law. Those who are already familiar with these matters may wish to skip the remainder of this Introduction.

Article 3 is the descendant of a very old body of law that has, at various times, gone under the names "the law of commercial paper," "the law of negotiable instruments," or "the law of bills and notes." Article 4 deals with certain aspects of the process by which the most common species of negotiable instrument—checks—are collected by banks. Do not feel bad if you have trouble understanding the difference between Articles 3 and 4. The problem is not you, it's the law. The peculiar line of division between Articles 3 and 4 is one consequence of the problem of anachronism that plagues this area of the law and that is explored throughout this book.

So, what is a "negotiable instrument"? If we want a rough and ready answer, we'll just say that "negotiable instrument" includes checks and promissory notes. If we want more detail, we would have to work through the rather complex definitional rules that are found in Part 1 of Article 3. In essence, Article 3 defines a negotiable instrument as an unconditional promise or order to pay a fixed sum of money, provided that the instrument is payable to order or to bearer, comes due on demand or at a set time, and contains no other promise or order. A "promissory note," or, more simply, a "note," is a *promise* to pay. For example, if John borrows $100 from Mary, he might sign a note in which he promises to pay the $100. Negotiable instruments law would refer to John as the *maker* of the note and Mary as the *payee*.

A check is an *order* to pay. For example, suppose that John repays his debt to Mary by giving her a check for $100. The check can be interpreted as a special form of letter, using highly stylized language, by which John directs his bank to pay $100 to Mary. Ordinary people have little occasion to notice or bother about the identity of John's bank. But, for purposes of negotiable instruments law, that is an important matter. Suppose that John maintains his bank account at Atlantic Bank. John will have pre-printed check forms identifying Atlantic Bank. When he fills out the check, it will be an order from John to Atlantic Bank, ordering Atlantic Bank to pay $100 to Mary. Negotiable instruments law would refer to John as the *drawer* of the check, Atlantic Bank as the *drawee* or the *payor bank,* and Mary as the *payee*. The words drawer and drawee come from the fact that a check is treated as a subspecies of the category known to negotiable instruments law as a *draft* or *bill of exchange*. (Those two terms mean the same thing.) A draft is an order (that is, an instruction) given by the drawer to the drawee, directing the drawee to make payment to the payee. The term draft refers to an order directed to *anybody* to make a payment; the term check refers to an order directed to a *bank* to make a payment. As we will see later on, in former times it was common for drafts to be drawn on entities other than banks.

To qualify as a negotiable instrument, the note or draft must be payable either *to bearer* or *to the order of* a certain person. Suppose that when John borrows $100 from Mary, he writes on a piece of paper "I, John, promise to pay $100 to Mary on December 1, 2010. /s/ John." That is not a negotiable instrument, because it is not payable either *to bearer* or *to the order of* a certain person. It would be a negotiable instrument if it said that John would pay the money "to bearer" or that he would pay the money "to the order of Mary." If you look at your blank check forms, you will see that they say that the bank is supposed to pay the money to "the order of" the person whose name you write in as the payee.

The basic assumption of negotiable instruments law is that one should be able to figure out exactly what the instrument requires merely by reading the fairly simple words of the note or draft. As the old saying put it, a negotiable instrument should be "a courier without luggage."[1] Thus to be a negotiable instrument, the note or draft must specify the precise amount to be paid, it must direct that the payment is to be made at a determinable time, and it must not contain any undertaking other than the payment of the money. The time for payment might be either on demand—like the usual form of a check—or at a stated time—like December 1, 2010 in the example above. However, a writing that says that John will pay Mary $100 two weeks after some other event occurs would probably not qualify as a negotiable instrument. Similarly, a writing that says that John will pay Mary a sum of money that is to be calculated on the basis of

1. Overton v. Tyler, 3 Pa. 346, 347 (1846).

some formula that turns on other events would probably not qualify as a negotiable instrument. So too, a writing that says that John will pay Mary a certain sum of money and also will build a house for her would not qualify as a negotiable instrument.

The requirements for classification as a negotiable instrument are all related to a very basic idea—that negotiable instruments are routinely transferred from person to person. The most significant concept of negotiable instruments law—the holder in due course concept—reflects this focus on transfer. Under the general law of property, a person to whom an item of property is transferred receives only such title as the transferor had. So, for example, if a thief steals goods and sells them to a buyer, the buyer gets no title because the thief had no title. Or, suppose that a contractual right is assigned from assignor to assignee. The assignee generally gets only whatever rights the assignor had. So, if the person obligated on the contract had some defense to her liability, the assignee would receive the contractual right subject to the defense that the obligated party could have raised against the assignor. The holder in due course doctrine is an exception to these rules. If a transferee of a negotiable instrument qualifies as a holder in due course, the transferee takes the instrument free from any claims and free from most defenses. So, if a promissory note is stolen and transferred to someone who qualifies as a holder in due course, the true owner's claim of ownership would be cut off. Similarly, if the maker of a promissory note had some defense that she could have raised against the original payee, that defense would be cut off if the note is transferred to someone who qualifies as a holder in due course.

The rules on holder in due course are fairly complex. But the basic idea has two components: (1) the transferee must take the instrument through the appropriate method of transfer, and (2) the transferee must give value for the instrument, unaware of any claims or defenses. The appropriate means of transfer is described as a "negotiation," and the effect of taking through a negotiation is that one will qualify as a "holder." For instruments that are payable to bearer, or that have been indorsed in blank, all that is necessary for negotiation is delivery of the written instrument. For instruments that are payable to the order of a specified person, negotiation requires delivery and indorsement by the person to whom the instrument was previously payable. For example, suppose that an instrument payable to the order of Jones is stolen by Scalawag. Scalawag forges Jones' indorsement and transfers the instrument to Smith. Smith will not qualify as a "holder," because Smith took through a forged indorsement. Accordingly, whether or not Smith was aware of the theft, Smith cannot qualify as a holder in due course. By contrast, suppose that Scalawag steals from Able an instrument that had originally been made payable to bearer. If Scalawag transfers the instrument to Baker, Baker can qualify as a "holder." If Baker gave value for the instrument, took it in good faith, and took it without awareness of any claims or defenses, then Baker can qualify as a "holder in due course" who would take free from Able's claim of ownership.

Although the holder in due course concept has commonly been seen as the centerpiece of negotiable instruments law, that concept came under attack in some settings by the latter part of the twentieth century. But the problems with this body of law run far deeper. The problem is not simply that the holder in due course concept produces some inappropriate results about the rights of some transferees. Rather, the entire edifice, which is built on notions of transfer, no longer makes sense. A major point of this book is that the focus on transfer is no longer useful. Notes and checks are no longer passed around from person to person outside the banking system. As we shall see, that fact accounts for much of the confusion that besets the current law of checks and notes.

1

The Sorry State of Modern Payment Systems Law

When we buy things or pay for services, we need to use some system for making payment. Today we use checks, credit cards, debit cards, and various other electronic or semi-electronic payment systems. As anyone who has ever discovered an unauthorized charge to a bank account or credit card account knows, much can go wrong. One would assume that the legal system has developed a sensible, coherent body of law to deal with payment system problems. One would be wrong. The modern American law of payment systems is, to put it politely, rather untidy. To be honest, it is a mess. An anecdote told by a leading teacher of payment systems law aptly illustrates the problem.[1] The professor was approached by a law faculty colleague who wanted to know whether he could refuse to pay a bank charge for an Internet purchase that went awry. The colleague was astonished to find that his rights depended on how the transaction was processed. As it happens, entirely different bodies of law apply to various different ways of "paying a bill electronically."[2]

1. Ronald J. Mann, *Making Sense of Payments Policy in the Information Age*, 93 Geo. L.J. 633, 634 (2005).
2. Stephanie Heller, *An Endangered Species: The Increasing Irrelevance of Article 4 of the UCC in an Electronics-Based Payments System*, 40 Loy. L.A. L. Rev. 513 (2006).

I. PAYMENT SYSTEMS LAW IN THE TWENTIETH CENTURY

Not long ago, things seemed much simpler. In the mid-twentieth century, the only significant payment system was the check system. Law school courses covered the check system as part of what lawyers called the law of "bills and notes." The law taught in those courses was the law of "negotiable instruments" as set out in Articles 3 and 4 of the U.C.C. The subject had a long history. Treatises on the law of bills and notes appeared by the late eighteenth century. In the late nineteenth century, this body of law was codified in statutes: the English Bills of Exchange Act of 1882[3] and the American Uniform Negotiable Instruments Law of 1896 (N.I.L.).[4] Half a century later, the content of the N.I.L. was included, with no basic rethinking, as Article 3 of the U.C.C.[5] Article 4, dealing with the

3. 45 & 46 Vict. c. 61. The process began in 1878, when Mackenzie D. Chalmers published a short volume in which he attempted, with remarkable success, to reduce all of the learning contained in some 2500 cases on bills and notes to about 300 numbered black letter rules, accompanied by brief illustrations, explanations, and citations to the principal cases. MACKENZIE D. CHALMERS, A DIGEST OF THE LAW OF BILLS OF EXCHANGE, PROMISSORY NOTES AND CHEQUES (1878). Two years later, he proposed that his effort be adopted as a statutory codification. As he noted in the introduction to his *Digest*, Chalmers was inspired in his codification effort by the example of the codes adopted by the English imperial authorities in India, with which he had become familiar during a tour of duty in the Indian civil service from 1869 until 1872.

4. The Uniform Negotiable Instruments Law was proposed by the National Conference of Commissioners on Uniform State Laws in 1896, and soon thereafter was enacted in all American jurisdictions. There was a bit of controversy about its details at the time the N.I.L. was proposed. James Barr Ames of the Harvard Law School published a very critical article, seemingly motivated at least in part by his sense of pique at not having been consulted in the drafting. James Barr Ames, *The Negotiable Instruments Law*, 14 HARV. L. REV. 241 (1900). No one, however, seems to have questioned the need for the statute nor disputed any of the basic concepts or rules that it codified.

5. Karl Llewellyn, who led the U.C.C. project, entrusted the drafting of Article 3 to an eager young scholar with essentially no familiarity with the subject, William Prosser, who would later earn fame as the leading scholar of the law of torts. Donald J. Rapson, *Book Review*, 41 BUS. LAW. 675–676 (1986) (reviewing FRED H. MILLER & ALVIN C. HARRELL, THE LAW OF MODERN PAYMENT SYSTEMS AND NOTES (1985)). Not surprisingly, Article 3 made no fundamental changes in the basic concepts and rules of the N.I.L.

process of collection of checks by banks, was the subject of somewhat greater controversy at the time the U.C.C. was drafted, but it too was rapidly assimilated into the profession's sense that this was a rather technical and fairly well-settled area of the law.

In the latter part of the twentieth century, this sense of simplicity evaporated. Even with respect to the check system, the dominance of the U.C.C. faded fast. In 1987, Congress adopted the Expedited Funds Availability Act (EFAA),[6] in response to what was perceived as a limited problem of banks placing unduly long holds on the availability of funds for checks deposited by customers. As in so many situations, Congress did not decide what the problem really was and solve it. Instead, Congress told an administrative agency—the Federal Reserve Board in this case—to identify the problem and decide how to solve it. The Board found that the task was not simply to tell the banks to let people have their money more quickly. Rather, the problem was to find a way that depositary banks could safely make funds available more promptly. It would have been irresponsible for the Fed to say that banks must make funds available quickly if that meant that banks might suffer significant losses by allowing customers to withdraw funds for checks that ended up bouncing. To solve that problem, the Fed had to devise a new framework for the process of the return of dishonored checks. The result is that the law of the check system is no longer found exclusively in Articles 3 and 4 of the U.C.C. Instead, much of the relevant law is found in Regulation CC, promulgated by the Fed under the authority of the EFAA.[7] Working through the relationship between the U.C.C. and Reg. CC can be challenging. For example, while the U.C.C. describes

6. 12 U.S.C. §§ 4001–4010.

7. 12 C.F.R. Part 229. For detailed analysis of EFTA and Reg. CC, see Barkley Clark & Barbara Clark, The Law of Bank Deposits, Collections and Credit Cards ¶¶ 7.01–8.13 (2009).

settlements made on forward collection as "provisional,"[8] Reg. CC makes settlements made between banks on forward collection "final," though the settlements may, in effect, be undone if a dishonored check happens to be returned through the same banks that processed it on forward collection.[9] To anyone not intimately familiar with check collection law, that last sentence will be incomprehensible. That is the point. The law of checks has become increasingly difficult as a result of the complex relationship between federal and state law.

Turning to payment systems other than the check system, we see further complexity in the sources of law. As the credit card system developed, Federal law dealt with certain aspects of the use of credit cards as a consumer payment system.[10] The development of the automated teller machine (ATM) card and various other consumer electronic banking systems prompted the enactment in 1978 of the Federal Electronic Fund Transfer Act (EFTA) specifying some aspects of consumer rights in electronic banking systems.[11] In recent decades, the fractionalization of payment systems law has increased. From its humble origins as an access device for ATM transactions, the card now known as a "debit card" has developed into a major consumer payment system.[12] A variety of systems have now developed by which consumers can pay their bills electronically. A consumer might authorize a merchant or utility to charge her bill to her credit card account. Or, the consumer might authorize the merchant or utility to charge her bill to her bank account. If so, the merchant or utility might obtain that payment in a variety

8. U.C.C. § 4-201.
9. 12 C.F.R. § 229.36(d).
10. 15 U.S.C. §§ 1642 (prohibition on unsolicited distribution), 1643 (limitation of cardholder liability for unauthorized use), 1666i (assertion of claims and defenses).
11. Electronic Funds Transfer Act, 15 U.S.C. § 1693–93r.
12. Donald I. Baker & Roland E. Brandel, The Law of Electronic Fund Transfer Systems ¶ 7.02 (2006).

of ways, such as by generating a remotely created paper item[13] or by initiating an Automated Clearing House (ACH) debit transaction.[14] Or, the consumer might contact her own bank and direct it to make payment to the merchant or utility.[15] Even though in my professional life I specialize in payment systems law, in my personal life I usually have to stop and think for a while before I can sort out exactly how a certain "electronic payment" that I have authorized will actually be implemented. There is no way that the average user could understand the major differences in legal rights that may flow from slight variations in the way a payment is made.

Developments have been equally dramatic in payment transactions among businesses. By the late twentieth century, checks were no longer the major payment system for business-to-business transactions. Rather, large dollar payments were routinely made by electronic wire transfers. For a while, the banks that provided electronic payment services seemed to feel that there was no need for any special statutory treatment. That sense of complacency was unsettled by a court decision in the early 1980s that raised the prospect that banks were potentially liable for ruinous damages if their failure to complete a transfer resulted in consequential damages to a user.[16] The banks then decided that they needed a statute, and the result was U.C.C. Article 4A on wholesale wire funds transfers.

At various points in recent years there have been suggestions for unification. In the late 1970s and early 1980s, the sponsors of the U.C.C. considered an ambitious plan to promulgate a uniform law that would unify the private law of all payment systems. A major conference was held on that project in Williamsburg, Virginia in 1978.

13. Clark & Clark, *supra* note 7, at ¶ 10.02[2] (2009).
14. Baker & Brandel, *supra* note 12, at ¶ 4.02.
15. *Id.* ¶ 10.02[3].
16. Evra Corp. v. Swiss Bank Corp., 673 F.2d 951 (7th Cir. 1982).

The reception was decidedly cool. Lawyers for banks felt that the proposal was too radical. The general feeling seems to have been that, at most, some changes were needed in the in law governing particular payment systems, rather than a wholesale rethinking of the law. The U.C.C. sponsors relented.[17] A more modest set of revisions to Articles 3 and 4 were drafted, along with a new Article 4A on wholesale wire funds transfers. Recently, there has been a revival of the suggestion that the time has come to reconsider unification.[18] It is, however, unlikely that anything concrete will come from this suggestion in the near future. Some have suggested that while it may not now be politically feasible to undertake an ambitious statutory revision project directed to a unification of all of payment systems law, it might be desirable to undertake a more limited project considering possible revisions to present Articles 3 and 4 that might be appropriate in light of developing methods of electronic collection of checks.[19] Even that suggestion has not generated much enthusiasm.

It is possible that at least part of the problem will go away with the passage of time. The law of check collection embodied in U.C.C. Article 4 plays an increasingly limited role as methods of electronic collection of checks are developed.[20] Indeed, checks may sometime become a relic of the past. A banking industry group in the United

17. Fred H. Miller, *U.C.C. Articles 3, 4 and 4A: A Study in Process and Scope*, 42 Ala. L. Rev. 405 (1991).

18. *Symposium: Rethinking Payments Law*, 83 Chi.-Kent L. Rev. 475 (2008).

19. Memorandum, March 16, 2009, from Fred H. Miller, Chair, Study Committee on Payments Issues and Linda J. Rusch, Reporter, "Request for Comments on Issues under UCC Articles 3 and 4," *available at* http://www.nccusl.org/Update/CommitteeSearchResults.aspx?committee=327. One lesson of this book is that one should be skeptical about the wisdom of that approach. As a matter of historical development, the law of the check system happens to have developed as a branch of the law of bills and notes. Yet if one were to start from scratch, there would be no reason to adopt that approach. So it is doubtful that another revision of a body of law that is thoroughly anachronistic would provide a useful step in working toward a modern law of payment systems.

20. *See* Heller, *supra* note 2.

Kingdom has proposed that checks be eliminated by 2018.[21] Whether that happens remains to be seen. It is, however, unlikely that payment systems law will be generally modernized until we come to realize how odd and anachronistic the law of bills and notes has become. Lawyers on both sides of the Atlantic still seem to assume that the law of negotiable instruments—U.C.C. Articles 3 and 4 in the United States and the Bills of Exchange Act in the United Kingdom—remains a sensible body of law, suitable to at least some modern transactions.

This book explores one little-understood aspect of the problems that confront the modern law of payment systems—the pernicious impact of history. Most discussions of payment systems law start from the implicit assumption that so far as the traditional paper-based check system is concerned, there is nothing essentially wrong with the current law, as set out in Articles 3 and 4 of the U.C.C. The thought is that the need for change comes only from the evolution of new payment technologies. In fact, this assumption is unfounded. The system of law for checks and notes found in the U.C.C. is itself centuries behind commercial development. It is a law for practices that ceased to occur generations ago. It is doubtful that there is anything of value in this statutory body of law. Repeal or radical revision would probably be the best solution. That is, of course, a fairly bold claim. The burden of this book is to prove the point.

II. WHAT IS NEGOTIABLE INSTRUMENTS LAW?

Much of the trouble with modern payment systems law comes from confusion engendered by the concept of "negotiability." Pick up a

21. Payments Council, The Future of Cheques in the UK (2009), *available at* http://www.paymentscouncil.org.uk.

piece of play money. Chances are it will be stamped "not negotiable." One will find the same legend on such things as copies of bank checks, phony checks issued as advertising gimmicks, or large-sized images of checks presented in fund-raising ceremonies. In colloquial legal speech, one encounters a version of this usage. Lawyers and judges interested in impressing people with their fancy language often speak of someone "negotiating" a check when all that they really mean is depositing it for collection with a bank. In a somewhat similar vein, judicial opinions sometimes use the phrase "not negotiable" to mean only that a check was submitted for collection but was not paid. In all of these usages, the core meaning of the phrase "not negotiable" is that although an item may look like currency or a good check, it really isn't.

In more precise legal usage, the term "negotiable" refers to the transferability of the instrument. Sometimes the term is used to mean only that the instrument either is or is not transferrable. For example, U.S. Savings Bonds and certain forms of bank certificates of deposit are sometimes said to be "non-negotiable," in the sense that they cannot easily be transferred from person to person.[22] In the narrowest sense, however, "negotiable instrument" refers to a writing, typically a promissory note or check, that is governed by Article 3.[23] In particular, a negotiable instrument is a writing that is governed by the pre-eminent concept of Article 3—the holder in due course doctrine. In that sense, a negotiable instrument means a writing that not only is readily transferrable, but also is governed by the rule that

22. Steven L. Harris, *Non-Negotiable Certificates of Deposit: An Article 9 Problem*, 29 UCLA L. Rev. 330 (1981).

23. Article 3 also applies to several less common species of instruments; however, for purposes of this book it will suffice to focus on checks and notes.

a good faith transferee for value takes it free from any claims and free from most defenses.[24]

So U.C.C. Article 3 is the body of law that governs certain forms of instruments and sets out detailed rules on the transfer of the instruments and the rights of transferees. Let us ask what at first may seem a silly question about this body of law: Why does it exist? To any lawyer familiar with commercial law, the answer will seem obvious. Checks and promissory notes are commonly used in business and financial affairs. It is, therefore, hardly surprising that there is a body of law governing the rights and responsibilities of people who use checks and notes. That, however, is not really a sufficient answer. Checks are instructions directing the transfer of funds through the banking system. Promissory notes are written contracts embodying someone's promise to pay money to another. Why should these two quite different devices be treated in the same statute?

One might also note the odd phenomenon that the scope of Article 3 is quite limited. Article 3 applies only to an "instrument," which Section 3-104(b) tells us means "negotiable instrument." Section 3-104 provides a very narrow and formalistic definition of "negotiable instrument," as "an unconditional promise or order to pay a fixed amount of money" that is "payable to bearer or to order," is "payable on demand or at a definite time," and "does not state any other undertaking or instruction by the person ordering payment." That definition is further explicated in a variety of highly technical

24. In an extreme version of this view, an influential nineteenth-century commentator insisted that the term "negotiable" should limited to instruments payable to bearer or instruments payable to the order of a certain person that had been indorsed in blank by that person. WILLIAM WILLIS, THE LAW OF NEGOTIABLE SECURITIES 6–14 (1896). In Willis's view an unindorsed order instrument was not "negotiable" because a transferee who took though a forged or ineffective indorsement could not qualify as a holder in due course.

provisions in Part 1 of Article 3.[25] The introductory passages of books on Article 3 generally work thorough some of the details of this definition. Thus, a writing payable "to the order of John Jones" is governed by Article 3, but one payable "to John Jones" is not. A writing promising or ordering payment of a set sum is governed by Article 3, but one directing payment plus performance of some other act is not. Some of the rules are extremely technical. For example, a writing can be a negotiable instrument even though the time for payment is the earlier of a stated date or the time that a certain person dies. On the other hand, a writing promising payment six months after a person dies is not a negotiable instrument. The odd definitional provisions exclude some instruments that have major commercial significance. For example, it is routine for lending transactions to be documented by a comprehensive loan agreement. Lawyers often also have the borrower execute a separate note, but the note will invariably state that the terms of the parties' undertakings are spelled out in the loan agreement. That cross-reference usually has the effect of disqualifying the note from treatment as an Article 3 instrument. Section 3-106 says that an instrument fails the unconditional promise requirement if it states that it is "subject to or governed by another record." Not surprisingly, the case law attempting to interpret that provision is in hopeless disarray.[26]

The provision on the scope of Article 3 is unlike anything else in the Uniform Commercial Code. For example, Article 2 on the

25. U.C.C. §§ 3-106 (unconditional order or promise); 3-107 (instrument payable in foreign money); 3-108 (payable on demand or at a definite time); 3-109 (payable to bearer or to order).

26. An instrument can, however, qualify as a negotiable instrument if it merely contains "a reference to another record for a statement of rights with respect to collateral, prepayment, or acceleration." U.C.C. § 3-106. The case law attempting to interpret that provision is terribly messy. *See* Fred H. Miller & Alvin C. Harrell, The Law of Modern Payment Systems 150–52 (2003).

sale of goods begins by saying that "unless the context otherwise requires, this Article applies to transactions in goods . . . ."[27] Similarly, Article 9 on secured transactions begins by saying that "this article applies to a transaction, regardless of its form, that creates a security interest in personal property of fixtures by contract."[28] It would be easy for Article 3 to have a similar scope provision. For example, the statute might say that it applies "to any writing that is intended to embody a promise or order for the payment of money." If Article 3 really were the repository of the significant rules governing checks and promissory notes, that would be the only sensible approach.

The explanation for these oddities cannot be found in anything about modern financial practice or law. Rather, one must look to history. Article 3 of the U.C.C. is not designed as a body of law for modern financial transactions. If one looks closely at the prefatory passages of the books on Article 3, one sees that the statute is not intended to provide the governing law for all instruments embodying debts or directions for payment of money. Rather, it is intended to apply only to those instruments that are readily transferable and may pass freely from person to person. Transfer is the central concept of Article 3. The statute is intended to cover instruments that are intended to be readily transferrable, and to state the special rights of transferees of these instruments. The key to the transfer rules in Article 3 is the "holder in due course" doctrine. A transferee who qualifies as a holder in due course takes the instrument free from claims of ownership, even if the instrument has passed through the hands of a thief. Moreover, a holder in due course may enforce the instrument against a party liable on it even if that party would have

27. U.C.C. § 2-102.
28. U.C.C. § 9-109(a).

had defenses that could have been asserted against the party to whom the instrument was initially issued.

This pattern of the organization, scope, and focus of Article 3 would make sense if checks and notes were routinely transferred from person to person as a medium of exchange. If that were the case, then one could also understand the common usage of the phrase "not negotiable" to mean something like "looks like money but really isn't." The things that we call "negotiable instruments" would be things that passed from hand to hand as currency. At one time, that orientation made sense. The law of negotiable instruments developed long before anything like the modern currency and banking system. In the era in which negotiable instruments law evolved, negotiable instruments were not only transferred, but that system of transfer was essential to the payment system. At that time, people did not make payment by instructions to banks for the transfer of bank credit. Rather, people's liquid balances were held in the form of claims upon a variety of non-bank entities. Issuance and transfer of negotiable instruments was the mechanism by which these claims were transferred as a medium of exchange. That is no longer the case. The problem with the current law of checks, and hence with a major part of modern payment systems law, is that the legal profession has never fully realized that the basic concepts and organization of negotiable instruments law have not made sense for at least a century.

III. WHY IS PAYMENT SYSTEMS LAW ANACHRONISTIC?

Proof of the assertion that the law of checks and notes is thoroughly anachronistic will occupy the balance of the book. At the outset, however, it is worth speculating a bit about why the subject of negotiable instruments law has produced this odd situation.

In part, the phenomenon may be a severe manifestation of a risk that confronts any legal system based on fidelity to precedent. Both statutes and judicial decisions come into being as a response to the conditions that prevail at a given time. The fact that courts generally defer to legislation and are reluctant to overturn prior decisions provides a degree of stability and continuity in a legal system. Yet those principles also make the legal system particularly subject to the danger of anachronism. There is, of course, a substantial and rich body of literature on how a legal system should deal with these problems. With respect to the approach that courts should take to outdated statutes, Guido Calabresi has provided the classic discussion of such problems as whether the courts should take action on their own, leave the problem to the legislature, or attempt to goad the legislature into action.[29] Yet, however one resolves those problems, there is a prior question. How can we tell whether a statute or law has outlived its usefulness? Usually that is fairly obvious. But in the area of the law of bills and notes, the problem is that the profession has generally not even noticed that the law has become profoundly anachronistic. Why is that?

Part of the answer may lie in patterns of legal thought and argument that are so much a part of our intellectual arsenal that they are easy to overlook. Suppose that we have a question of interpretation of a certain statute. We typically approach the problem by asking which possible interpretation will best advance the purposes of the statute. That is a pattern of thought that is so ingrained that we often do not notice how absurd it can be. For example, in connection with the Statute of Frauds, one often encounters suggestions that we need to be fairly rigorous about the requirements for an adequate writing, or else people will not be careful to ensure that their agreements are

29. Guido Calabresi, A Common Law for the Age of Statutes (1982).

evidenced by clear written agreements.[30] A bit of reflection reveals how odd that argument is. Anyone who actually thought about the problem of proving his or her case in litigation would get a written agreement. One would do that no matter what the legal rules were on whether a written agreement is absolutely required. Who would choose to run all the risks of years of litigation over possible disputes about an oral agreement when the whole problem could be avoided by getting a written agreement?

But, there is another problem with our unthinking inclination toward such functionalist arguments. How do we decide what the purposes of a given statute might be? Sometimes we can find useful evidence in legislative history, but that is often not the case, especially for older statutes. Even so, the argument often proceeds in a backwards fashion. Theoretically, we should start with the purposes and then reason toward a conclusion about the interpretation that best advances those purposes. In fact, however, we often start with the desired conclusion and then work backwards to see what purpose we should assume to justify an interpretation that yields that conclusion. Then, we either just assume that such was the purpose, or we dig through legislative history in an effort to find some shred of evidence that might support a claim that the purpose of the statute is what we want.[31] Curiously, we rarely consider one answer to the question of legislative

30. As a comment to a statute of frauds provision in a section of the U.C.C. once put it, "More harm than good would result from allowing creditors to establish a secured status by parol evidence after they have neglected the simple formality of obtaining a signed writing." Former U.C.C. § 9–203 cmt. 5.

31. As a young lawyer, I was once given the task of finding some evidence to support an argument that a certain state constitutional provision was intended to advance something that the lawyer had already decided was the purpose that best fit his argument. I spent a delightful week or so in a historical society archive leafing through old newspaper accounts of the state constitutional convention in an effort to find some shred of evidence that would support the contention. I sometimes wonder whether that experience was what soured me on legal practice and prompted my interest in legal history.

purpose—quirks of history. Maybe the statute was enacted for reasons that made sense at the time it was passed, but which have long since ceased to have any relevance. As we shall see, that is quite commonly the case with provisions of Article 3. Much of Article 3 was a perfectly sensible response to genuine problems in the eighteenth or nineteenth centuries, but those issues have no modern significance.

A deeper part of the problem explored in this book may be that the legal profession no longer takes commercial law seriously. That may be an overstatement, but it contains enough truth that it is something that needs to be considered. A century ago, commercial law was assumed to be a matter of everyday importance. The major law schools not only taught courses in the subject, but actually had professors who wanted to teach those courses and who wrote articles and books on commercial law. Professors were interested not just in commercial law, but in the law of bills and notes. Today, although secured transactions and bankruptcy still attract a bit of attention, commercial law has largely become an academic backwater.[32] If one wants to escape a conversation at a gathering of legal academics, all one need do is announce that you work on the law of bills and notes.

In part, this may be an unnoticed consequence of the well-known *Erie Railroad* case in 1938, where the Supreme Court ruled that federal courts in diversity cases cannot develop their own rules, but must follow the law of the state where they sit.[33] In the pre-*Erie* era of *Swift v. Tyson*,[34] matters of general commercial law were treated seriously by the United States Supreme Court and other federal courts. Indeed, *Swift v. Tyson* was itself a bills and notes case. In the late nineteenth century, the Unites States Supreme Court was the

32. Larry T. Garvin, *The Strange Death of Academic Commercial Law*, 68 Ohio St. L.J. 403 (2007).
33. Erie R.R. v. Tompkins, 304 U.S. 64 (1938).
34. 41 U.S. 1 (1842).

pre-eminent commercial court in the country. Since *Erie*, issues of commercial law have been regarded solely as matters of state law, and hence not worthy of the attention of the Supreme Court. Can one imagine a nominee for the United States Supreme Court being grilled in her Senate confirmation hearings about her views on commercial law? When the justices of the Supreme Court do have to deal with commercial matters, usually in the setting of disputes about the interpretation of Federal bankruptcy law, one has the sense that they do so with a distinct lack of interest.[35]

Even in those courts that still have to deal with commercial disputes, one has the sense that judges approach commercial law with a considerable lack of enthusiasm. It is easy to understand the stakes in disputes about landlord and tenant, products liability, criminal procedure, school funding, employment discrimination, health law, and so forth. Even some matters of business law, such as securities fraud or subprime mortgage financing, are readily seen as matters of genuine modern concern. But—and I readily admit that this is a rather subjective and impressionistic sense—I think that when the subject is commercial law, and bills and notes in particular, even a conscientious judge has a hard time staying awake. In that setting, there is a nearly irresistible tendency to fall into a fairly standard mode of reasoning. The judge will say that in matters of commercial law, certainty is of the utmost importance. Therefore, in any matter governed by a commercial law statute, we must simply apply the statute as it is written. We never need to ask whether that interpretation really makes any sense, or whether the statute itself really makes any sense. That mode of argument is so routine in commercial law cases that it goes all but unnoticed. Suppose one were to make a

35. *See* Robert K. Rasmussen, *Creating a Calamity*, 68 OHIO ST. L.J. 319, 328 (2007) (commenting that the Supreme Court's handing of a bankruptcy issue "betrays a certain disdain for commercial law").

similar argument in other areas of the law. Can one imagine a court deciding a constitutional law case saying "it doesn't really matter what the rule is, it only matters that the rule be certain"?

Recent events have shown the danger of failing to give serious attention to matters of business law that may initially seem dry and arcane. In the 1990s, few people had even heard of "securitization." The financial crisis of 2007 made that ignorance seem quaint. Today, even the popular news media are filled with stories about the details of the system of issuance of mortgage-backed securities and the law governing such financial practices. The payment system and the law of the payment system, by contrast, are still quite obscure. It would be nice if it could stay that way. Suppose, however, that a payment system develops in which an unregulated, uninsured entity incurs substantial obligations to payment system users. Suppose that the provider of that system becomes insolvent. It seems unlikely there will be opportunity for long study of the problems. Rather, there is likely to be political pressure for some rapid "solution." If we have not even realized how anachronistic the current law is, we are unlikely to be in a good position to make sensible law for the future. Ignorance of the past is, therefore, quite risky.

IV. WHAT IS THE ANACHRONISM: NEGOTIABILITY OR NEGOTIABLE INSTRUMENTS LAW?

One aspect of the law of negotiable instruments has received considerable attention in recent years—the application of the holder in due course doctrine to consumer sales. One consequence of the traditional concepts of negotiable instruments law was that a consumer who signed a promissory note for the price of goods would have to pay, even though the goods were defective, if the note had been transferred to a financer who qualified as a "holder in due course." In the latter part of the twentieth century, many scholars argued that the application of the holder in due course doctrine in the consumer sales setting was unjustifiable,[36] and some suggested that the doctrine had no legitimate modern application.[37] That particular problem was resolved in the 1970s by a Federal Trade Commission rule that effectively abrogated the holder in due course doctrine in the setting of consumer sales.[38] Yet, as will be explored in more detail in Chapter 4, the holder in due course doctrine still yields unjustifiable results in other areas. Moreover, the problem of anachronism runs far deeper. Let us assume that we are in agreement that the holder in due course concept has outlived its usefulness. A different question then arises. What, if anything, is left of negotiable instruments law after negotiability? People do, of course, still use promissory notes and checks. So it is hardly surprising that legal issues concerning notes and checks arise. The question is not whether there should be some body of law governing notes and checks, but whether there is any reason to have a body of law of the sort that we now find in U.C.C. Article 3. Does the basic structure of Article 3 remain viable, or does basing the law of checks and notes on the traditional concepts of negotiable instruments law make as little sense as inviting a vegetarian to dinner at a steak house?

36. Edward J. Murphy, *Another "Assault Upon the Citadel": Limiting the Use of Negotiable Notes and Waiver-of-Defense Clauses in Consumer Sales*, 29 Ohio St. L.J. 667 (1968); Albert Rosenthal, *Negotiability—Who Needs It*, 71 Colum. L. Rev. 375 (1971); Vern Countryman, *The Holder in Due Course and Other Anachronisms in Consumer Credit*, 52 Tex. L. Rev. 1 (1973).

37. Grant Gilmore, *Formalism and the Law of Negotiable Instruments*, 13 Creighton L. Rev. 441 (1979); James Steven Rogers, *The Myth of Negotiability*, 31 B.C. L. Rev. 265 (1990); M.B.W. Sinclair, *Codification of Negotiable Instruments Law: A Tale of Reiterated Anachronism*, 21 U. Tol. L. Rev. 625 (1990); Ronald Mann, *Searching for Negotiability in Payment and Credit Systems*, 44 UCLA L. Rev. 951 (1997).

38. Preservation of Buyers' Claims and Defenses in Consumer Installment Sales, 36 Fed. Reg. 1211 (Jan. 1971). The current version of the rule is in 16 C.F.R. § 433.

2

The Puzzling Persistence of the Law of Checks and Notes

Before undertaking the task of assessing modern law, it is necessary to survey a bit of the history of negotiable instruments law. That is a subject that I have explored in detail elsewhere. For present purposes, it is sufficient to present only a brief account.[1]

Consider the following excerpt from a treatise on the law of bills and notes published in London in 1789:

> To make a bill or note negotiable, it must be payable to order, or bearer. A bill or note payable to J.S. or order, is payable to order; a bill or note payable to J.S. or bearer, to the bearer. . . .
>
> The person who makes a bill is called the drawer, the person to whom it is addressed the drawee, and the person in whose favour it is made the payee. The person who makes a note is called the maker, the person to whom it is payable the payee.

1. Though the phrase "puzzling persistence" seems to have come into common use in recent years, Larry Tribe deserves credit for that delightful locution. Laurence Tribe, *The Puzzling Persistence of Process-Based Constitutional Theories,* 89 Yale L.J. 1063 (1980).
The material in the next two sections is adapted from James Steven Rogers, *The Myth of Negotiability,* 31 B.C. L. Rev. 265 (1990). More extensive treatment of the history is presented in James Steven Rogers, The Early History of the Law of Bills and Notes (1995).

> Bills and notes must be for the payment of money only; an order or promise to pay money and do some other act is no bill or note.[2]

The striking thing about this passage is how familiar it would seem to a modern lawyer schooled in the law of checks and notes. Indeed, one could find the same content, and virtually the same expression, in many modern law books.

That seems quite odd. Is it really likely that a body of law developed by the end of the eighteenth century remains suitable for the modern world? Surely no one could fail to notice that the methods of business, finance, and commerce have undergone significant change over the centuries. The period when negotiable instruments law emerged predates the development of nearly every important institution of the modern business and financial world: incorporated banks, business corporations, developed capital markets, the Industrial Revolution, governmentally regulated or controlled monetary systems, and on and on. Perhaps the merchants and jurists of the late Middle Ages and Renaissance were so prescient that they developed a body of law so universal that it could be applied without significant change no matter how much the commercial world might change. That hardly seems likely. We must, then, look at bit more closely at the books on negotiable instruments law in an effort to understand why the law of bills and notes seems to have endured over the centuries with so little change.

2. John Bayley, A Short Treatise on the Law of Bills of Exchange, Cash Bills, and Promissory Notes 1–2 (1789).

I. THE TRADITIONAL ACCOUNT OF NEGOTIABILITY

Works on negotiable instruments law in the mid-twentieth century generally began by explaining the concept of "negotiability." In legal usage, that concept refers to the principle that a transferee of a negotiable instrument can qualify as a holder in due course who acquires its interest in the instrument free from adverse claims and free from most defenses that could have been raised by the original obligor. The books typically explain how the concept of negotiability differs from the general rules of assignment applicable to others forms of property and why this special concept is essential to commercial transactions. The following passage is typical:

> Negotiability is the property by which certain choses in action, that is, undertakings to pay, pass from hand to hand like money. The common law knew nothing of that; or rather the common law repudiated entirely the notion that a promise by A to B could be treated as a promise extending also to C. The utmost which the law allowed was assignment; and that only after long debate and serious misgiving. Assignment merely works the appointment of another as beneficiary of the assignor's rights; the assignee "takes the shoes" of the assignor. That would never have served the purpose of circulating paper; that purpose required a denial of the maxim *Nemo dat quod non habet*. The new taker of a bill of exchange must have a perfect right, if his purchase of it was in due course, a right in no way to be affected by the rights of him from whom he bought it.[3]

3. Melville M. Bigelow, Elements of the Law of Bills, Notes, and Cheques, and the English Bills of Exchange Act 2–3 (1893).

The chapter or chapters devoted to the holder in due course will be the major part of the books, and all other chapters will emphasize the relationship between the matters under discussion and the holder in due course doctrine. The discussion of the formal requirements of negotiable instruments will typically explain that the point of the definitional rules is to specify the requirements that an instrument must meet if a purchaser is to qualify as a holder in due course. The treatment of transfer rules will explain that unless the transfer takes the proper form, the transferee will not be a holder who can qualify as a holder in due course. The discussion of defenses will consist primarily of a differentiation of the "personal" defenses which cannot be asserted against a holder in due course from the "real" defenses which can. Indeed, a major twentieth-century American book on the subject stated explicitly that the holder in due course rule "is, by far, the most important principle in the whole law of bills and notes."[4]

The books commonly also give at least a brief historical account of the development of the holder in due course doctrine. It is generally assumed that one of the main functions of bills of exchange or other negotiable instruments has always been to serve as freely transferrable evidences of indebtedness that could be used as currency substitutes. The holder in due course rules seem to be essential if debt instruments are to be used as currency substitutes. It is commonly asserted that the principle of negotiability developed as part of the "law merchant" as early as the Middle Ages, but that English law was slow to recognize this economically essential concept. The following passage, from an early twentieth-century

4. William Everett Britton, Handbook of the Law of Law of Bills and Notes 25 (1943).

American treatise on the law of bills, is typical of the story that has become familiar to generations of lawyers:

> Originally all instruments, including bills of exchange, promissory notes and bank checks were non-negotiable—in the sense that the maker could, when asked for payment, deduct from the amount due on the instrument any just claim that he had against the original owner. Such a claim was termed a counter-claim, or set-off. In the revival of commerce in Italy, in the eleventh century, merchants and traders, feeling the need of a commercial instrument, similar to a bank bill that could be used in their barter and trade and commercial transactions, and realizing that no such instrument could be passed from hand to hand or sold readily, no matter how good the financial standing of the maker was, if he, the maker, could always insist on adjusting accounts with the original owner—adopted a custom later known as the law merchant, under which notes, checks, drafts, and bills of exchange, drawn in certain prescribed forms, and in the hands of a bona fide purchaser, could be enforced to their full extent against the maker, regardless of certain defenses or counterclaims that the maker might have against the original holder. Such instruments were negotiable and such was the origin of negotiability.[5]

In fact, the traditional account is almost entirely wrong as a matter of history. Let us briefly survey the actual content of the law of bills and notes in the period from the late eighteenth century until sometime in the mid- to late-nineteenth century, a period that might be termed the classical era of the law of bills and notes.

5. James Matlock Ogden, The Law of Negotiable Instruments 9–10 (1909).

II. THE LAW OF BILLS AND NOTES IN THE CLASSICAL ERA

Consider a common form of trade in the late Middle Ages, such as the shipment of spices from Italy to Bruges for redistribution through northern Europe. A Venetian merchant would not have shipped his cargo to someone in Bruges who had already agreed to buy the goods. Rather, he shipped to a merchant in Bruges who acted as a commission agent, selling the goods for the account of the Venetian merchant. The local sales by the commission agent might be for cash or on credit, but it was not those sales that gave rise to bills. Rather, bills arose out of the relationship between the commission agent and his principal. Once the commission agent in Bruges had sold the goods, he was holding funds for the account of his principal. Bills of exchange developed as a mechanism by which merchants could make use of the funds lying in the hands of their agents in distant locations.[6]

In the simplest form of bill transaction, suppose that some other merchant in Bruges had shipped goods, such as English wool, to his representative in Venice who had sold them on commission. The Venetian agent of the Bruges wool merchant had funds due to the Bruges wool merchant, just as the Bruges agent of the Venetian spice merchant had funds in Bruges due to the Venetian spice merchant. If the amounts involved were equal, everyone's accounts could have been squared by having the Bruges representative of the Venetian spice merchant pay money to the Bruges wool merchant, and the Venetian representative of the Bruges wool merchant pay money to the Venetian spice merchant. The following diagram illustrates the mechanism by which a bill was used to accomplish this result.

6. Rogers, Early History of the Law of Bills and Notes 32–43.

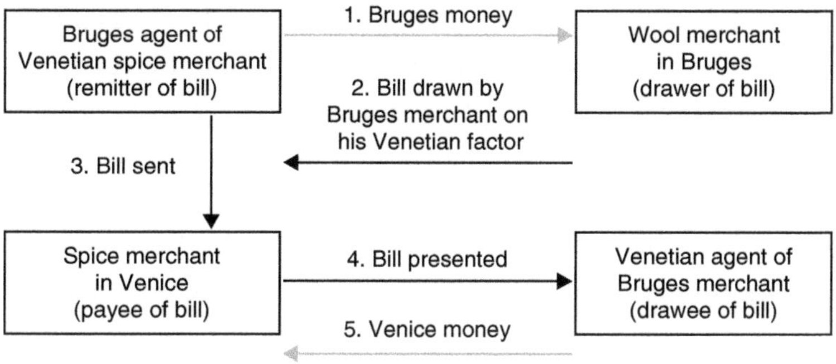

Figure 1 Exchange Transaction.

The process would have been as follows: In Bruges, the Bruges agent of the Venetian spice merchant would deliver money, in local Bruges currency, to the wool merchant. The wool merchant in Bruges would draw a bill of exchange on his agent in Venice, payable to the Venetian spice merchant. The Bruges wool merchant would have been the *drawer,* and his agent in Venice would have been the *drawee.* The bill would have directed that the payment was to be made to the Venetian spice merchant, the *payee.* (The Bruges agent of the Venetian spice merchant would not have actually been a party to the bill, but would have been referred to as the remitter.) The bill would be sent to the Venetian spice merchant, who would present it for payment to the Venetian agent of the Bruges wool merchant. On presentment of the bill, the Venetian agent of the Bruges wool merchant would pay money, in local Venetian currency, to the Venetian spice merchant. So, in Bruges, the agent who had collected money on the sale of the Venetian merchant's spices would have paid that money to the Bruges wool merchant. In Venice, the agent who had collected money on the sale of the Bruges merchant's wool would have paid that money to the Venetian spice merchant. In effect, the Bruges wool merchant's outward cargo became the Venetian spice merchant's return cargo, and vice versa.

The bill of exchange was an outgrowth of the development of a system of trade in which the characteristic form of business organization was the shipment of goods from one merchant to his representative in a distant location for sale by the foreign representative on commission for the account of the shipping merchant. This form of business organization was by no means confined to the Italian merchants who developed it. Rather, the system of trade through commission agents which evolved in Italy in the fourteenth century spread throughout Europe, and later other parts of the world with which Europe traded. It remained the predominant form of business organization until developments in communications and transportation in the nineteenth century made possible other forms of business organization.

Thus, the paradigmatic commercial transaction giving rise to bills was not a credit sale of goods from seller to buyer. Rather, the archetypal bill transaction was a merchant drawing on his factor for the proceeds of goods sold on commission. The relationship between drawer and drawee was not, though, confined to that of a merchant drawing on his factor. Rather, any situation in which one person had or might have funds in his hands belonging to another might form the basis of a bill transaction. One commonly encounters cases in which an English importer's foreign factor buys goods for the merchant's account, paying or reimbursing himself by drawing a bill on his principal.[7] There are many cases of bills drawn against funds in another's hands arising out of other sorts of financial affairs, such as bills drawn on one's banker or other person who, as the contemporary phrase went, "kept one's cash."[8] Indeed, one might have funds in another's hands in non-mercantile situations. For example,

7. *E.g.*, Francis v. Rucker, 27 Eng. Rep. 436 (Ch. 1768).
8. *E.g.*, Grant v. Vaughan, 97 Eng. Rep. 957 (K.B. 1764).

the case usually cited as the first reported decision on an inland bill, *Edgar v. Chut*,[9] was one in which a parson in Norfolk who had funds in London drew a bill on his London friend and gave it to a local butcher who needed London funds to pay for cattle. There are also a fair number of cases of profligate sons surprised to find that dear old dad had finally had enough and dishonored the bills they had drawn on him.[10] Although in these cases the relationship between drawer and drawee may not have been merchant and factor, all involve essentially the same form of underlying transaction—the drawee has, or is hoped to act as if he had, funds of the drawer in his hands. Unlike the model of bill transactions assumed in the twentieth century treatises, these were not cases in which bills were given as embodiments of obligations to pay for goods sold on credit.

The realization that bills characteristically arose not out of credit sales, but out of the obligation of a commission merchant to return funds held for his principal, sheds a great deal of light on the role of the transferability of bills. The picture one gets from most modern law books is that merchants have long wanted some form of transferable paper instrument and found that bills of exchange met the need. That is putting the cart before the horse. In the era in which the commission merchant system of distribution predominated, merchants would invariably find that they had balances due to them from their correspondents in various locations around the country or the globe. Bills of exchange were the mechanism by which they could make use of these distant balances in the era before the development of a specialized financial system. That the bills were transferrable facilitated this system, but it was not the essential key to it. Indeed, one finds many cases in the classical era in which a bill is used as a payment

9. 83 Eng. Rep. 1130 (K.B. 1663).
10. *E.g.*, Witherly v. Sarsfield, 89 Eng. Rep. 491 (Exch. Ch. 1686).

device without any transfer of the bill itself. For example, suppose that a merchant in Bristol had funds in the hands of his factor in London, and needed to make a payment to someone else in London. The Bristol merchant could do so by drawing a bill on his London factor, payable to his London creditor. The London creditor, as payee, could simply present the bill to the drawee and receive payment. No transfer or indorsement would be involved, but the bill would have served an essential role as a payment mechanism.[11]

To be sure, bills were commonly transferred, but the characteristic of transferability is perhaps best understood not as an end in itself, but as a mechanism by which bills could be used to enable a merchant to make use of funds in the hands of correspondents in distant locations. For example, a Bristol merchant might be able to make a payment to his creditor in Bristol by giving him a bill drawn on his factor in London. The creditor would be willing to accept such a payment whether or not he had immediate need of funds in London, because he knew that many other people would have need of funds in London. The well-known case of *Peacock v. Rhodes*[12] is a perfect example. Rhodes, in Halifax, in western Yorkshire, drew a bill on his London bankers payable to Ingham or order. The bill passed through several hands before being stolen from Joseph Fisher at York, about forty miles northeast of Halifax. We next find the bill forty miles further to the northeast at the coastal port of Scarborough where it was taken by a mercer in payment for cloth. From Scarborough, the bill presumably was sent down to London by the regular coastal shipping routes, but was dishonored by the

11. For a nineteenth-century American example, see Aymar v. Beers, 7 Cow. 271 (N.Y. Sup. 1827) where a Virginia farmer travelled to New York to sell his crop of wheat. The buyer paid by giving the farmer a bill drawn on his correspondent in Richmond, which the farmer took back with him when he returned home.

12. 99 Eng. Rep. 402 (K.B. 1781).

London bankers. Thus, from the bare facts of the report, we can literally trace the physical path of the bill through a series of transfers closer and closer to the drawee.

Understanding the characteristic transactions that gave rise to bills also provides the basis for understanding the issues that were a major focus of the law of bills and notes in the classical era. Consider, for example, the rules on presentment, dishonor, and notice of dishonor, that is, the precise steps that a person must follow in making a demand for payment on the obligor and notifying others if that payment is not made. Modern books either skip over these dull subjects or treat them with a sense of reluctant obligation. In the classical era, however, these issues were the heart of the law. Why?

Accustomed as we are today to modern payment systems, it is hard for us fully to appreciate the consequences of the principle that the drawer and indorsers of a bill are liable in the event of nonpayment by the drawee. In the commercial world of the eighteenth century, any merchant would regularly have to take bills as a form of payment, since there frequently was no other available payment medium. Then, in order to pass on the bills, the merchant would be called upon to indorse them. Though the merchant might well have considered any specific such transaction closed long ago, any indorser through whose hands the bill had passed might find himself called upon to pay it months later as a result of the failure of some other merchant perhaps wholly unknown to him. For example, in 1795 an ambitious young Tennessee man travelled to Philadelphia where he sold some land to a Philadelphia merchant, taking the latter's note as payment. In turn, he bought goods, paying by indorsing over the note, and returned to Tennessee intending to set up business as a general merchant with the stock purchased in Philadelphia. Shortly after returning to Tennessee, however, the young man—one Andrew Jackson—learned that the Philadelphia merchant had failed, and Jackson was forced to pay the note, thereby losing the great bulk of his fortune.[13]

The plight of indorsers called upon to make good bills that had passed through their hands explains a great deal of the law of bills and notes. Consider, for example, all of the rules about such matters as the exact time for payment that drearily occupy many chapters of law books on the subject. Is a presentment at seven o'clock in the evening sufficient if the regular clerks had left for the day but another servant was present?[14] If a bill is drawn payable six days after sight, does the day of sight count as one of the six?[15] Are "days of grace" allowed on promissory notes as well as bills of exchange?[16] If the date for payment is a Sunday or holiday, does the bill become due on the day before or the day after?[17] Does commencement day at Harvard College count as a holiday in Massachusetts?[18] Why would anyone spend money to have lawyers argue about such things if the dispute were with the principal obligor? Why not just wait until Tuesday to file suit rather than worrying about whether you could have sued on Monday?

The answer is that the disputes that gave rise to so many of the picayune bills and notes rules were not suits against the principal obligor, but efforts by the holder of a dishonored bill to collect it from an indorser or drawer. Once the economic context is understood, it becomes clear that the arcane disputes about presentment, dishonor, and notice were not the product of mindless pettifoggery

13. John Spencer Bassett, The Life of Andrew Jackson 34 (1931); Marquis James, The Life of Andrew Jackson 74–78 (1938); 1 James Parton, Life of Andrew Jackson 242–44 (1860).
14. Garnett v. Woodcock, 105 Eng. Rep. 1159 (K.B. 1817).
15. Coleman v. Sayer, 94 Eng. Rep. 206 (K.B. 1728).
16. Brown v. Harraden, 100 Eng. Rep. 943 (K.B. 1791).
17. Tassell v. Lewis, 91 Eng. Rep. 1397 (K.B. 1695).
18. City Bank v. Cutter, 20 Mass. (3 Pick.) 414 (1826).

but of the understandable desperation of people facing the prospect of financial ruin when called on to pay bills that passed through their hands months before in long-forgotten transactions. Indeed, an indorser who paid without quibbling would have been thought unusually honest. For example, Andrew Jackson did pay the notes of the failed Philadelphia merchant, which so impressed people of that era that in his later years it was said that Jackson's indorsement was better security than that of men ten times richer than he.[19]

III. TRANSFER OF BILLS AND NOTES IN THE EIGHTEENTH AND NINETEENTH CENTURIES

By the eighteenth or nineteenth centuries, one sees patterns in negotiable instruments dealings that look somewhat more like the model assumed by most modern lawyers. In some such circumstances, it certainly did make sense to say that a transferee of a bill or note took it free from most claims and defenses. Perhaps the strongest case for the traditional rules of negotiable instruments law was presented when instruments were circulated as a form of currency.

Open up your wallet and take out a dollar bill. Do you happen to remember exactly where and from whom you got that specific dollar bill? Probably not. Even if you do, do you have any idea where the person from whom you took it got it? Almost certainly not. How about the person from whom the person from whom you got it, and so on? When you took that dollar bill, did it occur to you that perhaps you should make inquiries about its history? Of course not. Suppose, though, that I look over your shoulder at that particular dollar bill, examine the serial number carefully, and announce

19. Parton, *supra* note 13, at 249–50.

"Ahah! That's mine. That is the exact same dollar bill that was stolen from me six months ago when I was held up by a mugger." Suppose further that I really can prove this. Should I be able to recover that dollar bill from you? In English and American law, it is well settled that the true owner of ordinary chattels can recover his stolen property from any immediate or remote transferee from the thief, regardless of the transferee's good faith or lack of reason to know or suspect of the theft. Money, however, is an exception. A person who takes money takes it free from any adverse claims, even if the specific item of currency can be identified as having been stolen from its true owner.[20]

Today, we encounter negotiable instruments either in the form of promissory notes used in loans, often from banks, or in the form of checks used to direct funds transfers by banks. The instruments then, represent either promises to pay money or directions for the transfer of money. The law of negotiable instruments, however, is profoundly influenced by the fact that in former times negotiable instruments were used in a rather different way: they *were* money. The story is often told of how in Lancashire in the early nineteenth century bills of exchange were sometimes found with a hundred or so indorsements made as they passed from hand to hand.[21] In the first half of the nineteenth century, currency in the United States consisted of engraved notes issued by individual banks and other mercantile entities, rather than by the government.[22] Those notes

20. *E.g.*, City of Portland v. Berry, 739 P.2d 1041 (Or. Ct. App. 1987).
21. L. S. Presnell, Country Banking in the Industrial Revolution 172–73 (1956).
22. Although bank notes were the most common form of circulating currency, promissory notes made by any person or company regarded in the community as financially sound might well be circulated as a form of currency. For example, notes issued by several insurance companies were the principal currency used in Chicago and surrounding areas in the mid-nineteenth century. F. C. James, The Growth of Chicago Banks 201–04 (1938).

were negotiable instruments, governed by the usual rules on bills and notes.

Today, of course, banks do not issue circulating notes. Before the late nineteenth century, however, the issuance of circulating notes was a standard part of banking. Indeed, note issuance was commonly considered the essence of the business of banking, so that regulation of banking typically took the form of regulation of the issuance of bank notes. When one deposited money (specie) in a bank account, or took out a loan from a bank, one received not credit in an account at the bank, but notes *issued by that bank*. The notes were simply promissory notes issued by the bank embodying the bank's promise to pay the note (in real money, that is, specie) to the bearer. The person who received such notes from the bank could use them in making payment for other transactions. Anyone who received the bank notes could, of course, take them directly to the bank and demand payment in specie; however, so long as people in the community had confidence in the solvency of the bank, there would be little reason to do that. The paper bank note, after all, was more convenient to carry around than silver or gold coins and could simply be passed along to others as a sort of private currency. Indeed, a banker was likely to regard it as an insult for someone actually to present a note for redemption in specie. As one authority notes, "[I]t had become the habit of bank officers and others to regard the presentation of notes for *redemption* in specie as an act to reprobated, manifesting a desire to injure the bank and through it the community where it was located."[23]

Circulating private bank notes have long since passed into history. In the United States, the Civil War era National Bank Act effectively put an end to issuance of bank notes by state banks by

23. A. Barton Hepburn, A History of Currency in the United States 166 (1915).

imposing a prohibitive tax.[24] From the middle of the nineteenth century until the early twentieth century, the circulating currency used in the United States consisted in large part of notes issued by national banks.[25] In form, these notes were promises of the individual banks that issued them, that is, the text of the notes said that a certain bank, such as the First National Bank of Boston Massachusetts, would pay ten dollars to the bearer on demand. In economic reality, however, the notes did not represent only the credit of the issuing bank. National banks were permitted to issue circulating notes only if they had deposited with the United States Treasury certain classes of United States government bonds, and the bank notes were redeemable at the Treasury.[26] Thus in economic effect, the currency represented a claim on the Federal government, even though in precise legal terms, the notes were promises of individual banks. The National Bank Act had detailed provisions on these circulating notes, regulating their form as well as specifying precisely the requirements for deposit of the government bonds that backed the currency. With the creation of the Federal Reserve System in 1913, the older system of national bank notes became obsolete.[27] By the 1930s, the United States retired all of the classes of government bonds that were eligible to serve as security for national bank notes, so that, in practice, it became impossible for national banks to issue

24. Bray Hammond, Banks and Politics in America 718–39 (1957); Veazie Bank v. Fenno, 75 U.S. 533 (1869) (upholding constitutionality of prohibitory tax on state bank notes).

25. Hepburn, *supra* note 23, 306–41.

26. Charles F. Dunbar, Theory and History of Banking 158–90 (2d ed. 1909).

27. W. Randolph Burgess, The Reserve Banks and the Money Market 71–88 (rev. ed. 1936).

notes.[28] Today, state and national bank notes are of interest only to currency collectors.[29]

A slightly different form of circulation of notes lasted somewhat longer than the bank note era. Suppose that one mercantile firm was owed money by another firm. The creditor might want cash rather than having to wait until the maturity of the debt. Suppose that the creditor firm had received a note or bill representing the obligation of the debtor firm. The creditor firm could obtain cash by transferring the instrument to someone else. In the early nineteenth century, the practice of "discounting" mercantile notes and bills was common. Indeed, the business of banking was commonly described as a process by which banks discounted notes, and the lending decisions of banks were described as a matter of deciding which notes offered for discount they were willing to take.[30] Mercantile notes and bills might have been offered directly to banks, but there were

28. Milton Friedman & Anna Jacobson Schwartz, A Monetary History of the United States 1867–1960 at 442 (1963).

29. Curiously, the statutory provisions establishing and regulating the system of note issue by national banks endured long after the notes themselves. When I began teaching payment systems law in the 1980s, the federal statutes still contained all of the provisions on the issuance of circulating notes that had been enacted in the Civil War era. If one looked only at the text of the statutes, one might have assumed that national banks could and did still issue circulating notes. But no lawyer or judge had any occasion to look at the National Bank Act provisions on circulating notes anytime after the early part of the twentieth century. Certainly these statutory provisions were not taught in law school courses, save, perhaps, for a passing reference in a historical introduction in course books on banking law. The National Bank Act provisions on circulating notes simply sat there as an irrelevancy until they were repealed in 1994 as part of an effort to tidy up the federal statutes by eliminating obsolete provisions. Notice the anomaly. With the demise of the national bank note system, the law governing that system was recognized as obsolete and the statutes have now been repealed. The system of privately issued instruments that circulated from party to party also passed into history long before the twentieth century. But, we still have, in Article 3 of the U.C.C., a statute on negotiable instruments.

30. Charles F. Dunbar, *supra* note 26, at 9–19; Henry Dunning Macleod, The Elements of Banking 121–34 (1878). An entertaining account of the practices of banks in discounting notes can be found in J. S. Gibbons, The Banks of New York 199–213 (1859).

other intermediaries who might be more willing to take instruments, particularly those of somewhat doubtful credit. Perhaps the most colorful exemplar of this function were the so-called "hat band brokers," who bought notes from mercantile firms and carried them around tucked into the bands of their high hats until they could find a bank or other person willing to buy them.[31]

In its original form, the practice of discounting involved a note or bill that had been issued as payment for an actual commercial transaction, such as the sale of goods. Much of eighteenth- and nineteenth-century banking theory was based on the notion that lending should be confined to the discount of such "real bills." The theory was that this would ensure that bank lending would be confined to prudent transactions. Moreover, at the macro level, the idea was that limiting bank lending to the discount of real bills would automatically regulate the aggregate level of increase in the money supply that necessarily comes with bank lending.[32] Not surprisingly, borrowers wanted to make it look as though they were offering real bills for discount, even if they were simply borrowing money for other purposes. In the late eighteenth and early nineteenth centuries, both economic theory and legal doctrine had to deal with the problems created by the practice of circulation of "accommodation bills," that is, instruments drawn up to appear to have been issued in genuine mercantile transactions even though they were simply a means of borrowing.[33]

31. Albert O. Greef, The Commercial Paper House in the United States 86–87, 97 (1938).

32. 2 Adam Smith, The Wealth of Nations, c. II (1776). Shortly after its foundation, the Federal Reserve System attempted to reproduce in the United States the conditions that had given rise to the real bills theory in England, however, adherence to the real bills theory soon lapsed. Friedman & Schwartz, *supra* note 28, at 189–96.

33. Rogers, History of the Law of Bills and Notes 223–49. One aspect of the controversy about accommodation bills is considered in Chapter 8 of the present book.

By the later part of the nineteenth century or early part of the twentieth century, the practice of raising money by discounting instruments that had been issued to the borrower was largely replaced by the practice of having the borrower itself appear as the person obligated to pay. For one thing, discounting notes received in mercantile transactions presented the simple problem of the irregularity of the denominations. A given firm might have received notes or bills from its customers in various odd amounts. It might well be more convenient, both for the borrower and the lender, to have the borrower issue a note for a single round sum. For this and other reasons, "single name" commercial paper largely replaced "double name" commercial paper by the early twentieth century.[34]

There is, of course, still a "commercial paper" market. But the practices of that market no longer have anything to do with the body of law known as the law of "commercial paper" as set out in Article 3 of the U.C.C. In the first place, the firms that have access to funding through the commercial paper market are a far cry from the miscellany of hardware wholesalers, dry goods merchants, meat packers, lumber merchants, brewers, textile mills, and so forth that once were the principal issuers of commercial paper.[35] The modern commercial paper market is dominated by financial firms such as banks, finance companies, and investment bankers, as well as a smaller number of very large industrial firms.[36] The discount of commercial paper is no longer part of the day-to-day affairs of ordinary businesses.

34. Greef, *supra* note 31, at 65–78; Margaret G. Myers, The New York Money Market 315–25 (1931); Don M. Dailey, *The Early Development of the Note-Brokerage Business in Chicago*, 46 J. Polit. Econ. 202, 212–13 (1938).

35. Greef, *supra* note 31, at 78–85.

36. Federal Reserve Bank of Richmond, Instruments of the Money Market, 105–27 (7th ed. 1993); Pu Shen, *Why Has the Nonfinancial Commercial Paper Market Shrunk Recently?*, 88 Fed. Res. Bank Kansas City Econ. Rev. 55 (2003); Thomas K. Hahn, *Commercial Paper*, 79 Fed. Res. Bank Richmond Econ. Q. 45, 49–50 (1993).

Rather, the commercial paper market is a highly specialized segment of the financial system. To be sure, small to medium-sized mercantile and industrial firms still need financing to enable them to sell to their customers on credit. But, today that need is typically met by some form of financing arrangement in which the firm borrows from a bank or finance company, granting a security interest in its receivables as collateral for its obligation to pay. That is a form of financing transaction familiar to all modern lawyers who have studied Article 9 of the U.C.C. The modern form of receivables financing, which is a development of the twentieth century, has now almost entirely displaced the commercial paper discount model of earlier times.

Even with respect to the firms that still have access to the commercial paper market, the term "commercial paper" is today nothing more than a reflection of history. There is no longer any paper. Today, all significant issues of commercial paper in the United States are held through a special purpose securities depository, The Depository Trust Company, in purely electronic form.[37] The issuer, acting through a commercial paper dealer, borrows money from the investor. The borrower's promise to pay, however, is not represented by an actual physical piece of paper that might be handed around from one investor to another. Rather, the investor's position is reflected solely by electronic records maintained by DTC. Theoretically, that investment is transferrable. However, because of its short term, commercial paper is usually held by the initial investor until maturity. Accordingly, it is rare for commercial paper to be sold from one investor to another.[38]

37. Depository Trust & Clearing Corporation, *Discussion Paper: Issues and Recommendations Regarding Commercial Paper Settlement Practices,* March 2003, *available at* http://www.dtcc.com/downloads/leadership/whitepapers/cppaper.pdf

38. Hahn, *supra* note 36, at 53.

The history of financial practice is a story of dramatic change. Business people would hardly find that surprising. But, lawyers commonly assume that the law set out in Article 3 of the U.C.C. captures unchanging verities that remain as significant today as they were in the eighteenth century. In part, that may be a product of confusion over language. The term "commercial paper" is commonly used to describe the notes and other instruments that were commonly discounted in the eighteenth and nineteenth centuries. In legal parlance, by the twentieth century, that term became the common title for books on the law of the field previously known as the law of bills and notes. In business and financial parlance, the term commercial paper is still used to describe the market in which certain firms can raise capital by issuing short term unsecured debt instruments. But the fact that the same term is used in these various settings is the source of nothing but confusion.[39]

IV. ORIGINS OF THE MYTH OF NEGOTIABILITY

The main thrust of this book is that it no longer makes any sense to organize the law of notes and checks around the concept of negotiability that is the centerpiece of Article 3 of the U.C.C. As a matter of legal history, we encounter a different puzzlement. How did the

39. A similar problem involves the word "discount." In earlier times that term was used to refer to the sale of notes or bills. Today the term survives in the metaphorical phrases "discount window" and "discount rate" used to refer to one of the means by which the Federal Reserve System makes credit available to banks. "Discount" advances by the Fed must be secured by a pledge of various forms of eligible collateral, principally government securities. No one—with the possible exception of a lawyer puzzled about U.C.C. Article 3—would think that discount lending has anything to do with the old practice of circulation of commercial notes and bills. For information on the modern discount window, see FEDERAL RESERVE BANK OF RICHMOND, *supra* note 36, at 22–33; Federal Reserve System Discount Window website, www.frbdiscountwindow.org.

concept of negotiability come to play such a central role in the profession's thinking about the law of bills and notes? Why did lawyers feel the need to explain why there was a special body of law of bills and notes? Why was negotiability its central concept? In the eighteenth or early nineteenth centuries, it is unlikely that anyone would have asked why there should be a law of bills and notes. The answer would have been obvious: There was a law of bills and notes because people used them in everyday financial dealings. Indeed, by the early nineteenth century, there was a market for vest pocket-sized guides to the law of bills and notes intended for the ready reference of people engaged in business.[40]

The classical law of bills and notes dealt with all of the various sorts of problems that arose from the actual transactions and practices of merchants who used bills and notes in the seventeenth, eighteenth, and early nineteenth centuries. Major portions of the treatises were devoted to such topics as the Stamp Act duties on bills and notes, agency law questions that might arise in connection with the use of bills and notes, issues of pleading, evidence, and proof in actions on bills, questions of proof and treatment of claims on bills in bankruptcy proceedings, criminal law issues concerning forgery of bills and notes, etc. This was an important body of law because the use of bills and notes was important to commerce as then conducted.

40. John I. Maxwell, A Pocket Dictionary of the Law of Bills of Exchange, Promissory Notes, Checks, &c. (1808); Robert Muir, A Practical Summary of the Law Relating to Bills of Exchange and Promissory Notes, Intended Chiefly for the Use of Merchants (1836); John Rolle, Pocket Companion to the Law of Bills of Exchange, Promissory Notes, Drafts, Checks, &c., (2d ed. 1815). As the preface to Rolle's book put it: "The extensive operation which these instruments have obtained in commercial transactions renders it unnecessary to expiate on the utility and importance of a publication like the present. In the whole of British law there is not perhaps, any branch (exempting those which regulate our civil rights and liberties) of more extensive import than that which regulates the effect and operation of Bills of Exchange and Promissory Notes."

The specific issues that were important were those that arose from the actual transactions, not from some jurisprudential theory.

By the late nineteenth century, one senses a transformation in the profession's sense of this entire body of law. The concept of negotiability came to occupy a greater and greater role. When the law was codified, England retained the traditional nomenclature, adopting a statute entitled the Bills of Exchange Act. In the United States, by contrast, the statute was adopted under a title that moved the concept of negotiability to the forefront: the Uniform Negotiable Instruments Law. One also sees evidence of the change in the titles of the treatises. The full title of Byles' 1829 treatise was *A Practical Compendium of the Law of Bills of Exchange, Promissory Notes, Bank-Notes, Bankers' Cash-Notes and Checks.* The titles of all of the other treatises of that era take essentially the same form: "The law of . . .," where the ellipsis is filled in with a list of then-current forms of instruments. By the end of the nineteenth century, however, one begins to see treatises called something like the *Law of Negotiable Instruments.*[41] The descriptive laundry list of forms of instruments used in mercantile practice has been replaced by a collective noun defined by the legal characteristic of negotiability. The emphasis on negotiability continues when one opens the books. As has been noted already, the treatises of the late nineteenth and early twentieth centuries commonly began with a theoretical explanation and justification of the concept of negotiability and discussed all other issues in light of the impact of the rules on the rights of holders in due course.

41. *E.g.*, James Matlock Ogden, The Law of Negotiable Instruments (1909). Ogden did, however, retain the laundry list in the subtitle, which read *Including Promissory Notes, Bills of Exchange, Bank Checks and Other Commercial Paper with the Negotiable Instruments Law Annotated.* The titles of other books of that era dropped the list altogether. *E.g.*, Alfred W. Bays, The Law of Negotiable Paper (1911); John W. Daniel & Charles A. Douglas, The Elements of the Law of Negotiable Instruments (1903); Samuel Williston, Negotiable Instruments (1915).

The topics covered in the treatises of the modern era also reflect this fundamental difference in approach. Many of the topics that accounted for major parts of the treatises of the classical era, such as bankruptcy, procedure, evidence, and the like, completely disappeared by the time of the treatises of the late nineteenth and early twentieth century, presumably because they did not fit into the conception of this as a body of law centered around the concept of negotiability. Moreover, the material that still was included had been reorganized. Where a classical era treatise would have had separate lengthy chapters dealing with all questions of legal capacity and agency that might affect parties' obligations on bills, a twentieth-century treatise would cover only parts of these topics in the course of discussion of the distinction between "real" and "personal" defenses. Perhaps the most striking change, though, is the treatment of the cases and rules about the rights of holders of lost or stolen instruments. In the classical era treatises, these topics were generally treated in a separate chapter, usually quite short and found in the back of the book with other miscellany of relatively little importance. By contrast, in the twentieth-century books, *Miller v. Race*,[42] which held that a good faith purchaser of a stolen instrument took that instrument free from the owner's claim, became the case that defined the law of negotiable instruments, for it represented the quintessential instance of the distinction between negotiability and mere assignability. The law had turned inward, so to speak, looking to its own legal concepts and categories as the points of major significance, rather than defining itself and concerning itself with problems and concerns drawn from an actual body of commercial practice.

In part, this transformation may be the result of the profession's failure to take account of changes in commercial practice. The subject

42. 97 Eng. Rep. 398 (K.B. 1758).

of the classical era law of bills and notes was the system in which payments were made by means of balances held with other non-bank entities. One might have made payment by drawing a bill on one's correspondent payable to one's creditor, or by transferring to one's creditor a bill or note that one had received from someone else. By the late nineteenth century, that payment system had passed into history. Payments were made either in governmentally issued currency or by transfer of bank balances. Had the significance of this change been fully recognized, it seems likely that negotiable instruments law would have withered and been replaced by a body of payment systems law that grew out of the actual methods of payment that were in use. Instead, however, the profession seems to have been captivated by one aspect of bills and notes law—the concept of negotiability.[43]

There is an intriguing coincidence between the transformation of the law of bills and notes and developments in the study of legal history. The concept of negotiability seems to have come to prominence in the legal literature at about the same time that lawyers began to be fascinated by the history of commercial law and the "law merchant." The first work that set out the now familiar story of a special mercantile law that was applied in the fair and staple courts and then eventually was adopted by the common law in the eighteenth century seems to have been an introduction to a general work on commercial law published by John MacDonnell in 1890.[44]

43. Grant Gilmore surmised the holder in due course doctrine endured because bankers found it advantageous to apply the old concepts of negotiable instruments law to a new form of transaction—finance of consumer purchases of durable goods. Grant Gilmore, *Formalism and the Law of Negotiable Instruments*, 13 Creighton L. Rev. 441, 451–61 (1979). The dispute over negotiability in consumer finance will be examined in Chapter 4. Gilmore's thesis is attractive, but it probably takes too much of the blame away from the legal profession. The problem was not so much that bankers cleverly pulled the wool over the eyes of judges, but that lawyers failed to realize that the world had changed.

44. John Macdonell, *Introduction* to John W. Smith, Compendium of Mercantile Law (10th ed. 1890).

That was followed within a few years by Thomas Scrutton's influential book on mercantile law and Edward Jenks essay on the history of negotiable instruments law.[45] Within a decade, virtually all of the treatises on the law bills and notes incorporated the results of these works on legal history. A summary account of the evolution of the law merchant and its triumphant struggle with the common law has been a standard accoutrement of the treatises on bills and notes ever since. In part, this may be a function of the common human tendency to exaggerate the importance of whatever one is doing. It is hard to resist the temptation to describe one's field as embodying concepts that are essential to commerce.

So the law of bills and notes that we find in the statute books in the early twenty-first century is essentially the same law that was put into statutory form at the end of the nineteenth century. Moreover, that law was itself the law of the past. As the distinguished twentieth-century commercial law scholar Grant Gilmore put it, the codification of negotiable instruments law captured the past "like a fly in amber."[46] The challenge that we face in the twenty-first century is how to escape from this past.

45. Thomas E. Scrutton, The Elements of Mercantile Law (1891); Edward Jenks, *The Early History of Negotiable Instruments*, 9 L.Q. Rev. 70 (1893).

46. Gilmore, *supra* note 43, at 461.

3

Paperless Paper

The aspect of negotiable instruments law that has attracted the most attention in recent years is the holder in due course doctrine, examined in the following chapter. This chapter considers an even more fundamental principle: the idea that the paper instrument is the indispensible embodiment of the obligations that it represents. The principle has been referred to as "reification"—that is, the underlying rights are reified in the paper—or as the "paperizing principle."[1] In current Article 3, the reification principle is reflected in a number of statutory rules. A person incurs a legally enforceable obligation merely by signing the instrument.[2] While the instrument

1. Robert Charles Clark, *Abstract Rights versus Paper Rights Under Article 9 of the Uniform Commercial Code*, 84 Yale L. J. 445, 476 (1975); James Steven Rogers, *Negotiability as a System of Title Recognition*, 48 Ohio St. L. Rev. 197, 200 (1987); Dale A. Whitman, *Reforming the Law: The Payment Rule as a Paradigm*, 1998 BYU L. Rev. 1169, 1169–71 (1998). Characteristically, Grant Gilmore express the point in delightful prose: "The other idea which, the first time you run into it, sounds like nonsense—the legal mind at its worst—was even more basic to the structure and indeed was what gave the completed edifice its pure and almost unearthly beauty. That was the idea that the piece of paper on which the bill was written or printed should be treated as if it—the piece of paper—was itself the claim or debt which it evidenced. This idea came to be known as the doctrine of merger—the debt was merged in the instrument." Grant Gilmore, *Formalism and the Law of Negotiable Instruments*, 13 Creighton L. Rev. 441, 449 (1979).
2. U.C.C. § 3-308(b). However, as is explained more fully in Chapter 8, unless the instrument gets into the hands of a holder in due course, the obligor can raise any defense that would be available if no instrument had been issued.

is outstanding, the underlying obligation is suspended.[3] Transfer of the rights embodied in the instrument requires physical delivery of the instrument.[4] The obligation can be discharged by destruction of the physical instrument.[5]

A simple example will illustrate why the reification principle once made sense, but no longer does. Consider airline tickets in the mid-twentieth century. When the time came for the plane to depart, the gate employees had to determine who was entitled to board. In a world before computers and modern telecommunications, that was a significant problem. The problem could be solved having a definitive paper ticket issued at the time the reservation was made. Then the personnel at the airport gate could simply ask a person who presented herself for travel to surrender the original paper ticket. That's convenient for the airline, but it can be a nuisance for the traveler. Anyone of a certain age will well remember how annoying it was to keep track of that piece of paper, and how much one worried about what would happen if one lost it. Today, definitive paper airline tickets are a relic of the past. Why? Because modern communication methods make it an easy matter for the airline to have instantaneous communication between the ticketing function and the personnel at the check-in counter or gate. One can print out a boarding pass from an Internet site in advance, but no one would think that that piece of paper had any magical significance. If you lose it, you simply print out another one.

That is a simple illustration of the problem that plagues modern negotiable instruments law. The old system of airline tickets was

3. U.C.C. § 3-310(b).
4. U.C.C. § 3-203(a).
5. U.C.C. § 3-604. As is explained more fully in Chapter 5, the notion that destruction or alteration of the instrument can discharge the underlying obligation provides fodder for what would otherwise be seen as obviously frivolous defenses.

based on the notion that it made sense to regard the paper ticket as the indispensible embodiment of the right to fly on the plane. That may have been a useful technique in the early days of air travel, but it makes no sense today. Fortunately for the airline industry, no body of statutory law had developed about paper tickets. So, when the paper ticket became a hindrance, it was a simple matter for the industry to dispense with it. If only the situation were that simple for negotiable instruments.

I. REIFICATION AND DOCUMENTS OF TITLE

Before examining the problems that reification presents for the modern law of payment systems and debt contracts, it is worth seeing how these problems have been treated in other areas of the law. Consider the law and practice of documents of title.[6] A document of title is a piece of paper issued by a bailee to indicate that goods have been delivered to the bailee. A document issued for storage is called a warehouseman's receipt; one issued for transport is called a bill of lading. A document of title is, in one respect, simply a contract between the owner of the goods and the bailee. Negotiable documents of title, however, play another role. The document becomes a reification of rights in the goods. The bailee engages that it will surrender the goods only upon presentation of the original document. Prior to delivery, the document can be transferred from party to party by a process of indorsement, akin to the transfer process for negotiable instruments. But, unless that piece of paper gets to the

6. Ray D. Henson, Documents of Title Under the Uniform Commercial Code (2d ed. 1990).

party who is to receive the goods, the bailee will not surrender the goods.[7]

Treating the piece of paper as a reification of rights to the underlying goods used to be quite useful. Goods covered by a negotiable bill of lading could proceed, probably rather slowly, by an ocean-going freighter on their way to the destination. All the while, parties could deal in the goods by dealing with the piece of paper. The goods in transit could be bought and sold numerous times, with each transaction implemented by delivery of the document. Any owner of the goods could borrow using the goods as collateral by physically delivering the document to the lender in pledge. This was all based on the assumption that it would be quicker and easier to deal with the paper document than with the goods themselves. The recent history of the document of title is largely a matter of figuring out what to do about the fact that this basic assumption is often no longer true.

In certain forms of transport, negotiable documents never became significant. For example, in the air freight business, it was obvious from the outset that it might take longer to move a piece of paper from one entity to another than to get the goods to their destination. Accordingly, negotiable bills of lading never came into common use for goods transported by air carriers. In recent years, the same problem has come to plague the traditional centerpiece of the bill of lading device—ocean transport of bulk goods. Today it is

7. The concept of reification applies only to negotiable documents of title. A non-negotiable document of title is simply a contract between the owner and the bailee. Surrender of a non-negotiable document is not necessary for receipt of the goods from the bailee. A negotiable document states that the goods are to be delivered to "the order of" a certain person. A non-negotiable document states that the goods are to be delivered to a certain person. For railroad bills of lading, there was an even easier way to distinguish the two types: federal regulations required that negotiable bills be printed on yellow paper and non-negotiable bills on white paper. *Id.* § 2.13.

not at all uncommon for goods shipped by ocean carriers to arrive at their destination before the paper document of title can be forwarded to the intended recipient. A variety of devices have emerged to meet this problem. Some have suggested that the traditional negotiable bill of lading be abandoned in favor of a nonnegotiable waybill.[8] Various other systems have been proposed to replace the paper bill of lading with some form of electronic registry, though no such system appears to have yet achieved widespread adoption.[9] The fundamental problem is that the assumptions that underlie the traditional system of negotiable documents of title no longer make any sense.

II. REIFICATION AND SECURITIES

Developments in law and practice concerning investment securities provide another illustration of the general point that reification of abstract rights into pieces of paper no longer serves a useful function in the modern world. The history of commercial practice concerning security certificates is somewhat complex.[10] By the early to

8. William Tetley, *Waybills: The Modern Contract of Carriage of Goods by Sea*, (Pts. 1 & 2), 14 J. Mar. L. & Com. 465 (1983), 15 J. Mar. L. & Com. 41 (1984); Anthony Lloyd, *The Bill of Lading: Do We Really Need It?*, Lloyd's Mar. & Com. L.Q. 47 (Feb.1989). Short of that, a "letter of indemnity," can be used to get around the problem created by the negotiability of bills of lading. In order to obtain possession of the goods upon arrival, a buyer who has not yet received the bill of lading can give the shipper an indemnity to protect the shipper against liability for misdelivery if someone else later shows up with the original bill of lading. William D. Hawkland, *Documentary Transactions: New Solutions to Old Problems*, 18 UCC L. J. 291, 304–06 (1986).
9. Susan Beecher, *Can the Electronic Bill of Lading Go Paperless?*, 49 Int'l Law. 627 (2006); Marek Dubovec, *The Problems and Possibilities for Using Electronic Bills of Lading as Collateral*, 23 Ariz. L. Int'l & Comp. L. 437 (2006).
10. For a brief account of the history of the law of investment securities, see James Steven Rogers, *Negotiability, Property, and Identity*, 12 Cardozo L. Rev. 471 (1990).

mid-twentieth century, however, it seems clear that paper securities certificates had come to be regarded as reifications of the underlying rights.[11] Ironically, by about the time that the legal system had overcome the obstacles to treating paper security certificates as embodiments of the underlying rights, the problems with that technique began to be apparent. The fact that debt securities could be transferred simply by delivery of the paper certificate meant that there need not be any record of the transfers. That provided a perfect mechanism for hiding transactions from the prying eyes of the taxman or other governmental authorities. For such reasons, crime control authorities have urged the elimination of large denomination currency.[12] But, gilt-edged securities in bearer form could play a similar role. Not only were bearer securities themselves an ideal subject of theft, but they also provided a convenient means of settling the payment side of drug deals or other illicit transactions. Accordingly, the United States stopped issuing Treasury securities in paper form and effectively eliminated the issuance of new corporate securities in bearer form by a provision of the tax code that

11. In the late nineteenth and early twentieth centuries, debt securities came to be regarded more and more as embodied in paper certificates. In the early stages this development took place by squeezing debt securities into the categories of traditional bills and notes law and, somewhat later, into the language of the Uniform Negotiable Instruments Law. Equity securities required separate treatment, in the Uniform Stock Transfer Act of 1910, and Article 8 of the U.C.C. The original version of Article 8 of the U.C.C. was intended to solidify these developments. As Soia Mentschikoff, who served as Reporter for Article 8, noted "Originally this Article of the Code was intended to deal only with the requirements for creating a 'holder in due course' with respect to non-commercial paper. The basic problem was one of defining the types of investment paper which should be the subject-matter of protection in the hands of such a holder." Preliminary Tentative Draft No. 1—Article V (April 22, 1946), *reprinted in* 3 Uniform Commercial Code Drafts 1, 7 (Elizabeth S. Kelly ed. 1984).

12. Steve Scherer, *500-Euro Bill Lifts Crime Risk, Bank of Italy Says*, Bloomberg Businessweek, Apr. 20, 2010, *available at* https://www.bloomberglaw.com/link/load/document/L165J21A74E9.

denies the issuer the deduction for interest paid if debt securities are issued in paper form.[13]

Even if we confine attention to legitimate transactions, the paperizing principle has serious limits. To settle securities trading, one needed to move an enormous volume of paper among major brokerage firms and banks.[14] By the late 1960s this "paper crunch" had reached such a critical state that on numerous occasions the New York Stock Exchange had to close trading early in the day to give the back-office paper processing system an opportunity to catch up.[15] During the 1970s, the legal profession worked on these problems with the thought that the paper certificate could be eliminated in favor of a system in which issuers would create completely uncertificated securities.[16] The industry, however, could not wait for the lawyers. Instead of eliminating paper certificates, the industry made them irrelevant. Just as active traders had long left their securities with their brokers, brokers and other custodians developed a system in which all paper certificates were delivered to a central securities depository. That has made it possible to settle trades by entries on the records maintained by the central securities depository. No movement of paper certificates is needed.[17]

The development of the indirect holding system for securities produced a result not unlike that which currently confronts payment systems law. The law of securities transfers, as set out in U.C.C.

13. Marcia Stigum, After the Trade 86–90 (1988); 26 U.S.C. §§103(b) & 163(f); S. Rep. No. 97-494, at 242–44, (1982), *as reprinted in* 1982 U.S.C.C.A.N. 995–98.

14. Richard B. Smith, *A Piece of Paper*, 25 Bus. Law. 923 (1970); Richard B. Smith, *A Piece of Paper Revisited*, 26 Bus. Law. 1769 (1971).

15. Walter Werner, *The Certificateless Society: Why and When?*, 26 Bus. Law. 605 (1971).

16. Martin J. Aronstein, *The Decline and Fall of the Stock Certificate in America*, 1 J. Comp. Corp. L. & Sec. Reg. 273 (1978).

17. Charles W. Mooney, *Beyond Negotiability: A New Model for Transfer and Pledge of Interests in Securities Controlled by Intermediaries*, 12 Cardozo L. Rev. 305, 316–30 (1990).

Article 8, was based on the notion that paper certificates were the embodiment of the underlying rights and that transfers would be implemented by delivery of the paper certificates. In practice, however, no paper certificates were actually delivered to settle securities trades. That fact was reflected, rather poorly, by various provisions in old Article 8 concerning securities held through intermediaries, and by the usual lawyer technique of "deeming." For example, when paper certificates were eliminated for U.S. Treasury securities, the federal law governing Treasury securities had to be amended. That was done by providing that the actual record-keepers—the Federal Reserve Banks—should be treated as if they had possession of certificates representing the Treasury securities. That way, transfers could be analyzed as if there were still paper certificates. That was never a particularly tidy technique, and it became all but incomprehensible once state law was amended to provide for both certificated and uncertificated securities. Which body of law governs non-existent pieces of paper that are deemed to exist? Is the law of actual paper certificates or the law of uncertificated securities?[18]

Eventually the strains produced by the disconnect between the realities of the marketplace and the basic concepts of the commercial law of securities transfers proved intolerable. The crunch came at the time of the October 1987 stock market crash when financial system regulators were urging banks to provide emergency liquidity to securities firms. The banks were willing so long as they could obtain assurance that they would have a perfected security interest in the securities positions held by the borrowing firms. The bankers

18. At one point during the course of the project that produced the 1994 revision of Article 8, one of the participants in the drafting committee meetings, Professor Charles Mooney, aptly observed that questions of this sort lie more within the expertise of a faculty of theology than of law.

turned to the lawyers for assurance on that point, and were not happy with the answer. As one knowledgeable observer remarked, 'That's an interesting question' is not an acceptable answer to questions about the legal rights of securities market participants at a time when the prospect of the collapse of the financial system is a matter of more than theoretical concern.[19]

The response was the law revision project that produced the 1994 version of U.C.C. Article 8.[20] The indirect holding system rules of Revised Article 8 are based on the newly devised concept of a "security entitlement." That is the term used to describe the rights of a person who holds a position in a security through an account with an intermediary. The key to the approach taken in Revised Article 8 was the abandonment of the effort to state the law for modern practices by forcing new commercial practices into the ill-fitting categories of earlier law. Unlike prior law, Revised Article 8 is not based on the idea that rights are embodied in pieces of paper.

Experience with Revised Article 8 over the past fifteen years proves the wisdom of the basic approach taken in that project. The old commercial law rules were designed for the system in which delivery of physical certificates was the key to the securities transfer process. Trying to use those rules for the modern system of securities holding through intermediaries is like trying to use an old electric system for a modern building; it can be done, but it takes a lot of effort and provides little protection against emergencies. Eventually, one must bite the bullet and discard legal concepts drawn from the commercial practices of the past.

19. My recollection is that the remark was made by Ernest T. Patrikis, then General Counsel of the New York Federal Reserve Bank.

20. James Steven Rogers, *Policy Perspectives on Revised U.C.C. Article 8*, 43 UCLA L. Rev. 1431 (1996).

III. REIFICATION AND NOTES

Now let us turn to the reification principle as applied to negotiable instruments law. The reification concept made perfect sense at a time when negotiable instruments circulated as a form of currency. To see why, imagine that I walk into a store and want to buy an item for ten dollars. Suppose I say to the storekeeper "I have a ten dollar bill in my wallet. I hereby declare that henceforth I will hold that bill, separate from any other currency, in trust for you." Obviously the storekeeper is not going to hand over the goods. If I want the goods, I have to pay for them. Paying means handing over the currency. No amount of legal gobbledygook is going to substitute for the simple act of physically handing over the ten dollar bill.

Does the reification principal make sense as applied to modern transactions involving negotiable instruments? Consider routine bank loans to business enterprises. If the amount of the loan is large enough to warrant careful lawyering, the transaction will be documented by comprehensive and lengthy loan agreements. At the closing, representatives of the lender and borrower, along with their attorneys, will meet for the signing and delivery of all of the many documents involved in the transaction. Some of the documents may require signature by multiple human beings. If it is not feasible to have all of the people appear at one place, the documents may be executed in multiple counterparts. Even if all the people are to meet at the same place, each party, and each law firm, will want to have a fully executed copy of the agreement for their files. So, the closing ceremony will consist of the associates from the law firms handing the principals one piece of paper after another, saying "sign here . . . and here . . . and here." The agreements will all have a boilerplate clause saying something like "this Agreement may be executed in several counterparts, each of which shall be deemed an original and all of which shall constitute one and the same instrument."[21] Could any of these documents be negotiable instruments? If they were, the consequences would be severe. Each of the multiple copies might be separately enforceable. But it is obvious that these documents are not the indispensible embodiment of the deal, they are simply pieces of paper that record the parties' deal. As a senior member of the Boston bar told me in the late 1980s, "I've been doing bank and insurance company lending work for thirty years and I've never had occasion to look at Article 3. The only effect it has on our work is that we always draft the papers to make sure that Article 3 does not apply."[22]

Consider another common modern transaction: mortgage lending. Here it is still common for loan documentation to include a definitive promissory note which is, at least in some circumstances, drafted with the thought that it might qualify as an Article 3 instrument.[23] How likely is it that the borrower realizes that? A modern

21. Another common boilerplate provision permits the bank to photocopy, microfilm, or scan the agreement and then destroy the original. If one treated the agreement as a negotiable instrument, one would have to worry about whether the destruction of the original might discharge the underlying obligation.

22. In one of the standard forms of documentation for such loans, the bank and borrower execute a detailed loan agreement, and the borrower also executes a short form of promissory note. Since the terms of deal between the parties are fully described only in the loan agreement, the note invariably will include words along the lines of "This Note is subject to the terms of a Loan Agreement of even date." To some extent, the use of the note may be superfluous, but it remains common. The lawyers assume that the "subject to loan agreement" legend will keep the note from being a negotiable instrument, and therefore they need not worry about anything in Article 3. At one point in the project that resulted in the 1990 revision of Article 3, the draft had rather complex scope provisions that might have been read to include virtually any loan agreement. Fortunately, those provisions were dropped and revised Article 3 retains a fairly tight scope provision.

23. Whether routine mortgage notes qualify as Article 3 instruments is, however, a matter of some doubt. Scholars who have examined modern mortgage notes through the lens of traditional negotiable instruments law have commonly concluded either that the instruments do not qualify as negotiable instruments, or that one can reach no confident conclusion on that score. Ronald Mann, *Searching for Negotiability in Payment and Credit Systems,*

mortgage note is not the simple instrument imagined by traditional negotiable instruments law. It is a multi-page document containing all kinds of provisions, and referring, in various ways, to many of the other documents presented to the borrower for signature. The borrower is confronted with a large stack of papers, many of which consist of recitals, certainly false, that the signer has read and understood the previous documents. The borrower might pause a moment before signing the note, but that is only because doing so drives home the fact that the borrower is promising to pay an astonishingly large amount. Grit your teeth, think about how nice the house is, and sign that note along with the scads of other papers. Some of the documents are to be signed in multiple copies, others are not. It seems inconceivable that any significant number of borrowers realize that one of those pieces of paper is of a completely different nature than the others.[24]

Now consider the flip side of the mortgage transaction. Today it is rare for the note to be held until maturity by the initial lender. Rather the mortgages are securitized. The originator makes the initial loans, receiving notes and mortgages from the borrowers. The notes and mortgages are combined into pools and transferred through one or more entities to an entity that issues securities representing rights to receive the income and principal from the mortgages.[25] In the old-style world of circulating instruments, it was easy to determine who

44 UCLA L. Rev. 951, 971–73 (1997); Dale A. Whitman, *How Negotiability Has Fouled Up the Secondary Mortgage Market, and What To Do About It*, 37 Pepp. L. Rev. 737, 747–54 (2010).

24. The problems created by the possibility of applying the holder in due course doctrine to mortgage notes are considered in Chapter 4.

25. The literature on securitization is enormous. Useful overviews can be found in Tamar Frankel, Securitization: Structured Financing, Financial Assets Pools, and Asset-Backed Securities (1991) and Steven L. Schwarcz, Structured Finance: A Guide to the Principles of Asset Securitization (3d. ed. 2007).

was entitled to enforce the obligation embodied in the instrument. Either one did or did not have the instrument in one's hands. Nothing could be further from the truth in the modern world. Dale Whitman has pointed out that the requirement of physical production of the note currently operates as a major obstacle to efforts to foreclose mortgages.[26] In a very large percentage of the cases, no one can find the actual original note signed by the borrower. Accordingly, the complaint includes a "lost-note affidavit" certifying that the foreclosing party is unable to produce the actual piece of paper. Needless to say, that provides an attractive basis for defense of foreclosure actions.

Even if the original note can be found, there are likely to be problems about who actually has possession of it. One will know that the borrower signed a note. One will know that that mortgage note was pooled with others and formed the basis of a securitization. A half-dozen or so different legal entities may well have been involved in the securitization. The lawyers doing the deal may, or may not, have endeavored to invoke concepts of negotiable instruments law by some form of "deeming" possession of the notes to have been transferred, even though the actual physical piece of paper may have stayed with the originator, or some other servicing company. That servicing entity would be the party who actually had physical possession—or who would probably have had physical possession if we could find the original piece of paper. But, that servicing entity would have been acting only as "agent" for someone else who held the economic interest. Courts disinclined to see borrowers losing their homes are going to have no difficulty finding ways of saying that whoever is suing has failed to prove that it is actually the holder of the note.[27]

26. Whitman, *supra* note 23.

27. The problems are particularly acute in connection with mortgages handled through "MERS," the Mortgage Electronic Registration System. A few courts have ruled against

Thus, for whatever reason, the actual operation of the modern mortgage lending business just does not comport with the fundamental concept of negotiable instruments law that the underlying obligation is reified in the physical instrument.

IV. REIFICATION AND CHECKS

Now consider the concept of reification as applied to checks. A check is a way of instructing banks to make a payment from one person to another. There are many other means of doing that. One could appear at one's bank in person and ask that funds be transferred to someone else who maintained an account with that bank, or, if the bank was prepared to do so, to someone who banked at another bank. One could do the same thing by a telephone call to one's banker. Turning to more commercially significant payment systems, one can direct a payment by means of a debit card handed to a merchant that makes it possible for the merchant to receive funds from one's bank account. Alternatively, one can send an electronic message to one's own bank directing that an electronic funds transfer be made to someone's account at another bank. In none of

foreclosure actions by MERS. *E.g.*, LaSalle Bank v. Lamy, No. 0300049/2005, 2006 WL 2251721 (N.Y. Sup. Ct. 2006). For discussion of the problem, including cases reaching results contrary to *LaSalle Bank*, see Whitman, *supra* note 23, at 763–66. In Massachusetts, efforts to foreclose mortgages have run afoul of a somewhat different snafu. A recent controversial decision held that even one with possession of the original mortgage note is not entitled to foreclose if an assignment of the mortgage had not been recorded in the land records prior to initiation of the foreclosure action. U.S. Bank. N.A. v. Ibanez, 458 Mass. 637 (2011). The *Ibanez* decision is probably wrong as a matter of interpretation of the U.C.C., *see* Permanent Editorial Board for the U.C.C., Draft Report U.C.C. Rules Applicable to the Assignment of Mortgage Notes and to the Ownership and Enforcement of Those Notes and the Mortgages Securing Them (March 29, 2011), but the case illustrates the difficulty of squaring the Article 3 rules with modern financial practices.

these systems would the means by which the payment was directed be regarded as legally equivalent to the instruction itself.

Suppose that a business directs that an electronic funds transfer be made from its bank account to a certain person. Suppose that a nefarious interloper causes the funds to transferred to someone else. U.C.C. Article 4A has a comprehensive system for adjudication of such disputes. But, no one would ever think that the sensible way to resolve the problem would be by asking questions about who had good title to the electronic message that somehow got to the bank. Yet, because the U.C.C. treats checks as a species of negotiable instrument, that is the way that such questions are analyzed in the check system.

The actual operation of the check system is hardly consonant with the notion that the piece of paper on which the check is written is the indispensible embodiment of the instruction. Consider what actually happens to a check in the process of collection. After it leaves the hands of the payee, there is usually only one step where any human being actually looks at the check. That is in the proofing department of the depositary bank.[28] The clerks sit at large machines, key in the amount of the check, and the machine prints that amount in the MICR (magnetic ink character recognition) line of the check.[29] The clerks operate under significant time pressure, so their examination of the checks will necessarily be quite limited. Once that step has been taken, it is somewhat odd to talk about the check. All that

28. For checks deposited in person at bank, there may also be a human examination by the teller. Also, checks that have some problem preventing them from being read by a sorter may be subject to manual examination. In cases of payees who receive a large volume of checks, the MICR encoding may be done by the payee before the checks are sent to the depositary bank.

29. There is an entertaining account of the traditional check collection process in Martin Mayer, The Bankers: The Next Generation 95–100 (1997).

is needed to process the payment are the three items of information encoded on the MICR line: (1) the identification of the payor bank, (2) the drawer's account number, and (3) the amount. All of the processing thereafter proceeds on the basis of these three items of data. As a physical object, the check is largely irrelevant.[30]

Once one realizes that a check is nothing more than the carrier of the three items of data shown on the MICR line, the oddity of the check collection system becomes apparent. Negotiable instruments law is based on the idea that abstract rights are embodied in a piece of paper, and that people deal with the abstract rights by physically delivering the paper. In the check system, all that really matters is the abstract information, that is, the instruction from the user to the banking system to transfer a certain amount of bank credit to someone else. That information, not the physical object, is the basis of the payment system. Consider other means of transferring information. Today, most communication from person to person occurs via e-mail rather than by old-fashioned letters. We may print out e-mail messages when we receive them, but no one would think that the printed copy has any special significance. What matters is the information, not the medium. Now suppose that communication by e-mail was subject to a legal regulation devised in the distant past. Suppose that one element of that old law had the effect that every time someone sent an e-mail message, the sender's computer also had to print out a paper copy and mail it to the recipient. That would be truly weird. Yet, that's the traditional check system.[31]

30. In the unusual case where something goes wrong, it may become necessary to look at the check itself to see whether the payment was processed in a fashion consistent with the instruction embodied in the check. For the routine check collection process, however, the check is simply the carrier of the MICR line information.

31. As Mayer notes, "[T]he question of who processes checks and how they are processed ought not to be asked at all, because the checking system—all 65 billion checks a year, and

Bankers have been working for decades on various truncation systems to minimize or eliminate the flow of paper. There are, however, at least two problems. First, in the United States we have thousands of different banks. A check drawn on any of those banks may be deposited for collection at any other one. Some of the banks may be less willing than others to invest in new technology. Even if they account for only a small percentage of the total, the banks that are not prepared to receive electronic presentment make it impossible for the system as a whole to move to a fully electronic means of processing payments initiated by checks.[32] Second, there is the sense that at least some bank customers attach special importance to getting back their actual cancelled checks.

The most recent effort at reform of the check system, the Check 21 Act adopted by Congress in 2003,[33] addresses both of these problems. Under Check 21, banks handling checks for collection can make an electronic image of the check and proceed with the collection process on the basis of that electronic record. Then, if the particular payor bank on which the check was drawn is unable or unwilling to accept electronic presentment, the presenting bank can create a "substitute check" and present that for payment. The "substitute check" is a paper reproduction of the original, containing the MICR line information, printed on paper of size and quality similar to an original check, "suitable for automated processing in the same manner as the original check."[34] The concern about bank customer

counting—should be a dodo in an age of data processing." MAYER, *supra* note 29, at 106.

32. For simplicity, the discussion herein focuses on the forward collection process. My understanding is that the process for return of dishonored checks has, thus far, proved to be more resistant to efforts to eliminate paper flow.

33. 12 U.S.C. §§ 5001–5018. For an overview of the act, see Alvin C. Harrell, *Introduction to Check Truncation*, 58 CONSUMER FIN. L.Q. REP. 362 (2004).

34. 12 U.S.C. § 5002(16).

resistance is addressed by a provision that a substitute check shall bear the legend "This is a legal copy of your check. You can use it the same way you would use the original check."[35]

Check 21 has made it possible to process payments initiated by check without actually moving all of the pieces of paper. But it has done so in a somewhat peculiar fashion. Check 21 attempts to strike a balance between the fact that paper is irrelevant in the modern payment system and the fact that traditional law and lore about the check system treats paper as significant. The act does not actually eliminate paper checks, rather it attempts to find some way of preserving the traditional reverence for paper even after the paper has become essentially irrelevant. Under Check 21, if anyone actually wants a paper check, a substitute check can be created from the electronic information that is actually the basis of the payment system.[36]

35. 12 U.S.C. § 5003(b)(2). It is not entirely clear what it means to say that a substitute check is a "legal copy" of the original. As an undergraduate, I was taught by a professor of linguistic philosophy that a good test of whether a proposition was nonsense was to ask whether its opposite made any sense. Could there be an "illegal copy" of a check? Presumably the thought behind the "legal copy" legend is that if someone needs to prove that she really did make a payment, producing a substitute check has the same effect as producing an original cancelled check. Of course, nothing in Check 21 specifies what evidentiary effect a cancelled check has. Suppose the payee contends it did not actually receive the check so that any purported indorsement must be a forgery. The drawer may have a "legal copy" of an original document, but that will mean nothing if the original had a forged indorsement.

36. Most of Check 21 seems to be based on the notion that the reconversion will be done by presenting banks, not payor banks. That, presumably, is why the statute requires that a substitute check be in paper and of a format that is "suitable for automated processing in the same manner as the original check." That makes sense from the perspective of dealing with payor banks that are not capable of receiving electronic presentments. It is less clear from the text of the act that a payor bank could use the Check 21 substitute check device as a way of responding to customers' requests for some form of paper representation for payments made by the bank on the basis of an electronic presentment. An odd definition buried in the regulations adopted by the Federal Reserve Board seems to be designed to permit the application of Check 21 to a paper first produced by the payor bank. The term "transfer" is, counterintuitively, defined to include "delivery of the substitute check . . . by a bank to a person other than a bank." 12 C.F.R. § 229.2(ccc)(1). Thus, one might conclude that the transfer warranties established by Check 21 apply to the relationship between a payor bank

Indeed, under Check 21, it is possible that more than one paper substitute check will be created at different points in the collection process if so requested by the participants. In essence Check 21 says "You want paper? OK, we'll print paper. That's easier than persuading you that paper is unnecessary."

Now consider that approach from the standpoint of the reification concept of negotiable instruments law. If an underlying obligation has been embodied in a paper negotiable instrument, then that piece of paper has special legal significance. It is not merely the medium that conveys the information; it is itself a complete embodiment of the underlying rights. No one would think that a negotiable instrument can be destroyed without the possibility that doing so would affect the underlying obligation. Certainly no one would think that we could make an electronic image of the paper, and then create as many paper copies as we might later need if someone asked for a paper instrument. Think again of currency. Suppose that I find myself in possession of a large quantity of U.S. currency. I become worried about having all that currency around in paper form. Suppose I say, "Gee, I have a simple solution. I'll just scan the currency into my computer and destroy the originals. Then, if I actually need the paper currency, I'll just print out a copy." That's what Check 21 does. The act may be an appropriate response to the needs of the modern payment system, but it is fundamentally inconsistent with the idea that it makes sense to treat checks as negotiable instruments.

and its own customer. Curiously, however, something qualifies as a Check 21 "substitute check" only if it is printed on paper of size and quality similar to an original check and is "suitable for automated processing in the same manner as the original check." A paper copy produced by a payor bank would have been generated long after all processing has been completed.

V. METAPHOR AND REALITY

Underlying much of the oddity of negotiable instruments law is our unthinking assumption that paper matters. In the era in which negotiable instruments law developed, it seems to have been fairly obvious that something remarkable was happening when paper came to be regarded as the embodiment of valuable rights. The preface to an early nineteenth-century handbook on negotiable instruments law remarked that "Paper is now become the grand currency in commercial dealings, and an ample substitute for cash; insomuch that it has almost superseded the circulation of specie. We are convinced of the propriety of what has been asserted by a certain exalted character, 'That we eat and drink paper, and live upon paper.'"[37] Similarly, at the time when the stock market developed in Amsterdam, numerous satirical engravings show some personification of folly scattering paper shares of stock to the eager crowd. Indeed, the depictions could be far cruder than that, as in an eighteenth-century Dutch portrait showing a broker eating money and excreting shares of stock.[38]

The idea that the paper on which words are written has significance beyond the words themse.lves is not unknown in other contexts. For example, at one time people seem to have treated parchment charters with particular reverence. In accounts of colonial America, one often hears discussions of charters suggesting that the important thing was not what the document said, but the actual physical object on which the words were written. There is, for example, the story, perhaps apocryphal, of the Connecticut colonists' response in 1687 to the demand of the King's representative that

37. Edward W. Manning, The Law of Bills of Exchange, Promissory Notes, Bank-Notes, Bankers Notes, Drafts, and Checks iii (1801).
38. Simon Schama, The Embarrassment of Riches 367 (1987).

they surrender their charter. They blew out the candles in the room where the confrontation occurred and tossed the parchment out of a window. It was then taken off to be hidden in a cavity of a tree, ever since known as the "Charter Oak."[39]

That attitude is not wholly confined to history. Think of the once common practice of holding a party to celebrate the day when one had finally completed payments on a mortgage and owned the house free and clear. The highlight of the event was the ceremonial burning of the original physical paper on which the mortgage was written. That practice seems to have largely died out, though one may wonder whether that is a result of a diminished sense of the mystical significance of the original mortgage document or merely the fact that no one ever finishes paying off a mortgage anymore. Think of the attitude we take toward the deed for our property. We still tend to think that the physical piece of paper is especially significant. I am sure I am not the only one who has that piece of paper carefully secreted away in a safe deposit box. We still do that even though once recording acts were developed, the important thing is not the physical object itself, but the fact that there is a copy of it on record in the registry of deeds.

39. Albert C. Bates, Charter Oak (1907), reprinted from Encyclopedia Americana, *available at* http://www.archive.org/texts/flipbook/flippy.php?id=charteroak00bate. Some of the significance once attached to original documents might simply be the product of the difficulty—in a world before anything like modern office machinery—of determining whether something was, in fact, an accurate copy of the original document. At one time, when someone borrowed money, a wooden stick was notched to indicate the amount, and then the stick was split in two lengthwise, with debtor keeping one side and the creditor getting the other side. The debtor could verify that the side of the stick presented by a creditor was genuine by seeing whether the two sides matched, or "tallied." It is said that the destruction of the Parliament buildings in 1834 was caused by a fire that started in a storehouse of ancient tallies. W. T. Baxter, *Early Accounting: The Tally and the Checkerboard*, 16 Acct. Hist. J. 43–83 (1989).

With respect to monetary matters, it seems harder for us to escape the image of paper. We constantly speak of governments "printing money." Every television news story on inflation is accompanied by stock footage of the printing presses at the Bureau of Printing and Engraving churning out sheets of twenty-dollar bills. We all have burned into memory the images of people toting around wheelbarrows full of bank notes in Weimar Germany. We simply cannot think about money without thinking about pieces of paper. That is the case even though currency is now only a small portion of the money supply. "Money" today really means demand deposits held with banks. But it would hardly make for good TV to have the inflation story backed up by a chart of the components of M2 drawn from a dry Federal Reserve Board publication.

To come even closer to the subject of negotiable instruments law, consider the phrase "commercial paper." Today, that term simply means a promise to repay a short term unsecured loan extended to a highly creditworthy enterprise. Such obligations are no longer represented by paper. Rather, as was noted in the preceding chapter, the obligation is recorded in the records of the Depository Trust Company and transactions are implemented merely by making appropriate entries in those electronic records. But we still talk about investors "buying commercial paper" as if there were an actual piece of paper involved. We even speak of a "piece" of commercial paper, and ask such questions as whether the "paper" was sold or redeemed.

Thus, in various contexts, we still talk about "paper" even though there no longer is any paper. We treat the paper that represents an obligation as having a symbolic significance beyond the meaning of the words recorded. In most contexts, however, we probably recognize at some level that the sense of reverence that we give to some documents is largely a matter of symbolism. In the law of payment systems, however, we have still not made that transition. The physical object—the negotiable instrument—still plays a special role in the law of the check system and the law of promissory notes. One cannot help but wonder whether the sorry state of current payment systems law is in part attributable to our seeming inability to distinguish between metaphor and reality.

4

Reports of the Death of the Holder in Due Course Doctrine Are Greatly Exaggerated

In the twentieth century, the major controversy in the law of bills and notes was the struggle to avoid application of the holder in due course doctrine in cases involving credit sales to consumers. As a matter of the general law of assignments of contractual rights, an assignee generally gets only whatever rights the assignor had. So, if the person obligated on the contract had some defense to her liability, the assignee would receive the contractual right subject to the defense that the obligated party could have raised against the assignor. The holder in due course doctrine is an exception to that rule. If a transferee of a negotiable instrument qualifies as a holder in due course, the transferee takes the instrument free from most defenses. So, if the maker of a promissory note had some defense that she could have raised against the original payee, that defense would be cut off if the note is transferred to someone who qualifies as a holder in due course.

As we shall see in this chapter, the problem created by the application of the holder in due course doctrine in the setting of a sale of goods or services to consumers was resolved by the late twentieth century. But the holder in due course doctrine remains problematic in other areas. Thus, the subject of the holder in due course doctrine merits attention both to see the way in which anachronism has distorted the understanding of the issue and to see how courts might deal with the remaining problems caused by the holder in due course doctrine.

I. THE DEMISE OF HOLDER IN DUE COURSE DOCTRINE IN CONSUMER SALES

Perhaps the classic case in the story of the demise of the holder in due course doctrine in consumer sales is *Unico v. Owens.*[1] Mr. and Mrs. Owen were persuaded by a representative of Universal Stereo Corporation to sign up for a plan under which they were to receive a free record player when they agreed to buy 140 records albums over a period of about five years. The documents the Owens signed included a promissory note. That note was immediately transferred to Unico, a company related to Universal. Universal defaulted on its obligation to deliver the records, and the Owens stopped making payments. The transferee of the note, Unico, brought suit against the Owens, contending that it was a holder in due course of the note and accordingly took free of any defenses that the Owens might have raised if they had been sued by the original payee, Universal.

In a lengthy opinion, the New Jersey Supreme Court refused to allow Unico the usual rights of a holder in due course. The precise doctrinal basis of the decision is not entirely clear. The court emphasized the close connection between Universal and Unico, which might have been the basis for a conclusion that Universal was merely the

1. 232 A.2d 405 (N.J. 1967).

agent of Unico. If so, then we would have a simple two-party scenario in which the holder in due course doctrine would be irrelevant. Alternatively, the facts about Unico's close involvement with the transaction might have been taken to preclude Unico from qualifying as a holder in due course on the grounds that it had notice of the Owens' potential defenses. In any event, it is clear that the court felt that Unico should not be entitled to holder in due course rights. The most straightforward reading of the case is that the court simply refused to apply the statute in the context of the consumer sales transaction involved in the case.

As the *Unico* court saw it, the problem was striking an appropriate balance between "the interest of the commercial community in the unrestricted negotiability of commercial paper" and "the interest of installment buyers . . . in the preservation of their normal remedy of withholding payment when . . . the seller fails to deliver as agreed."[2] The latter part of that balance seems, at least at first glance, easy to understand. The former part is not so obvious. What, one might well wonder, is the legitimate interest of commerce in "the unrestricted negotiability of commercial paper"? The court referred to the holder in due course doctrine as giving transferees "the tension-free rights considered necessary in a fast-moving, credit-extending commercial world,"[3] but never really considered what that commercial need might be.

The arrangement in *Unico* and other modern cases has little if any resemblance to the transactions that gave rise to the holder in due course rules. Unlike the scenarios in typical eighteenth- or early nineteenth-century cases, the Owens' note was not being used as a form of currency. Nor was the Owens' note a significant form of

2. *Id.*, at 411.
3. *Id.*, at 410.

investment for banks or other investors in the money market. Of course, Unico would have liked to be able to force the Owens to pay, but, standing alone, that hardly provides a justification for doing so. The basic problem in cases like *Unico* was simply that it did not make sense to apply to consumer sales a legal doctrine that was the product of a long-gone era.

The twentieth-century law books almost completely overlook the nature of this anachronism. What gave rise to the law of bills and notes in general, and negotiability in particular, was the circumstance that privately issued instruments circulated as a form of currency substitute. What kept that body of law alive in the nineteenth century was that mercantile notes and bills were still dealt with in the money market. But, by the time the legal profession became captivated by the idea of negotiability, it was no longer common for instruments to circulate as a form of currency, and the practice of discounting mercantile notes in the money market was dying out. So, when twentieth-century law books looked for examples of the settings in which negotiability was important, they drew upon the then-current financial practices. Indeed, one still finds such passages in law books. For example, it is commonly said that the reason for the holder in due course doctrine is that it is important that a bank be able to advance funds to a business, take an assignment of the business's right to payment for goods embodied in a negotiable note, and take that note free from defenses that the business's customer could have asserted against the business itself.[4] Even a moment's thought will reveal how implausible that explanation is. The form of finance depicted in common accounts of the holder in due course doctrine is, in essence, no different than secured lending

4. Lary Lawrence, An Introduction to Payment Systems 9–11 (1997) (describing utility of holder in due course doctrine in the setting of an equipment dealer selling to a business buyer on credit and then discounting the note to a finance company).

using a business's receivables as collateral. Receivables financing has become routine in the twentieth century, and no one has ever believed that it could survive only if the financing entity took its security interest in the receivables free from defenses that the account debtors could have raised against the borrower.[5] The bank simply assesses the likelihood that the receivables will prove to be uncollectable and makes an appropriate adjustment in its lending arrangement.

Were it not for the confusion about the origins of negotiability, the argument that the holder in due course concept is essential to financing could not have passed the straight face test. But, even with the misunderstanding of the history of negotiability, the holder in due course doctrine could not hold off attack in the setting of credit consumer sales. Many state courts reached decisions akin to *Unico,* refusing to apply the holder in due course rules to consumer credit sales, and some states abolished holder in due course rights in consumer credit sales by statute.[6] Finally, the Federal Trade Commission put the nail in the coffin by adopting a rule in 1971 making it a violation of federal law to use a negotiable instrument in a consumer credit transaction.[7]

5. One does sometimes encounter agreements in which an account debtor agrees not to assert against the financer defenses that it could have raised against the original debtor. *See* U.C.C. § 9-403. But receivables finance is routine even in the settings where such agreements are not used.

6. Fred H. Miller & Alvin C. Harrell, The Law of Modern Payment Systems 150–52 (2003).

7. Preservation of Buyers' Claims and Defenses in Consumer Installment Sales, 36 Fed. Reg. 1211 (Jan. 1971). The current version of the rule is in 16 C.F.R. § 433.

II. WHAT WAS REALLY WRONG WITH THE HOLDER IN DUE COURSE DOCTRINE?

Oddly, however, the movement to abolish the holder in due course doctrine never really answered the question of precisely what was wrong about the situation in cases such as *Unico*. Suppose that the Owens had paid cash in advance for the stereo and Universal's promise to deliver records over time. If Universal failed to perform, it is pretty obvious that the Owens could not go to the Federal Reserve Bank and say "Look, we used some of that currency you issued and it did not turn out well. Please give us some more."

Suppose that the Owens went to a store and wanted to buy a stereo, but the store said they would only sell for cash. Suppose that the Owens then went to a finance company and took out a personal loan, using the money that they borrowed from the finance company to pay for the stereo. Suppose that the stereo turned out to be completely defective. Obviously the Owens would have a breach of warranty action against the seller, but it is hard to see how they could refuse to repay the loan to the finance company on the grounds that the thing they bought with the proceeds of the loan was defective. Actually, however, there is at least one situation where they might have that right. Suppose that the seller and the finance company happened to be subsidiaries of the same holding company, though there was no other business connection between them, and the Owens knew nothing about their common ownership. Under the FTC rule, the seller has committed a violation of the rule if the seller accepts as payment the proceeds of a loan made by an entity that "is affiliated with the creditor by common control, contract, or business arrangement."[8]

8. 16 C.F.R. § 433.1(d).

The FTC rule takes the form of a disclosure rule, in that it provides that the seller must ensure that any credit contract used in the transaction include certain language. In reality, of course, the rule is one of substantive law, for the effect of the required notice is simply to preclude any holder from qualifying as a holder in due course. At the time that the rule was first promulgated, the Federal Trade Commission was criticized for making substantive law under the guise of a disclosure rule. There may, however, be some justification. Suppose we tried to write a disclosure rule. Would it work? Suppose that the rule required consumer credit sales contracts to state explicitly that the consumer would have to pay the seller's financer even if the goods or services were defective. If the consumer credit buyer really read and understood that disclosure, it might well be fair to allow the financer to obtain payment of the loan even if the goods were defective. On the other hand, one might think that, at least in any case where the consumer deals with the seller rather than the lender, the likelihood that the consumer will understand the situation is so low that no form of disclosure is likely to be adequate. In that case, there is something to be said for simply abolishing holder in due course rights.

The confusion about what was truly wrong with the holder in due course rule produced some surprising results. Suppose that the Owens had purchased their stereo from a store using a credit card. Suppose that the stereo was defective, and that the store refused to rectify the problem. Should the Owens be able to refuse to pay the bank that issued their credit card on the grounds that the store sold them defective goods? It is hard to see any compelling argument for the card user in that situation. If the buyer paid with cash, or by check, the consumer would be out the money and would have to pursue the seller. Why should the situation be any different if the consumer paid with a credit card? It is certainly not the case that the credit card user is likely to have been confused about the fact that he was borrowing from one entity and buying the stereo from a different entity. In fact, however, federal law generally gives the card user the right to refuse to pay the card issuer if the goods bought with the card turn out to be defective.[9]

Even more odd, if the consumer pays for the stereo with a debit card, she will have no such right. Why the difference? The answer is largely a matter of history. The chargeback right for the credit card system is set out in a federal statute adopted in the early 1970s as a response to concerns about consumer rights in credit transactions.[10] That was the tail end of the era in which the application of the holder in due course doctrine in consumer credit transactions had been one of the most contentious issues of commercial law. When Congress was considering the credit card bill, the fights over the holder in due course doctrine were very fresh in everyone's mind. It is clear from the legislative history that the chargeback right for credit card users was adopted because Congress felt that a person who buys goods on credit with a credit card should have the same right to refuse payment for defective goods as a person who gave a promissory note for the goods.[11] By contrast, by the time that Congress enacted the Electronic Funds Transfer Act[12] in 1978, concerns about the holder in due course doctrine seem to have passed into history. Although there was some discussion of the issue,[13] Congress did not feel the

9. 15 U.S.C. § 1666i; Barkley Clark & Barbara Clark, The Law of Bank Deposits, Collections and Credit Cards ¶ 15.07 (2009).

10. Pub. L. 93-495, § 170 (1974); 15 U.S.C. § 1666i.

11. S. Rep. No. 93-278, 93d Cong., 1st Sess. 9–11 (1973).

12. 15 U.S.C. §§ 1693–93r.

13. 2 National Commission on Electronic Fund Transfers, EFT in the United States 49–51 (1977).

need to adopt a reversibility right for electronic transfer analogous to the right established for credit card purchases.[14]

The fact that the consumer issue was basically a problem of anachronism also seems to have produced some amusing consequences. The traditional statement of the doctrine is that a holder in due course takes the instrument free from "claims and defenses." So, when the FTC set out to reverse that rule, it said that any holder takes the debt "subject to all claims and defenses which the debtor could assert against the seller."[15] By the time that the rule was written, few lawyers had any idea what was meant by the negotiable instruments concepts of "claims and defenses." To negotiable instruments mavens, that is fairly simple. A "claim" is an assertion of a property interest to an instrument. For example, if a nineteenth-century bank note was stolen from its owner and passed to an innocent party, the owner's "claim" of ownership could not be asserted against the holder. By contrast, a "defense" is a basis for resisting payment.

The "claims" aspect of the holder in due course doctrine was really not involved in the consumer credit dispute. But, the FTC rule said that any taker of a consumer credit sales note was subject to all "claims." Modern lawyers seeking to give some meaning to that phrase would naturally read it in a more colloquial sense, as meaning any right of action. So misunderstood, the effect of the FTC rule would be not simply that the debtor could resist payment to the holder of the note, but that the consumer might have an affirmative right of action to recover from the holder of the note damages that

14. It is also worth remembering that when EFTA was adopted in 1978, nothing akin to the current "debit card" system had developed. So, at that time, the fact that TILA has a reversibility right and EFTA does not may not have seemed all that anomalous. After all, reversibility is not an issue when cards are used simply for getting cash from an ATM machine.

15. 16 C.F.R. § 433.2.

the consumer might have been able to recover from the seller. There would, of course, be no basis for any such right aside from the FTC rule.[16] But, the FTC anti-holder in due course rule might well have been read to impose a different rule. Apparently concerned about the overkill potential, the FTC rule does say that the debtor may not recover from the holder any amount greater than the amount that the consumer has already paid.[17] Of course, were it not for confusion about the meaning of the negotiable instruments concept of "claim," the holder of the note would not be liable for any damages that the consumer might have been entitled to receive from the seller. Poetic justice perhaps?

III. CONTINUING APPLICATIONS OF THE HOLDER IN DUE COURSE DOCTRINE

After the FTC rule was adopted, the raging battles over the holder in due course rule seemed to have become a matter of purely historical interest. White and Summers, perhaps the leading commentators on commercial law, evidently thought so, remarking that:

> After the FTC rule, why study the holder-in-due-course doctrine? We are not certain of the answer to that question. Partly we retain it to explain the operation of the FTC rule, and partly we retain it because the holder-in-due-course doctrine still has viability in several important areas. It remains important in

16. Suppose that an employee assigns her right to wages. Suppose that the employee happens to have stolen money from the employer. The employer could use the theft as a counterclaim to avoid paying wages to the assignee, but obviously the assignee is not liable to the employer for damages from the employee's theft.
17. 16 C.F.R. § 433.2.

> commercial transactions where the consumer is not involved. Even in consumer transactions it remains important when one is speaking of checks and not consumer credit. Finally, we include this analysis of the holder-in-due-course because we suspect that knowledge of the doctrine, like knowledge of a variety of other legal doctrines of marginal utility such as the rule against perpetuities, will remain a badge of "the lawyer." So, for better or worse, here is the holder-in-due-course doctrine.[18]

But, rumors of the demise of the doctrine, like those of Mark Twain's death, proved greatly exaggerated.

One setting where the holder in due course doctrine continues to play a role involves investment schemes promoted at a time when tax law provides for accelerated depreciation. The promoter persuades people to invest in oil wells, movies, or whatever, with the explanation that in exchange for putting in a bit of cash, the investor will receive tax deductions worth even more than the amount invested. The investors sign a variety of documents, one of which is a promissory note payable to the order of the investment company. The promoter tells the investors not to worry, that note is just a formality. The investment company borrows most of the money needed for the project from a bank, and pledges the investors' notes as collateral. If the investment scheme collapses, the bank will seek to collect from the investors on their notes. The investors, of course, will respond with various forms of fraud allegations. The bank will assert that it qualifies as a holder in due course. Thus, though the

18. James J. White & Robert A. Summers, Handbook of the Law Under the Uniform Commercial Code 551 (2d. ed. 1980). The corresponding passage in current version of White and Summers recognizes more explicitly that the doctrine continues to have significant bite. James J. White & Robert A. Summers, Uniform Commercial Code 508 (5th ed. 2000).

investors may have a right of action against the promoter, that has no effect on the bank's rights to collect the note. The FTC rule is of no use to the investors, for the rule reaches only "any sale or lease of goods or services to consumers."

In one such case, *Centerre Bank v. Campbell*,[19] the court responded in a fashion that was routine in the early twentieth-century cases before the FTC rule—it twisted the rules in order to avoid applying the holder in due course doctrine. The bank could qualify as a holder in due course only if the instrument qualified as a negotiable instrument. The definition of negotiable instrument is, of course, highly technical and formalistic. The note involved in the *Centerre Bank* case provided for interest at a variable rate. Under the version of Article 3 then in effect, the court could and did rule that the note did not provide for payment of a "sum certain" and so was not a negotiable instrument.[20] Ironically, however, that particular avenue for dealing with the problem would not be available if the *Centerre Bank* case were to arise today. The 1990 revision of Article 3 provides that a variable interest rate note may qualify as a negotiable instrument.[21]

Consider another setting in which the holder in due course rules continue to be problematic. As has been noted, the classic twentieth-century holder in due course case was one in which a consumer who bought goods on credit was sued by a financial institution to which the credit seller had transferred a negotiable instrument. That is the setting where the case law, state statutes, and the FTC rule seem to have solved the problem. But, suppose that the credit buyer is not a

19. 744 S.W.2d 490 (Mo. Ct. App. 1988).

20. As Gilmore noted, hyper-technical interpretations of the requirements for an instrument to qualify as a negotiable instrument were the routine way that courts evaded the holder in due course doctrine in the late nineteenth and early twentieth centuries. Grant Gilmore, *Formalism and the Law of Negotiable Instruments*, 13 Creighton L. Rev. 441, 455–56 (1979).

21. U.C.C. § 3-112(b).

consumer buying a stereo or television, but a small business buying equipment on credit. A classic illustration of the problem is provided by a 1984 Ohio case, *Allis-Chalmers Credit Corp. v. Herbolt.*[22] In 1977, a farmer named Ross Herbolt went to his local farm equipment seller, Hillsboro Farmers Exchange, and agreed to buy an Allis-Chalmers combine for a total price of over $45,000. Hillsboro was willing to provide financing, so Herbolt signed a note payable to the order of Hillsboro for the credit price. Herbolt had many difficulties with the combine and raised breach of warranty contentions against both the seller, Hillsboro, and the manufacturer, Allis-Chalmers. After he failed to receive a satisfactory response from Hillsboro or the manufacturer, he ceased making his payments. Hillsboro, however, had transferred the note to Allis-Chalmers' finance company, Allis-Chalmers Credit Corp. The credit company contended that it was a holder in due course and as such was entitled to payment regardless of any alleged defects in the machine. Aside from the fact that the credit buyer was a farmer, the case is indistinguishable from any of the mid-twentieth-century consumer cases that led to decisions like *Unico*.

Herbolt, however, faced problems in seeking the same recourse that the Owens had found in their dispute about the stereo. Herbolt began with a fairly common sense argument. Whatever the precise basis of the *Unico* line of cases, it had by then become widely known as the "close connectedness" doctrine, that is, a holder who was closely connected to the seller would not be given holder in due course rights. So, if Allis-Chalmers Credit Corp. was "closely connected" to Allis-Chalmers, the manufacturer, then Herbolt would prevail. Herbolt's argument on this point amounted to something along the lines of "It's obvious that they're related." But, that was not

22. 479 N.E.2d 293 (Ohio Ct. App. 1984).

enough for the Ohio Court of Appeals which ruled that the "similarity in the names of a transferee and transferor" was not enough to even create an issue of fact about close connectedness.

Herbolt then sought to take advantage of an Ohio statute that abolished the holder in due course rule in "consumer transactions," defined as "a sale of goods to an individual . . . for purposes that are primarily personal, family, or household." That hardly seemed a plausible argument for Herbolt, since I dare say that few of us buy combines for household amusement. But, things were not so obvious to the Ohio court. Since the case had arisen on summary judgment, the precise issue was not whether the combine was a toy, but whether there was an issue of fact about that. The court's discussion of this point is priceless:

> The key issue in the cause sub judice is whether Herbolt's use of the combine was primarily for personal, family or household purposes. This court has thoroughly reviewed all of the evidentiary matter which was before the trial court on Allis-Chalmers Credit's motion for summary judgment including the affidavits, responses to interrogatories, admissions and pleadings, and it is simply impossible to determine whether Herbolt's use of the combine was for *primarily* personal or *primarily* commercial use. . . . Perhaps such information appeared obvious to the parties and the court below, but, as an appellate court, we must base our decision *solely* upon what is properly in the record before us and we cannot speculate as to Herbolt's occupation or his purpose for using the combine.[23]

23. *Id.*, at 303.

It is impossible to take this seriously.[24] Indeed, it is doubtful that one could find as silly an argument prevailing in a judicial opinion in any setting other than Article 3. That is the point. Judges instinctively recognize that the holder in due course doctrine frequently does not make sense in modern transactions. No matter what the statute says, they are not going to apply it. As the mid-twentieth-century commercial law scholar Fairfax Leary used to say, "A court legislated to against its will, will reach the same decision still."

IV. MORTGAGES AND THE HOLDER IN DUE COURSE DOCTRINE

Mortgage notes are another setting in which the holder in due course doctrine has continued to plague ordinary people. First, consider what we might call the "disorganized secondary mortgage market." A 1987 Virginia case, *Taylor v. Roeder*,[25] is illustrative. A property developer borrowed money from a mortgage company granting a mortgage on certain property. Later that property was sold to a buyer. The buyer's lawyer discovered the mortgage as part of the title search and requested information from the mortgage company about the outstanding balance. At the closing, the buyer's lawyer had a check sent to the mortgage company to pay off the loan. Unbeknownst to the buyer or the buyer's lawyer, that mortgage company no longer held the note. The mortgage company had sold the note and mortgage to a private investor, but did not bother to tell the buyer about that. Nor did the mortgage company pay over

24. As a dissenting judge noted, "Clearly one does not pay over $45,000 for a combine unless he is involved in commercial farming. . . . 'If it walks like a duck and quacks like a duck and swims like a duck, it's probably a duck.'" *Id.*, at 304.

25. 360 S.E.2d 191 (Va. 1987).

to the actual holder of the note the amount received from the buyer. When the holder of the note sued to foreclose the mortgage, the buyer was evidently quite surprised, for the buyer thought that mortgage had been paid off long ago. The holder of the note, however, responded that payment was just a defense, and that defense could not be asserted against a holder in due course.

From the perspective of old-style negotiable instruments law, the holder's argument made perfect sense. In former times, when instruments routinely circulated from party to party, no one would ever pay the obligation on a note unless the note was exhibited and surrendered for cancellation upon payment. But, in the modern world of mortgage financing, it is not at all surprising that people would not realize that possession of one of the thousands of pieces of paper signed at the closing of a real estate transaction has special mystical significance. In the *Taylor* case, the court responded in the usual fashion. Sensing that the holder in due course rules made no sense in this setting, the court sought a way out. As in *Centerre Bank*, the note involved in *Taylor* happened to have had a variable interest rate provision. That saved the day, for it enabled the court to rule that the note was not negotiable and therefore the property owner could raise the defense of payment.

The subsequent history of the problem involved in the *Centerre Bank* case provides a fine illustration of the oddities of modern negotiable instruments law. As noted above, when Article 3 was revised in 1990, it eliminated the possibility of avoiding the holder in due course rules for variable rate notes. But, at about the same time that the Article 3 revision project was wrapping up, the American Law Institute undertook a project to draft a Restatement of Mortgages. The Reporters for that project felt that it was bizarre that an owner of real estate would have to pay the mortgage debt twice as a consequence of fraud by the entity that received payment after selling the mortgage. In one draft of the Mortgages Restatement, the Reporters devised an imaginative argument to the effect that Article 3 could be interpreted to avoid requiring a double payment, even if the current holder of the note qualified as a holder in due course. Negotiable instruments mavens responded along the lines of "nice try, but no cigar." As a result, the Mortgages Restatement dropped the effort to protect the property owner in cases where the mortgage note qualified as a negotiable instrument.[26] But, the problem was kicked back to the U.C.C. sponsors. In 2002, further revisions to Article 3 were proposed that would have the effect of allowing the defense of payment, even against a holder in due course, unless the holder of the mortgage note has affirmatively taken steps to notify the mortgagor that the mortgage has been transferred and payments should be sent to the current holder.[27]

Note the irony. In cases such as *Taylor*, the courts avoided what was perceived to be an unjust result by the traditional technique of finding some way of saying that the note was not a negotiable instrument. The 1990 revision of Article 3 cut off that avenue by authorizing variable interest rates in negotiable instruments. The Mortgages Restatement tried unsuccessfully to solve the problem that had been exacerbated by the 1990 revision of Article 3. In response, a further revision of Article 3 was proposed, the effect of which would be to get us back to the place that courts, in cases such as *Taylor*, had reached by creative formalism.

Next, consider what we might call the "semi-organized secondary mortgage market." The mess left by the activities of Diamond Mortgage Corp. and Obie & Associates in the mid-1980s

26. Dale A. Whitman, *Reforming the Law: The Payment Rule as a Paradigm*, 1998 BYU L. Rev. 1169 (1998).

27. U.C.C. § 3-602(b), (d).

is illustrative.[28] Diamond originated mortgage loans, engaging in various forms of fraud against the borrowers who signed mortgages and notes, the simplest of which was failing to pay the borrower the money that was purportedly being lent. The mortgages and notes were typically transferred by Diamond to a related entity, Obie & Associates. The mortgages and notes were then sold to individual investors. Unlike modern securitized mortgage finance, the investors were purchasing individual mortgage loans rather than securities representing interests in pools of mortgage loans. When Diamond and Obie collapsed, the courts were left with cases presenting a stark choice. The borrowers were typically middle class homeowners defrauded by Diamond. The purchasers of the mortgage notes were typically middle class investors defrauded by Obie. No obvious villains here—other than, of course, the now insolvent Diamond and Obie.

Thus, the courts genuinely had to choose between two innocent victims. Traditional negotiable instruments theory would have made that a simple choice—the innocent purchaser of a negotiable instrument prevailed over an innocent maker because that was thought essential to the circulation of negotiable instruments. But, confronted with an actual choice involving actual innocent parties, the courts responded in a predictably messy fashion. In some of the cases, the court trotted out traditional negotiable instruments concepts to rule that the purchasers qualified as holders in due course and thus were not subject to the borrowers' assertions.[29] Yet in other, essentially identical, scenarios, the courts found some way to avoid

28. A detailed account of the Diamond-Obie fiasco can be found in Kurt Eggert, *Held Up in Due Course: Codification and the Victory of Form Over Intent in Negotiable Instrument Law*, 35 Creighton L. Rev. 363 (2002) and Kurt Eggert, *Held Up in Due Course: Predatory Lending, Securitization, and the Holder in Due Course Doctrine*, 35 Creighton L. Rev. 503 (2002).

29. Thomas v. State Mortgage, 439 N.W.2d 299 (Mich. Ct. App. 1989); Max v. Jordan, 463 N.W.2d 299 (Mich. Ct. App. 1990).

that conclusion. For example, in several cases where the originator had failed to satisfy disclosure obligation under the federal Truth in Lending Act (TILA), the courts ruled that the federal TILA trumped state negotiable instruments law.[30] That approach could well be fatal to purchasers in many such cases, given that it is often so easy to find some violation of the TILA requirements, as in one case where the originator had provided only one copy of a certain statement instead of the required two copies.[31]

Next, consider the modern organized market in which mortgages are securitized.[32] An enormous volume of mortgage-backed securities were issued in recent years, often in arrangements that, to put it mildly, raised questions about the legitimacy of the original transactions. When the real estate markets collapsed, many of the borrowers defaulted, wreaking havoc upon the securitized mortgage market.[33] It seems likely that in the coming years we will see many cases in which someone seeks to enforce such mortgages against the original borrowers, who will respond by contending that they were defrauded by the originators of the mortgages. The entities that claim to have the right to enforce the mortgages will contend that they qualify as holders in due course and so take free from the contentions that the borrowers could have raised against the originator.

We can anticipate that there will be some cases where the courts will simply rely on traditional concepts on negotiable instruments law. Consider, for example, *Midfirst Bank v. C.W. Haynes & Co.*[34]

30. Stone v. Mehlberg, 728 F. Supp. 1341 (W.D. Mich. 1989); Franck v. Bedenfield, 494 N.W.2d 840 (Mich. Ct. App. 1992).
31. Elsner v. Albrecht, 460 N.W.2d 232 (Mich. Ct. App. 1990).
32. The problems that negotiable instruments law presents to holders of securitized mortgages are discussed in Chapter 3.
33. For an overview, see Steven L. Schwarcz, *Understanding the Subprime Financial Crisis*, 60 S.C. L. Rev. 549 (2009), and the other articles in the Symposium issue of which that was the keynote address.
34. 893 F. Supp. 1304 (D. S.C. 1994).

In that case, the fraudster was not the originator, but the entity to which the originator transferred the loans. The fraudster adopted the simple technique of taking the loans but never getting around to paying the originator for them. When the scheme collapsed, the originator ended up in a fight with the parties to whom the loans had been transferred in the securitization. The transferee's claim of holder in due course status was met with a contention that the ancient rules of negotiable instruments should not be applied to the modern securitized mortgage market. The court responded that "if UCC Article Three should not apply in this case, and the holder in due course doctrine is no longer warranted, then any abolishment of that body of law should come from the legislature, not the court."[35] Of course, the *Midfirst Bank* case presented the issue in the easiest possible situation. It was not a case of a defrauded borrower facing a collection action. Rather it was a fight between two financial institutions, each of which claimed to have the right to enforce the mortgages.

What will happen when courts confront cases in which defrauded borrowers are told that they must pay up or lose their homes, even though they were the victims of egregious fraud? Kurt Eggert's vivid description of one of the Diamond-Obie cases gives a good picture of what such cases will look like:

> When George and Marjorie Mox signed loan documents for a $31,000 loan from the Diamond Mortgage Corporation, they probably did not realize that they were dealing with a dishonest lender engaging in a massive campaign of theft and fraud. Diamond never paid off any of the Moxes' senior loans as it had promised nor did it give the Moxes the balance of the proceeds.

35. 893 F. Supp. at 1312.

> Instead, Diamond sold the Moxes' loan and then went bankrupt, leaving thousands of victims who lost an estimated seventy-five million dollars. The Moxes were likely shocked to discover that they would still have to pay back the loan or face foreclosure, even though they did not receive a dime. A Michigan appellate court held that, because of the holder in due course doctrine, the Moxes had to pay back $31,000 that they had never received.[36]

Now imagine that courts are confronted with a massive number of such cases. It is one thing to trot out the old shibboleths of negotiable instruments law if the dispute is between two financial institutions, or if the case seems to present an isolated problem. It is quite a different thing to rely on hard-nosed negotiable instruments concepts when you have real human beings in front of you facing the prospect of financial ruin.

Actually, it is not at all difficult to predict what the case law will look like when more decisions appear. Some courts will say that that negotiability is the essential grease for the wheels of commerce, so the greater good requires sacrifice of the individuals in the case before them. Other courts will recognize the problem, but say that a solution must come from the legislature. But it seems likely that the most common judicial response will be the one that we have seen for over a century in various contexts. The courts will acknowledge that the holder in due course rules would cut off the borrowers' defenses, but they will find some way to refuse to apply those rules. As Grant Gilmore pointed out long ago, courts have ample experience with how to reach that result. They simply drop into a formalist mode and find that the particular note involved in the case does not happen to meet the requirements for qualification as a negotiable

36. Eggert, *supra* note 28, at 506.

instrument.[37] Given the complexity of the writings used in modern mortgage lending, that will not prove to be a difficult task. Common provisions in modern mortgage notes may well defeat negotiability.[38] Even if the time-honored technique of picayune application of the requirements for qualification as an Article 3 instrument is, for some reason, not available, the judge need only turn to the other side of the equation. Given the complexity of securitization practices, it will not be difficult for the judge to find that the entity bringing suit does not qualify as the holder of the physical note.[39] Alternatively, the judge can rely on the technique of finding that the entity seeking to enforce the mortgage had sufficient awareness of the dishonest practices of those involved in the origination of the loans to disqualify it as a holder in due course. All in all, it seems highly likely that the mortgage note case law of the early twenty-first century will look just like the consumer credit sales case law of the mid-twentieth century.

V. WHAT TO DO ABOUT THE REMAINING PROBLEMS CAUSED BY THE HOLDER IN DUE COURSE DOCTRINE

Thus in a variety of settings, the holder in due course continues to pose significant problems. What is a court to do in such settings?

37. Gilmore, *supra* note 20, at 441.

38. Ronald Mann, *Searching for Negotiability in Payment and Credit Systems*, 44 UCLA L. Rev. 951, 971–73 (1997); Dale A. Whitman, *How Negotiability Has Fouled Up the Secondary Mortgage Market, and What To Do About It*, 37 Pepp. L. Rev. 737 (2010).

39. The problem of determining who is entitled to foreclose a securitized mortgage is discussed in Chapter 3. For a recent example of picayune application of the Article 3 rules to defeat a foreclosure, see In re David A. Simpson, P.C., No. COA10-361, 2011 WL 1645699 (N.C. Ct. App. 2011) (indorsement to "Deutsche Bank Trust Company Americas as Trustee" did not sufficiently identify plaintiff, whose full name was "Deutsche Bank Trust Company Americas as Trustee for Residential Accredit Loans, Inc. Series 2006–QA6").

There is the disingenuous approach that we have seen in cases extending back over a century. But, would it not be better for courts to be open about what they have long been doing? That is, if it makes no sense to apply the holder in due course doctrine, just don't.

The usual answer would be that a judge cannot refuse to apply a statute simply because the result dictated by the statute does not seem just. But, in the case of Article 3, there is a little noticed way out of that conundrum. In the current revised version of Article 3, the text of the section stating the holder in due course rules now includes, in Section 3-302(g), the following statement: "This section is subject to any law limiting status as a holder in due course in particular classes of transactions."[40] As used in the U.C.C., the term "law" means not only statutes but also judicial decisions. So this statute represents a recognition and approval of the cases refusing to apply the statutory holder in due course rule. Moreover, though consumer cases were at the heart of the holder in due course dispute, the case law was not obviously limited to consumer transactions. Indeed, the comments to Section 3-302(g) make it clear that this subsection may apply to some business cases as well as consumer cases.[41] Section 3-302(g), however, makes no effort to describe what the "particular classes of transactions" are where the holder in due course doctrine should not be applied. This is a remarkable statute. Restated honestly, what it actually says to judges is "Apply this statute unless you think you shouldn't. We legislators leave it to you judges to figure out whether it does or does not make sense to apply the statute in any particular class of transactions."

40. U.C.C. § 3-302(g).

41. U.C.C. § 3-302 cmt 7 ("There is a large body of state statutory and case law restricting the use of the holder in due course doctrine in consumer transactions as well as some business transactions that raise similar issues. Subsection (g) subordinates Article 3 to that law and any other similar law that may evolve in the future.").

What is a judge who takes seriously the obligation of fidelity to legislative command to do when confronted with a case where a transferee asserts that it qualifies as a holder in due course and therefore takes an instrument free from defenses? The judge can no longer do either of the things that judges have routinely done in the past: (1) torture other provisions of the statute to avoid applying the holder in due course rules, or (2) apply the rules without regard to the justice of doing so, saying "the legislature told me to do this." The legislature has *not* said that the holder in due course rules should be applied mechanically. Quite the contrary, what the legislature has said is that it realizes that these rules often don't make sense and leaves it to judges to decide whether the rules should or should not be applied. Judges now have no choice. They are obligated to consider whether application of the holder in due course doctrine makes any sense in the particular setting of the case. Moreover, if they are to do so with any sense of integrity, they cannot simply wave their hands with a vague reference to the assumed long history showing the need for the holder in due course doctrine. The assumptions about history that provided the foundation for the late-nineteenth- and early twentieth-century law of holder in due course are simply false.

There may well be cases where application of the holder in due course doctrine continues to make sense. For example, in *A. I. Trade Finance, Inc. v. Laminaciones de Lasaca, S.A.*,[42] a Spanish company agreed to buy steel processing machinery from an American seller. The seller made arrangements for a trade finance company to provide financing for the transaction. The buyer signed a note initially payable to the seller, and the seller transferred the note to the finance company. When problems arose with the machinery, the buyer refused to make payment to the finance company. The court decided

42. 41 F.3d 830 (2d. Cir. 1994).

the case in a fairly conventional manner. It ruled that the finance company qualified as a holder in due course, that it was not disqualified from that status by virtue of any notice or lack of good faith, and that the *Unico* "close-connectedness" doctrine did not apply to a non-consumer transaction.

The *A. I. Trade Finance* case was governed by New York law, and New York has not yet adopted the 1990 revision of Article 3. Suppose, however, that the case arose under the revised version of Article 3, and suppose that the court took seriously the command of Section 3-302(g) that the court must itself consider whether it does or does not make sense to apply the holder in due course doctrine. It would not be at all surprising for the court to rule that, in the circumstances of the case, the buyer should not be able to raise the defense against the finance company. It was hardly a surprise to the buyer that the finance company was involved in the transaction. A representative of the finance company had attended the meetings at which the transaction between the buyer and seller was negotiated. Moreover, the buyer could hardly contend that the finance company was intimately aware of the details of the sellers business and the transaction. Indeed, the representative of the finance company apparently sat quietly through the negotiations between the buyer and the seller, because those negotiations were conducted in Spanish, a language that the finance company representative did not understand.[43] In such circumstances, it is hard to distinguish the case from one where the buyer borrowed money from the finance company and used that money to buy the equipment from the seller.

By contrast, it is hard to see any reason that the holder in due course doctrine should be applied in a case like *Allis Chalmers Credit*

43. 413 F.2d at 833.

Corp. v. Herbolt, which was indistinguishable from the classic scenario of consumer credit sales, except for the fact that the buyer was a farmer rather than a consumer. Nor does it seem justifiable to apply the holder in due course doctrine to problems in the modern securitized mortgage market. In these settings, it makes no sense for a court to make some vague reference to the assumed need for negotiability in business settings. As we have seen, the holder in due course doctrine evolved for private instruments that circulated as a form of currency. We have not seen transactions such as that for centuries.

To be sure, if courts were to take Section 3-302(g) seriously as a command to consider, in individual cases, whether it makes sense to apply the holder in due course doctrine, the law would hardly be certain. But, it is far from clear that this is a serious problem, or that there is really any choice. For more than a hundred years, courts have been refusing to apply the holder in due course doctrine in cases where it seemed to produce unjust results. They have simply done so through tortured reasoning about such matters as the requirements that an instrument must satisfy to qualify as a negotiable instrument. What would be wrong with being honest?

5

A Visit to the Museum of Negotiable Instruments Law

Some years ago, a well-known scholar of commercial law remarked that "what Article 3 really is is a museum of antiquities—a treasure house crammed full of ancient artifacts whose use and function have long since been forgotten."[1] That comment, however, has had little effect—perhaps because no one has documented the provocative assertion. Thus it may be worthwhile to step into the museum and examine how the some of the musty exhibits got there. The story we will find is, though sometimes amusing, hardly a source of pride for the profession. Lawyers all too often base arguments on assumptions about the purposes of law without considering the actual reasons that the rules found their way into the law books.

I. POSTDATING AND ANTEDATING

The impact of history on Article 3 is sometimes neither obvious nor particularly problematic. Consider Section 3-113, which provides that "An instrument may be antedated or postdated." That's nice.

1. Grant Gilmore, *Formalism and the Law of Negotiable Instruments*, 13 Creighton L. Rev. 441 (1979).

But why is there such a rule in the statute? There is nothing in the statute saying that an instrument may be written on white paper or yellow paper, but that is undoubtedly true. Why is antedating or postdating a matter of sufficient concern to warrant a place in the statute?[2] There is, after all, nothing dealing with antedating or postdating in other articles of the Code dealing with other forms of contracts, such as Article 2 on contracts for the sale of goods, Article 5 on letters of credit, or Article 9 on security agreements.

The answer is to be found in an unlikely seeming place: the Stamp Acts. Under the English Stamp Acts as in force in the early nineteenth century, the stamp tax was higher on an instrument payable at a future date than on a demand instrument.[3] Tax evasion is surely as certain as death, so it is not surprising that the drafters of the Stamp Act contemplated the possibility that parties might try to evade the stamp duty by writing an instrument as a demand instrument, but dating it at some future date. Thus, the Stamp Acts imposed fines on anyone doing so and provided that no such post-dated instrument could be received in evidence.[4] By the time that the English Bills of Exchange Act was adopted in 1882, that provision of

2. In unusual situations, some question might arise about the date of an instrument. For example, in Almich v. Downey, 48 N.W. 197 (Minn. 1891), the date written on a note was June 25, 1886, but the evidence indicated that the date was a mistake and that the note was actually made on June 25, 1887. The date mattered because the action was brought by a person who claimed status as a purchaser for value. If the date had been 1886, the plaintiff would not qualify as a holder in due course because he would have taken the note after maturity. The court sensibly concluded that evidence of the incorrect date could be admitted as in the case of any other contract. Even in such cases, it would not make any difference whether there was or was not anything in the statute about postdating or antedating.

3. 55 Geo. 3, c. 184, § 12 (1815). The act also exempted bank checks payable on demand from stamp duty.

4. *Id.*; John Barnard Byles, A Treatise on the law of Bills of Exchange 70 (8th ed. 1862). For representative cases refusing to permit the introduction into evidence of unstamped postdated instruments, see Serle v. Norton, 152 Eng. Rep. 131 (Exch. Pleas 1842); Field v. Woods, 112 Eng. Rep. 414 (K.B. 1836).

the Stamp Act had been repealed.[5] But, presumably out of an excess of caution, the Bills of Exchange Act explicitly provided that "a bill is not invalid by reason only that it is ante-dated or post-dated."[6] A version of that provision was included in the American Uniform Negotiable Instruments Law,[7] and was continued in the original version of U.C.C. Article 3.[8] The 1990 revision of Article 3 retains that rule in Section 3-113, though the comments attempt no explanation of why any such rule is needed.[9] It is simply a case of a rule remaining long after the need for it has passed into the mists of history.

II. SIGNATURES BY AGENTS

Consider the Article 3 rules on instruments signed by agents on behalf of their principals. The former version of Article 3 had a series

5. Mackenzie Chalmers, A Digest of the Law of Bills of Exchange 34 (5th ed. 1896) ("The Acts which for fiscal purposes prohibited the post-dating of cheques or bills payable on demand were repealed by the Stamp Act, 1870.") For representative post-repeal cases permitting actions on instruments despite stamp problems see Gatty v. Fry, L.R. 2 Exch. Div. 265 (Exch. Div. 1876); Royal Bank of Scotland v. Tottenham, [1894] 2 Q.B. 715 (A.C.).
6. Bills of Exchange Act, 45 & 46 Vict., Ch. 61 § 13(2) (1882).
7. The N.I.L. provision is worded in a way that gives a bit more guidance as to its purpose, providing that "The instrument is not invalid for the reason only that it is ante-dated or post-dated, provided this is not done for an illegal or fraudulent purpose." Uniform Negotiable Instruments Law § 12 (1896).
8. Former U.C.C. § 3–114(1) ("The negotiability of an instrument is not affected by the fact that it is undated, antedated or postdated.").
9. It is easy to see how one might fail to see the odd Stamp Act origins of the postdating rule. Even as fine a lawyer as Chancellor Kent missed the point. In the fifth edition of his *Commentaries*, he remarked that "In the late case in England of Serle v. Norton, 9 Meeson & Welsby, 309, a post-dated check was held altogether void. We may well demur to that decision." 3 James Kent, Commentaries on American Law 75 (5th ed. 1844). Parsons, who was presumably more familiar with the intricacies of bills and notes law, noted Kent's error, remarking that in *Serle*, "It was there held, that a post-dated check is altogether void, and cannot be received in evidence for any purpose. But this decision proceeded entirely upon a provision in the English Stamp Act. Chancellor Kent seems to have supposed that it was independent of any statutory provision." 1 Theophilus Parsons, A Treatise on the Law of Promissory Notes and Bills of Exchange 41–42 n.(b) (1863).

of elaborate rules that turned on the precise form of the signature.[10] The comments had a fairly extensive discussion of the difference between, for example, a signature of the form "Peter Pringle by Arthur Adams, Agent" and "Peter Pringle, Arthur Adams."[11] It is not easy for lawyers to see that none of this has anything to do with the really important question—whether the principal is bound. Former Article 3 was completely silent on that issue. The only point covered by the statute was whether the agent was personally liable.[12]

The 1990 revision of Article 3 does a better job of explaining what the corresponding section does and does not do. Revised Section 3-402 begins by stating that the question of whether the purported principal is bound is determined not by anything in Article 3, but by the general law of agency. The section goes on to simplify somewhat the provisions on the personal liability of an authorized agent who signs incautiously. The elaborate rules of the former section are replaced by a simple rule that the agent is not

10. Former U.C.C. § 3–403 provided that:

(1) A signature may be made by an agent or other representative, and his authority to make it may be established as in other cases of representation. No particular form of appointment is necessary to establish such authority.

(2) An authorized representative who signs his own name to an instrument: (a) is personally obligated if the instrument neither names the person represented nor shows that the representative signed in a representative capacity; (b) except as otherwise established between the immediate parties, is personally obligated if the instrument names the person represented but does not show that the representative signed in a representative capacity, or if the instrument does not name the person represented but does show that the representative signed in a representative capacity.

(3) Except as otherwise established the name of an organization preceded or followed by the name and office of an authorized individual is a signature made in a representative capacity. Section 3-402 of current law contains a somewhat simplified version of these rules.

11. Former U.C.C. § 3-403 cmt. 3.

12. See Former U.C.C. § 3-403 cmt. 1. Even on that question, former Section 3-403 dealt with only part of the story. If the agent was not authorized to act on behalf of the purported principal, then the agent was personally obligated as an unauthorized signer under former Section 3-404 regardless of the form of signature.

bound if the form of signature unambiguously shows that the signature was made on behalf of a principal. The new section also adds a provision intended to reject the result of many cases decided under the prior law that had held authorized agents liable for incautiously signing instruments that were obviously corporate checks.[13]

All this seems fine and sensible. But, consider what may at first seem an odd question. Why have any rule in Article 3 on signatures by representatives? The revised version does a better job than the former version of making clear that all questions of the liability of the principal are governed by general agency law rather than by any special negotiable instruments law rule. So, the only issue covered by the Article 3 rule is whether an authorized agent is also personally obligated. Subsection (b)(1) of revised Section 3-402 provides that if the form or signature shows unambiguously that the agent signed on behalf of the principal, then the agent is not personally obligated. Who would have thought otherwise? The last part of subsection (b)(2) provides that in the usual case of an action between the immediate parties to a note, if the form of signature is not entirely clear, then the issue is resolved by other evidence. Again, there is nothing special about Article 3 instruments here. The only part of this section that establishes any special rule for negotiable instruments is the provision in subsection (b)(2) that if the instrument does not clearly show that it is intended to bind only the principal, the agent is personally obligated if the action is brought by a holder in due course who took without notice that the representative was not to be liable.[14]

13. U.C.C. § 3-402(c).

14. The significance of that rule is further diminished by Section 3-402(c) which provides that in the case of checks that identify the principal, such as the routine case of a corporate check, the agent who signs as drawer is not personally obligated regardless of whether the agent adds words of agency to the signature.

Thus, the only point on which the Article 3 rule has anything to say that would not otherwise be obvious from general agency law is that if an instrument other than a check gets into the hands of a holder in due course, an authorized agent who signed incautiously is personally obligated. Whether it makes sense or not to have any special Article 3 rule, therefore, depends on whether it is or is not important or common for instruments by agents signed in a less than careful fashion to get into the hands of holders in due course. That focus is clear from most descriptions of the rule in secondary sources. For example, one of the leading U.C.C. sources gives an explanation of former Section 3-403 that strongly emphasizes the holder in due course concept, noting that

> When the agent fails to state both the name of the person represented, as well as the fact that the agent is signing in a representative capacity only, a purchaser of the instrument does not know whether the agent himself or only the principal is liable. Since the purchaser does not know precisely whose obligation he is purchasing, the free circulation of the instrument is impaired. Rather than requiring the purchaser to make an inquiry to determine whether the agent intended to be personally liable, subsection 3-403(2)(b) provides absolutely that the agent is liable.[15]

There is more than a bit of an air of unreality about such explanations. Suppose that an instrument has a form of signature that suggests that a person has signed as an agent, but is not clear on whether he has also incurred personal liability. Would the Article 3 rules have any effect on whether someone would be willing to give value for the instrument?

15. William D. Hawkland & Lary Lawrence, Article 3: Commercial Paper: Uniform Commercial Code Series § 3-403:4 (1999).

Suppose that I sign a note purportedly on behalf of my employer, Boston College. Imagine—though this is hard to do—that the payee of the note wishes to transfer it to someone else for value. The main thing that the hypothetical transferee would presumably care about is whether Boston College is liable on the note. Nothing in Article 3 provides any assistance. The assumed transferee must undertake an investigation to determine whether I did or did not have authority to bind Boston College. The Article 3 rules deal only with the question of whether I am personally liable. Would a potential transferee be willing to dispense with any investigation of Boston College's liability if he can be assured that I am personally liable? That seems very odd. Note that the Article 3 rules only matter if the form of the instrument is ambiguous on whether I did or did not incur personal liability. If the note is ambiguous, presumably the assumed transferee is just going to refuse to take it. After all, if the form of my signature is ambiguous, the transferee can be sure that I will put up a hard fight if the transferee attempts to hold me personally liable. Who, one wonders, is this transferee?

The picture that emerges from the cases casts further doubt on whether the rules on rights of holders in due course against representatives really make any difference. There have been about thirty published opinions involving revised Section 3-402.[16] As one might expect, the routine cases simply involve disputes among the original parties. Indeed, none of the revised Article 3 cases seem to involve the situation of a holder in due course who took the instrument without awareness of the representative status of the signer. As for cases under former law, the treatise quoted above cites ten cases for the proposition that an agent who signs incautiously is personally

16. The conclusion is based on a search performed in 2007 in the UCC-CS library on Westlaw for cases that cited Section 3-402.

liable to a holder in due course. Quite a few of the cases involve a corporate officer who signed a corporate check without clearly indicating that he had done so in a representative capacity.[17] Under former Section 3-403, such an officer could be liable to a subsequent transferee. Revised Section 3-402 rejects that result, on the sensible basis that "virtually all checks used today are in personalized form which identify the person on whose account the check is drawn. In this case, nobody is deceived into thinking that the person signing the check is meant to be liable."[18] Though some other of the cases do seem to involve parties who might have been genuine holders in due course,[19] the cases cited hardly bear out the suggestion that it is a routine matter for instruments signed by possible representatives to the transferred to unrelated parties.

Thus, it is hard to see that the Article 3 provision on signatures by agents adds anything except potential confusion. The only parts of the rule that would not be immediately obvious from general agency law are the parts dealing with the rights of holders in due

17. Carador v. Sana Travel Serv. Ltd, 700 F. Supp. 787 (S.D.N.Y. 1988); Am. Exch. Bank v. Cessna, 386 F. Supp. 494 (N.D. Okla. 1974); Fin. Assocs. v. Impact Mktg., Inc., 394 N.Y.S.2d 814 (N.Y. City Civ. Ct. 1977); Pollin v. Mindy Mfg. Co., 236 A.2d 542 (Pa. Super. Ct. 1967).
18. U.C.C. § 3-402, cmt. 3.
19. FDIC v. Galloway, 613 F. Supp. 1392 (D. Kan. 1985) (Corporate officer who signed various notes, some not clearly indicating that he did so as representative, personally liable to Federal Deposit Insurance Company as receiver of failed bank); Perez v. Janota, 246 N.E.2d 42 (Ill. App. Ct. 1969) (note signed by a corporate officer under the name of the corporation without any indication of representative status assigned by payee to someone else, in a transaction not otherwise described in the opinion); Gramatan Co. v. MBM, Inc., 5 UCC Rep. Serv. 865 (N.Y. Sup. Ct. 1968) (same). In the *Gramatan* case, however, the note was signed by a corporate officer twice, once under the name of the corporation. Accordingly, the plaintiff would presumably have lost even in an action by the payee itself, there being no plausible explanation of the double signature other than as a way of incurring personal liability.
Then there is the category one might describe as the reluctant holder in due course. In O.P. Ganjo, Inc. v. Tri-Urban Realty Co., 261 A.2d 722 (N.J. Super. Ct. Law Div. 1969), a subcontractor had fallen far behind in its obligations to its general contractor and persuaded the general to give it a bit more time by, among other things, indorsing over to the general a note that the subcontractor had nefariously obtained from another general contractor.

course. Yet, as is apparent from cases examined throughout this book, actual holders in due course are about as common as hens' teeth. Even if we assume that someone might be willing to give value in exchange for the transfer of an instrument, it is impossible to see how the Article 3 rules on agency could have any effect on the decision. It appears that we simply have rules that got into the law centuries ago and have not been given any serious thought since.

III. ALTERATION

In some situations, the historical anomalies that have produced rules in Article 3 are actually quite problematic. Section 3-407 provides that the obligation of a party to an instrument is discharged if the instrument is fraudulently altered, except that the instrument can be enforced if the plaintiff is a bank that paid the instrument, or a person who took it for value, in good faith, and without notice of the alteration. The reference to banks making payment or holders in due course merely coordinates the alteration discharge rule with the usual rules on holders in due course. So the heart of Section 3-407 is the rule that an alteration can discharge the debtor even in an action between the original parties. The puzzling thing is why we have such a statutory rule. If an instrument issued by a party is later altered, no one would suppose that the obligor was obligated for a greater amount, or on different terms, than he originally agreed. That is not the issue. Rather the point of Section 3-407 is that if someone commits the naughty act of trying to alter an instrument, then he loses the right to sue on the original terms. It is a bit like a child who tries to take two pieces of candy after being offered one. The parent might well say "All right, you tried to be greedy, so now you cannot have even the one piece of candy." Do we really need a statute to say that?

A review of the cases suggests that the statute does little good and a fair bit of harm. A search reveals about seventy-five cases since the revision of Article 3 in which an obligor raised the defense of alteration. In only two of those cases was the defense successful.[20] So, for the most part, the rule operates simply as an invitation to lawyers representing desperate debtors to advance arguments that realistically have no chance of success. To be honest, the two cases in which the defense was successful make little sense. In the first, *First National Bank v. Robertson*,[21] the obligors signed a note secured by a real estate mortgage. They had some other dealings with the bank in which they had granted the bank a security interest in certain personal property. At some point, the bank made a notation on the mortgage note indicating that it was also secured by the personal property. When the obligors defaulted and the bank tried to foreclose on the real estate mortgage, the obligors defended on the ground that the addition of the language about the personal property security was a fraudulent alteration. Surprisingly, they prevailed on that defense at trial, and the North Dakota Supreme Court

20. The conclusion is based on a search performed in 2007 in the UCC-CS library on Westlaw for cases that cited Section 3-407. There are also some cases allowing an alteration defense under statutes other than Article 3, which similarly provide that any fraudulent alteration of a written agreement discharges the obligation represented by the writing. *E.g.*, James Talcott, Inc. v. Dettelbach, 226 S.E.2d 309 (Ga. Ct. App. 1976); Haines Pipeline Const., Inc. v. Exline Gas Sys., Inc., 921 P.2d 955 (Okla. Civ. App. 1996). The *James Talcott* case was actually an action on a written guaranty rather than a negotiable instrument, so Section 3–407 did not actually apply, but the court affirmed a directed verdict for a guarantor on the grounds that the creditor's insertion of the name and address of the principal debtor on a guaranty was a "material alteration" that discharged the guarantor. Oddly, the court did not discuss the requirement of both Section 3-407 and the other Georgia statute, Ga. Code Ann. § 13–4-1, that the alteration be fraudulent as well as material. The case probably illustrates nothing other than the fact that courts often bend over backwards to allow guarantors off the hook. In some cases courts can avoid deciding whether an alteration was fraudulent, because the action is brought by a receiver of an insolvent bank that is granted the rights of a holder in due course by federal law. Amity Plumbing & Heating Supply Corp. v. J. A. L. Prop., Inc., 11 UCC Rep. Serv. 128 (N.Y. Sup. Ct. 1972).

21. 442 N.W.2d 430 (N.D. 1989).

upheld that judgment. The language of the security agreements quite clearly provided that the personal property was collateral for any other obligation, but the borrowers prevailed at trial on an argument that that provision had been waived by the parties' course of conduct. Then, having won on that rather strained argument, the obligors succeeded in the contention that adding the reference to the personal property security to the mortgage note amounted to a fraudulent alteration. The result was that instead of the issue being merely whether the mortgage note was also secured by the personal property, the obligors were relieved of any obligation to repay the mortgage note.

In the other case, *Stanfield v. White*,[22] there was enormous dispute between the parties to a rather informal lending arrangement by which one fellow assisted another in starting a small business. From the opinion it is apparent that the appellate court was quite skeptical of the plaintiff's contention that he was actually owed the principal amount of the note. The plaintiff had, however, won at trial, so it would have been hard for the appellate court to reverse on the facts. As it happened, however, there was evidence that at some point the plaintiff had made a notation on the note about an increase in the interest rate. That provided the basis—or excuse—for the appellate court to reverse, holding that the notation amounted to a fraudulent alteration.[23]

22. 535 So. 2d 753 (La. Ct. App. 1988).

23. The court even tipped its hand to indicate that the alteration issue was probably just a convenient way of reaching a result prompted by other factors, noting that "As is patently obvious, this factual scenario presents a number of complicated issues. However, because of the result we reach, the only issue with which we will deal is that of whether the note contains a fraudulent material alteration. We nevertheless have presented most of the factual detail because it illustrates the divergent factual position of each side and also illustrates the complex factual context in which the issue of the changed interest rate arose." *Id.*, at 755.

Aside from those two oddballs, all of the seventy-five cases display a rather predictable routine in which the debtor says that he should not have to pay because the creditor altered the instrument and the court rejects that argument. In quite a few of the cases, the asserted defense amounts to little more than a claim that the obligation was discharged because the loan officer doodled on the note. For example, in *Brown County Coop. Ass'n v. Rasmussen-King Cattle Co.*,[24] the court not surprisingly rejected the debtor's argument that "the addition of two telephone numbers, someone's initials, the words 'Rasmussen-King Cattle', and a fourteen-word longhand notation on the note constitute[d] a material and fraudulent alteration."[25] In many of the cases, the debtor points to some change on the face of the instrument that seems to fit within the listing in former Section 3-407(1) of the kinds of alterations that are "material." The court responds that Section 3-407 requires that the alteration be fraudulent, and that the alteration was not fraudulent even if it was material.[26]

24. 300 N.W.2d 265, 269 (S.D. 1980).

25. *Id.*, at 269. Similar cases include Johnson v. First Nat'l Bank, 238 S.E.2d 747, 748 (Ga. Ct. App. 1977) ("An officer of the bank testified that 'certain administrative information was added to the back of the forms marked "For Bank Use Only," but no changes have been made to the faces of the notes themselves.'"); Franco v. Bank of Forest Park, 165 S.E.2d 593, 597 (Ga. Ct. App. 1968) (marginal notations concerning credit life insurance); Citizens Bank of Windsor v. Landers, 570 S.W.2d 756, 763 (Mo. Ct. App. 1978) (writing expected payment dates of interest on demand note); Bank of New Mexico v. Rice, 429 P.2d 368, 372 (N.M. 1967) (amount due after partial payment written on note); Ellenville Nat'l Bank v. Nat Kagan Meat & Poultry, Inc., 385 N.Y.S.2d 197 (N.Y. App. Div. 1976) (creditor testified that the "markings on the note were for internal banking purposes only"); Gov't of Israel v. Am. Israel Basic Econ. Corp., 6 UCC Rep. Serv. 681 (N.Y. Sup. Ct. 1969) (jottings on note made in preparation for collection); Equitable Merch. Co. v. Papa, 5 UCC Rep. Serv. 1001 (N.Y. Sup. Ct. 1968) (computation of due date of note due 60 days after date).

26. Sterling Nat'l Bank & Trust Co. v. Fidelity Mortgage Investors, 510 F.2d 870, 875 (2d Cir. 1975); Bluffestone v. Abrahams, 607 P.2d 25, 28 (Ariz. Ct. App. 1979); Shinn v. First Nat'l Bank, 606 S.W.2d 154, 157 (Ark. Ct. App. 1980); Hutcheson v. Herron, 266 N.E.2d 449, 452 (Ill. App. Ct. 1970); Hughes v. Talley, 400 So. 2d 253 (La. Ct. App. 1981); Cent. State Bank v. Powar & Ferraioli Enters., 395 N.Y.S.2d 328 (N.Y. Sup. Ct. 1977); Mandel v. Sedrish, 3 UCC Rep. Serv. 524 (N.Y. Sup. Ct. 1966); Gaffin v. Heymann, 428 A.2d 1066, 1070 (R.I. 1981); Bank of Ripley v. Sadler, 671 S.W.2d 454, 458–59 (Tenn. 1984); Lawler v. FDIC,

There is another oddity. Currently, Section 3-407 says that for an alteration to discharge, it must be fraudulent. As has been noted, the cases are legion saying that a certain alteration might have been material, but it was not fraudulent. Why all the talk about materiality in the first place? Part of the answer lies in former Article 3, which provided for discharge if an alteration was made that was "both fraudulent and material" and laid out a detailed statutory rule on what sorts of alterations were material.[27] But why have a rule specifying what sort of changes are material if the issue is fraud, not materiality? After all, it is hornbook law that materiality is an element of a cause of action for fraud.

The puzzlement increases if one looks to the predecessor of Section 3-407. The analogous provisions of the N.I.L. provided that if an instrument was "materially altered" it could not be enforced by anyone other than a holder in due course. The statute then listed the things that counted as material alterations.[28] Unlike the U.C.C. provision, however, the N.I.L. provision did not require that the alteration be fraudulent as well as material. Accordingly, cases under the N.I.L. commonly allowed the defense of alteration even when the change was one that could only have been favorable to the debtor.[29]

538 S.W.2d 245, 247 (Tex. Civ. App. 1976). Sometimes the Section 3-407 argument just adds another level of silliness to an issue that is already fairly muddled by other parts of the Code, as in Wilcox Press, Inc. v. Beauty Fashion, Inc., 423 N.Y.S.2d 565 (N.Y. App. Div. 1980), where a check was cashed after the payee had crossed out the "tendered in full payment" legend placed on it by the drawer. The court first had to go through the gyrations necessary to reach the sensible conclusion that crossing out the legend had no effect, and then concluded on that basis that doing so was not a material alteration.

27. Former U.C.C. § 3-407(1) provided that: "Any alteration of an instrument is material which changes the contract of any party thereto in any respect, including any such change in (a) the number or relations of the parties; or (b) an incomplete instrument, by completing it otherwise than as authorized; or (c) the writing as signed, by adding to it or by removing any part of it."

28. N.I.L. §§ 124 & 125.

29. E.g., Johnson Farm Loan Co. v. McManigal, 288 F. 185 (8th Cir. 1923) (reduction of interest rate); Born v. Lafayette Auto Co., 139 N.E. 364, 368 (Ind. 1923) (reduction of interest rate).

There are several possible explanations for the curious results under the N.I.L. One is that slapping the wrist of the greedy child really is the basis of the rule. Some of the authorities so indicate. For example, Ogden's treatise states that "The reason that a material alteration of a negotiable instrument discharges a party who has not consented thereto is founded upon what is or was deemed to be a public policy, the law imposing this severe penalty as a safeguard against tampering with written instruments."[30] Or, it might be simply a formalistic rule, based on the notion that the writing has a certain magical significance that is lost by tampering.[31] In the old English decision in *Pigot's Case*,[32] that notion seems to have been decisive in the case of an action on a sealed deed,[33] and some of the early English

William Everett Britton, Handbook of the Law of Bills and Notes 1076 (1943) ("All material alterations, therefore, avoid the instrument whether they were made with fraudulent intent or without fraudulent intent, and whether they are beneficial or detrimental to the interests of prior parties."). Some commentators thought that the rule was unjust and should be changed to limit the discharge to cases of fraudulent alterations. James Matlock Ogden, The Law of Negotiable Instruments 349–50 (5th ed. 1947). For pre-N.I.L. cases similarly holding that non-fraudulent alterations discharged instruments, see Wood v. Steele, 73 U.S. 80 (1867); Draper v. Wood, 112 Mass. 315 (1873); Moore v. Hutchinson, 69 Mo. 429 (1879); Harsh v. Klepper, 28 Ohio St. 200 (1876). There was, however, authority for the proposition that although a fraudulent alteration would prevent recovery altogether, a non-fraudulent alteration would preclude an action on the instrument but not an action on the underlying debt. 2 Parsons, *supra* note 9, at 571–72; Joseph A. Joyce & Howard C. Joyce, A Treatise on the Law of Defenses in Actions on Commercial Paper §§ 270–71 (Daniel W. Crockett ed., 2nd ed. 1924).

30. Ogden, *supra* note 29, at 318–19.

31. Coburn v. Webb, 56 Ind. 96 (1877) ("We are of opinion that the insertion of the words indicated destroyed the note as to Coburn, because they changed, in a material matter, the legal effect of the note as signed by him . . . . This change of the note did not, perhaps, operate to the prejudice of Coburn. But that is not the legal criterion by which to determine whether an alteration of a note destroys it. The question is, is the note sued upon the same note, in legal effect, as that signed by Coburn?").

32. 77 Eng. Rep. 1177 (K.B. 1614).

33. *Id.*, at 1178 ("when any deed is altered in a point material, by the plaintiff himself, or by any stranger, without the privity of the obligee, be it by interlineation, addition, raising, or by drawing a pen through a line, or through the midst of any material word, that the deed thereby becomes void.").

cases involving bills of exchange seem to rest on the notion that the rule for bills should be the same as for sealed deeds.[34] But it seems odd to suppose that such a formalistic notion should have survived so long.[35]

There is, however, another possible explanation. The Stamp Act once again! Suppose that someone had issued a note or bill, duly complying with the law by paying the tax and placing the required stamp on the instrument. Then, when the instrument came due, the debtor was unable to repay. Suppose that the creditor was willing to extend the maturity of the loan. To do that, a new instrument should have been written, and a new stamp bought and placed on the new instrument. Why not save a few pence by just changing the due date on the original instrument? If that worked, it could have an impact on the revenue that the Stamp Act was supposed to generate. It is, therefore, hardly surprising that there were many cases holding that a creditor could not sue on an instrument that had been altered in such a fashion that a new stamp should have been used.[36]

34. Master v. Miller, 100 Eng. Rep. 1042, 1048 (K.B. 1791) (Ashhurst, J.) ("It seems admitted that, if this had been a deed, the alteration would have vitiated it. Now I cannot see any reason why the principle on which a deed would have been avoided, should not extend to the case of a bill of exchange.").

35. Corbin suggests that even in English law the rigor of the rule was tempered by the intervention of Equity. He firmly states that in modern law a non-fraudulent alteration to a written contract should not result in discharge. 6 ARTHUR LINTON CORBIN, CORBIN ON CONTRACTS § 1317 (1962).

36. Walton v. Hastings, 171 Eng. Rep. 71, 71–72 (K.B. 1815) (Ellenborough, J.) ("Upon the stamp laws I think the bill is void. . . . Here, when the date was altered, a new bill was drawn, and that could not be done without a new stamp."); Outhwaite v. Luntley, 171 Eng. Rep. 58 (K.B. 1815) (Ellenborough, J.) ("consent would not justify the alteration with a view to the stamp laws"); Bathe v. Taylor, 104 Eng. Rep. 900, 902 (K.B. 1812) (Le Blanc, J.) ("This question does not turn upon the assent of parties to the alteration of the bill, but upon the construction of a revenue law, according to which there can be no alteration of a stamped instrument after it has been used for one purpose. The question then is whether the bill so altered was not a new security, a substitution of a new contract in the place of that which the parties originally made?"); Knill v. Williams, 103 Eng. Rep. 839, 841 (K.B. 1809) (Grose, J.) ("The objection may press hard on the plaintiff, and one cannot but be sorry that the justice

In that setting, it made absolutely no difference whether the alteration was made in an effort to defraud the obligor. The person who cared about the alteration was the tax collector, not any of the parties to the instrument. So, if the sanction of invalidation of the instrument was to be effective, one could not limit it to cases of fraudulent alteration. Rather, any material alteration would have to result in discharge.

The Stamp Act was, of course, repealed long ago. But, the alteration rule curiously lives on. It took a particularly pernicious form in the English Bills of Exchange Act and the original Negotiable Instruments Law. Both statutes stated that any material alteration discharged the instrument, and both contained a list of the kinds of alterations that were "material." From the perspective of the Stamp Acts, that made perfect sense. An alteration was "material" if it represented the sort of change in the instrument that should have been documented by a new instrument with a new stamp.[37] But, once the Stamp Act was gone, it made little sense to have a rule allowing discharge for an alteration that was "material" in the old Stamp Act sense, if the alteration was not an effort to pull the wool over someone's eyes. It is a bit like saying that if at first the child says "No thanks, I don't want any candy," the parent should refuse to let her change her mind and take a piece. There might be some fairly

of the case as between these parties is defeated; but the very alteration shews that the parties themselves were not satisfied with the note in its original and general form . . . . This made it another note, and required a new stamp; for want of which it could not be received in evidence."). The nineteenth-century treatises make it quite clear that the Stamp Act was the principal impetus behind the rules on alteration. BYLES, *supra* note 4, at 298–304; JOSEPH CHITTY, A PRACTICAL TREATISE ON BILLS OF EXCHANGE 103 (7th Amer. ed. 1830). For example, the first sentence in the chapter on alteration in Bayley's treatise says "If a bill or note be altered in a material part (though by consent of all parties), after it has once issued, it requires a new stamp." JOHN BAYLEY, SUMMARY OF THE LAW OF BILLS OF EXCHANGE, CASH BILLS AND PROMISSORY NOTES 90 (2nd Amer. ed. 1836).

37. This presumably also explains why the provisions defining materiality are so odd. For example, former Section 3-407(1) said that an alteration was material if it "changes the contract of any party thereto in any respect." That seems to say that *any* change is material.

weak reason for doing that, but it does not even rise to the level of punishing the greedy child who tries to take two pieces.

By the time of the drafting of the U.C.C., the foolishness of the old cases allowing discharge for a non-fraudulent alteration had become apparent. Thus, the first draft of the ancestor of Section 3-407 provided that an alteration resulted in discharge only if the alteration was "both fraudulent and material."[38] The comments explain that "the requirement that the alteration be not only material but also fraudulent . . . is intended to get away from the rule, which Ames called a 'barbarous relic,' that beneficial alteration by a kind-hearted holder who wants to reduce the debt or give the obligor the benefit of a lower interest rate discharges the maker . . . ."[39] Unfortunately, no one seems to have noticed that once the change was made to limit the discharge to fraudulent alterations, there was no need to talk about material alterations. The statute could and should have been redrafted to refer simply to "fraudulent" alterations rather than to "fraudulent and material" alterations, and the provision specifying what sort of alterations were material should have been deleted. Those changes were made in the 1990 revision, but, as the review of post-1990 cases suggests, that change has had little effect. The silly litigation continues where a debtor tries to avoid payment of a debt by pointing out that the creditor wrote some words on the note. Probably the better course of action would have been simply to omit any mention of alteration in the statute. In those few cases where courts really want to punish the naughty child who tries to take two pieces of candy, one doubts that they would have all that much difficulty finding a way of doing so.

38. Tentative Draft No. 2—Article III § 96 (April 25, 1947), *reprinted in* 3 Uniform Commercial Code Drafts 101 (Elizabeth S. Kelly ed. 1984).

39. Notes and Comments to Tentative Draft No. 2—Article III § 96 (April 25, 1947), *reprinted in* 3 Uniform Commercial Code Drafts 222 (Elizabeth S. Kelly ed. 1984).

6

The Bank Always Loses

Thus far, we have seen various instances in which forgetting the past has produced some oddities and confusion, but these have largely been matters of risible detail. Ignorance of the origins of the law of checks and notes can, however, produce far more serious consequences. In this chapter we shall see how the entire orientation of the profession toward an important aspect of the law of the check collection system has been distorted by a failure to understand the odd history of this body of law.

Ask most lawyers what the rule is on disputes between banks and bank customers over check fraud and the answer is likely to be "the bank always wins." That will be uttered in a half mocking, half serious tone of voice. Partly the sentiment is that one has a vague recollection, either from a law school class or from a bar review course, that the rules were terribly complicated but that the outcome always seemed to be that the bank won. The remark may also reflect a somewhat schizophrenic attitude toward the law. We realize that the law often does reflect the interests of the powerful. Of course, if we ruled the world, things would be different. We don't, but by such snide remarks we can try to retain some sense of fidelity to our aspirations.

If asked where one got the sense that the rule is that "the bank always wins," most lawyers would probably not be able to point to any particular source. A few however, might say that they remember hearing something about the controversy at the time the U.C.C. was first drafted over the provisions on the check system. An even fewer might recollect a specific source—a 1952 article in which Frederick K. Beutel, then a well-known authority on the law of the check system, remarked:

> Article 4 on Bank Deposits and Collections is an unfair piece of class legislation maneuvered through the American Law Institute and the Commission on Uniform Laws by pressure groups favoring bankers over their customers. . . . This article is a deliberate sell-out of the American Law Institute and the Commission of Uniform Laws to the bank lobby in return for their support of the rest of the "Code." . . . Such a sell-out is beneath the dignity of both organizations and is a tremendous blow to their prestige as scientific bodies.[1]

Stirring stuff. But the lesson that most modern lawyers take from their recollections of this dispute is entirely wrong. The fundamental principle of the law on allocation of loss from unauthorized checks is that the bank always loses.

I. BASIC PRINCIPLE OF LOSS ALLOCATION

Consider two check fraud scenarios: forgery of the payee's indorsement on a genuine check and forgery of the drawer's signature on a bogus check. In the forged indorsement scenario, Drawer draws

1. Frederick K. Beutel, *The Proposed Uniform [?] Commercial Code Should Not be Adopted*, 61 Yale L.J. 334, 335, 362–63 (1952).

a genuine check to the order of Payee on its account with Payor Bank and sends it to Payee. Fraudster steals the check from Payee, forges Payee's indorsement, and deposits the check for collection at Depositary Bank. Depositary Bank forwards the check to Payor Bank, which pays it. Assuming no negligence, the loss rests with Depositary Bank.

The forged indorsement scenario can be diagrammed as follows:

Consider remedial routes that the Payee might pursue. Payee, as owner of the check, might bring a conversion action against Depositary Bank. Payee will prevail because Depositary Bank has "obtain[ed] payment with respect to the instrument for a person not entitled to enforce the instrument or receive payment."[2] Fraudster was not a person entitled to enforce, because the instrument was payable to Payee, not Fraudster, and Fraudster's indorsement in the name of Payee is ineffective.[3] The same result might also be reached by an alternative procedure. Since Payee has not received payment from Drawer, Drawer might have to make a second payment to

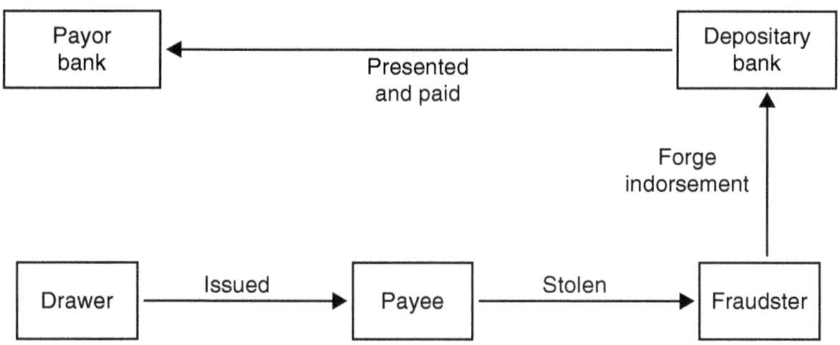

Figure 2 Forged Indorsement.

2. U.C.C. § 3-420(a).

3. U.C.C. Section 3–301 provides that "person entitled to enforce" means, generally, the "holder." U.C.C. Section 3-201(a) provides that "negotiation" is a transfer such that the transferee becomes the "holder," and U.C.C. Section 3-201(b) provides that negotiation of order paper requires indorsement by the holder.

Payee. Then, Drawer could recover from Payor Bank since Payor Bank did not make the payment to Payee that Drawer had directed. Payor Bank could then recover from Depositary Bank for breach of warranty.[4]

The result in this scenario might be explained by negligence law concepts. The notion would be that Depositary Bank was in the best position to have prevented the loss by demanding better identification from Fraudster. In fact, however, it is doubtful that negligence concepts are the basis of the loss allocation rule. The result in the

4. For detailed discussion of these remedial routes, all leading to the end result that the loss rests with the depositary bank, see JAMES J. WHITE & ROBERT S. SUMMERS, UNIFORM COMMERCIAL CODE § 15–3, at 553–555 (5th ed. 2000). Although English law is essentially the same as American law with respect to forgery of the drawer's signature, English law has taken a different approach to forged indorsements. In the early nineteenth century in England, checks were commonly made payable to bearer. By the middle of the nineteenth century, practice shifted, presumably as a result of changes in the applicable stamp duties, so that checks were commonly made payable to order, as in the United States. When checks were commonly made payable to bearer, payor banks faced no risk of liability if checks were stolen. Perhaps because bankers had become accustomed to facing no liability in paying checks, they were troubled by the prospect of liability for paying a check in order form if it turned out that the check had been stolen and the payee's indorsement had been forged. J. MILNES HOLDEN, THE HISTORY OF NEGOTIABLE INSTRUMENTS IN ENGLISH LAW 219–41 (1955). The 1853 Stamp Act eliminated that liability by providing that a payor bank was not liable for paying a check over a forged indorsement. 16 & 17 Vict., c. 59, § 19. The substance of that provision was subsequently included as Section 60 of the Bills of Exchange Act of 1882, 45 & 46 Vict., c. 61, § 60. Under the Bills of Exchange Act, a collecting bank, as distinguished from the payor bank, might have been liable for collecting a check bearing a forged indorsement, though the situation was somewhat different with respect to crossed checks. Bills of Exchange Act of 1882, 45 & 46 Vict., c. 61, § 82. The potential liability of collecting banks for handling checks bearing forged indorsements was, however, eliminated by the Cheques Act of 1957, 5 & 6 Eliz. 2, c. 36, § 4(1). Thus, as a starting place, English law appears to absolve banks from liability for handling checks bearing forged indorsements. That, however, is subject to a major qualification. Section 60 of the Bills of Exchange Act protects a payor bank only if it acts in good faith and in the ordinary course of business. Section 4(1) of the 1957 Cheques Act protects a collecting bank only if it acts in good faith and without negligence. BYLES ON BILLS OF EXCHANGE 298–334 (Frank R. Ryder & Antonio Bueno eds, 26th ed. 1988). Note also that the bank has the burden of proof on these issues. CHALMERS ON BILLS OF EXCHANGE 313 (David A. L. Smout ed., 13th ed. 1964). Thus, whether the actual results of English law and American law differ depends on how the English courts apply the requirements that the banks act in the ordinary course of business or without negligence. I lack sufficient familiarity with English case law to offer an opinion.

forged indorsement case is entirely consistent with ordinary concepts of property and conversion. Suppose that Fraudster had stolen a painting from Payee and sold it to Depositary Bank. Depositary Bank would be liable to Payee in conversion because Depositary Bank dealt with the painting for a person not its true owner. The liability of a person who takes stolen property from a thief is not in any sense based on negligence. Rather conversion liability rests simply on the fact that someone purchased property from a person who was not its true owner.

Now, consider the forged drawer's signature scenario. Fraudster steals a blank check from Drawer and makes it payable to himself or a confederate as Payee, forging Drawer's signature. Payee deposits the check for collection at Depositary Bank. Depositary Bank forwards the check to Payor Bank, which pays it. When Drawer discovers the loss, it complains to Payor Bank. Payor Bank is required to recredit Drawer's account, because Payor Bank has charged the account for the amount of an item that was not genuinely drawn by its customer.[5] The forged Drawer's signature scenario can be diagrammed as follows:

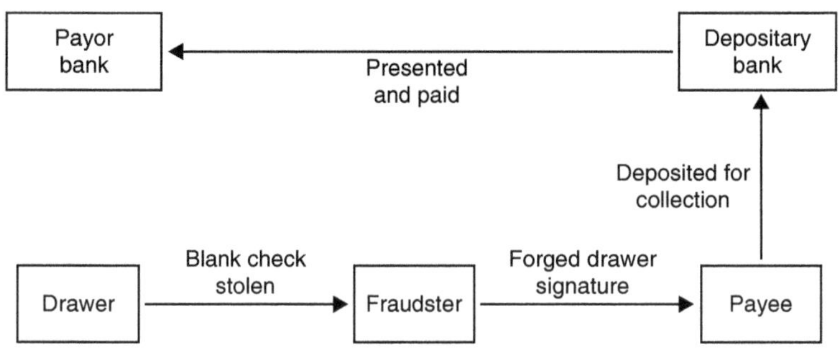

Figure 3 Forged Drawer's Signature.

5. White & Summers, *supra* note 4, § 18-3, at 657–665.

Now consider whether Payor Bank has any remedies. If Payor Bank seeks to pass the loss to Depositary Bank, its cause of action would be an action for restitution of money paid by mistake. Aside from the special rules for the check system, a bank that has paid out money to a person not entitled to receive it will prevail in a restitution action. For example, if a bank by mistake pays money to a person it erroneously believed was its customer, or erroneously overpays its actual customer, the bank is entitled to recover the money from the person who received the mistaken payment.[6] Yet in the setting of the check system, a Payor Bank that has paid a check bearing a forged drawer's signature will lose in an action against Depositary Bank, or any prior party. That is the significance of the eighteenth-century English case of *Price v. Neal*.[7] That case created an exception to the usual principle that money paid by mistake can be recovered. Under *Price v. Neal*, a drawee that pays a check on which the drawer's signature was forged cannot recover the money. Thus, in the case of forgery of the drawer's signature, the loss rests with the Payor Bank.[8]

The rationale for the rule of *Price v. Neal* has often been questioned. When the case was decided in the late eighteenth century, the result might have been justified by ordinary negligence concepts. The theory would be that the drawee, or payor bank, is expected to know the signature of the drawer. Therefore, the drawee was in the best position to have prevented the loss. As Lord Mansfield is reported to have said in the case itself, "It was incumbent upon the plaintiff, [the drawee] to be satisfied 'that the bill drawn upon him

6. Bank of Naperville v. Catalano, 408 N.E.2d 441, 446 (Ill. App. Ct. 1980); RESTATEMENT (THIRD) OF RESTITUTION AND UNJUST ENRICHMENT § 6 (Tentative Draft No. 1, 2001); 3 GEORGE E. PALMER, THE LAW OF RESTITUTION 174–181 (1978).

7. 97 Eng. Rep. 871 (K.B. 1762).

8. WHITE & SUMMERS, *supra* note 4, § 17-2, at 613–616.

was the drawer's hand,' before he accepted or paid it."[9] That rationale was noted, although with some skepticism, in the comments to former Article 3: "The traditional justification for the result is that the drawee is in a superior position to detect a forgery because he has the maker's signature and is expected to know and compare it."[10] Under modern conditions, however, that rationale is questionable and has frequently been doubted. Given the realities of modern high-volume check processing, it is quite unlikely that the payor bank will actually have any significant chance of detecting the forgery of the drawer's signature. Indeed, the weakness of this rationale has long been noted. Over a hundred years ago, James Barr Ames pointed out that "if the drawee's negligence were the test, he ought to be allowed to show, in a given case, that he was not negligent; for example, that the forgery was so skillfully executed as naturally to deceive him."[11] Writers on commercial law have frequently expressed skepticism about any negligence rationale for the rule.[12]

9. 97 Eng. Rep. at 872.

10. Former U.C.C. § 3-418 cmt. 1.

11. James Barr Ames, *The Doctrine of Price v. Neal*, 4 Harv. L. Rev. 297, 298 (1891). Ames also correctly notes that in other situations the negligence of a person who pays money by mistake is not a defense to an action in restitution to recover money paid by mistake. In a statement that says as much about changes in the profession's attitudes toward explanation of doctrine as it does about the issue itself, Ames concluded that "[t]he true principle, it is submitted, upon which cases like Price v. Neal are to be supported, is that far-reaching principle of natural justice, that as between two persons having equal equities, one of whom must suffer, the legal title shall prevail." *Id.*, 299.

12. William D. Hawkland & Lary Lawrence, Article 3: Commercial Paper, Uniform Commercial Code Series § 3-418:2 (1999) ("This rationale . . . does not withstand close scrutiny. The drawee bank may not always be able to detect a forgery, even by use of reasonable care. For instance, the forger may have obtained a facsimile of the drawer's signature, thereby making a perfect forgery."); White & Summers, *supra* note 4, § 17-2, at 614 ("If *Price v. Neal* is founded on the theory that any drawee who fails to discover a forged drawer's signature is negligent and thus is not entitled to recover payment, there should be an exception to that doctrine for those cases in which the signature is so cleverly forged that a banking employee using due care could not discover the forgery.").

The comments to former Article 3 suggested that "a less fictional rationalization is that it is highly desirable to end the transaction on an instrument when it is paid rather than reopen and upset a series of commercial transactions at a later date when the forgery is discovered."[13] That contention has fared no better with the commentators. As White and Summers observe, there is no apparent basis for permitting transactions to be reopened in forged indorsement cases yet precluding that result in cases of forgery of the drawer's signature.[14] Given the uniform and long-standing criticism of the rule of *Price v. Neal,* the surprising thing is that it has so long endured. It is, of course, possible that this is simply an example of inertia. But before abandoning any effort to justify the rule, it is worth giving the matter another thought.

In the forged indorsement scenario, the loss rests with the person who took the instrument from the Fraudster, that is, the Depositary Bank. The result seems consistent with basic negligence concepts and sound policy, in that the Depositary Bank is probably in the best position to have avoided the loss by exercising greater care before taking the instrument from the Fraudster. In the forged drawer signature scenario, the loss rests with the Payor Bank, under the rule of *Price v. Neal.* This seems rather peculiar since the Payor Bank did not deal with the Fraudster. Once one passes the unrealistic eighteenth-century concept that it was somehow negligent for the Payor Bank to fail to detect the forgery, one is left with little reason for placing the loss with the Payor Bank rather than with the person who took the instrument from the Fraudster. After all, the person who took

13. Former U.C.C. § 3-418 cmt. 1.

14. White & Summers, *supra* note 4, §17-2, at 612–616. *See also,* Lary Lawrence, An Introduction to Payment Systems 245 (1997) ("Why, you may ask, does the payor bank suffer the loss? I wish that I could give you some logical explanation. All of the proffered explanations appear to be more like rationalizations.").

the check from the Fraudster at least had some opportunity to prevent the loss by more careful dealing.

In considering whether the rule of *Price v. Neal* is in fact an anomaly, however, it is important to state the issue correctly. The issue is not who bears the loss if some party might be charged with negligence. Other provisions of the U.C.C. ensure that if someone's negligence substantially contributed to the forgery, that person will bear the loss.[15] Rather, the question is who bears the loss if there is no basis for concluding that anyone's negligence contributed to the loss. In other words, the issue is not who should bear the loss in most cases, but who should bear the loss in those cases where the loss was, as a practical matter, unpreventable. Once the issue is correctly framed, it seems doubtful that negligence principles help much in resolving it. The question is "who bears the risk of an unavoidable loss?" It is not much of an answer to say "the person in the best position to have avoided it."

Moreover, one must avoid the fallacy of confusing descriptions of the role that actors play in a particular transaction with descriptions of the parties themselves. There is no such thing as a "Payor Bank" or a "Depositary Bank." There are only banks. In some transactions, a given bank acts as payor of checks and in others the same bank acts as a depositary. The terms do not designate different actors or different categories of actors, but simply the role that the particular actor happens to have played in a particular transaction. There is a far more significant description of the banks, whether payor or depositary. They are the providers of the check payment system.

15. U.C.C. § 3-406(a) ("A person whose failure to exercise ordinary care substantially contributes to . . . the making of a forged signature on an instrument is precluded from asserting . . . the forgery against a person who, in good faith, pays the instruments or takes it for value or for collection."); U.C.C. § 3-405(b) (establishing "per se" negligence rule making employer responsible for fraudulent indorsements by responsible employees).

Thus, our diagrams of the forged drawer signature and forged indorsement scenarios might be recast as follows:

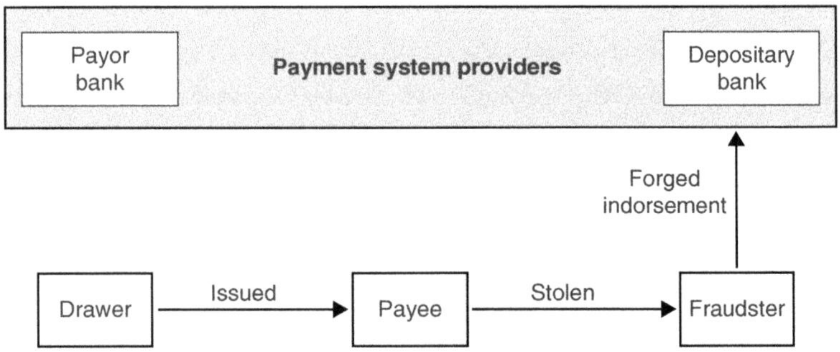

Figure 4 Forged Indorsement.

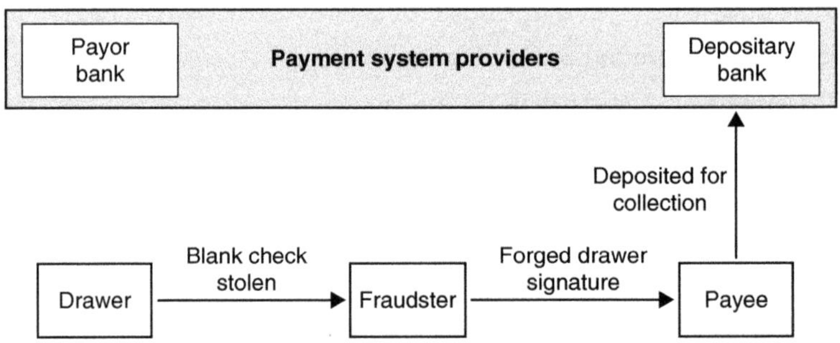

Figure 5 Forged Drawer's Signature.

Under the existing rules, the loss in the forged indorsement scenario is borne by the providers of the payment system. In the routine case, the scalawag forges the payee's indorsement and deposits the check in an account at a depositary bank. Either the payee brings a conversion action against the depositary bank, or the drawer proceeds against the payor bank and the payor bank passes the loss to the depositary back by a warranty action. As it happens, the depositary bank is the particular provider that bears the loss, but from the standpoint of overall allocation of the costs of forgery losses, that is a minor point.

Theoretically, it is possible that the loss from a forged indorsement might rest with someone other than a bank. Suppose that the fraudster who stole the check from the payee did not deposit the check in a bank account, but instead transferred it to someone else. That transferee would bear the loss.[16] But, as will be explored in detail in Chapter 7, checks are rarely if ever transferred from person to person outside the payment system. It is possible that the scalawag might obtain value for the check not by depositing it in an account at a bank, but by cashing it at a check cashing agency, grocery store, or the like.[17] If some such non-bank agency is willing to give money for the check, it is, in effect acting like a depositary bank. That entity has chosen to play the role of one of the providers of the payment system. So the slight possibility that the scalawag might cash the check at a grocery store or check cashing agency, rather than depositing it at a bank, is not really inconsistent with the principle that the loss from a forged indorsement rests with providers of the payment system.

Under the existing rules—specifically under the rule of *Price v. Neal*—the loss in the forgery of the drawer's signature scenario also rests with the providers of the payment system. In the forged drawer

16. The payee, as the true owner of the check, could bring a conversion action against the transferee. Alternatively, the payee might obtain a new payment from the drawer. The drawer could recover from the payor bank, which paid a check that was not properly payable. The payor bank could recover from the presenting bank for breach of the presentment warranty of good title. U.C.C. §§ 3-417(a)(1) & 4-208(a)(1). The presenting bank could pass the loss back to the depositary bank by actions for breach of the transfer warranty of good title. U.C.C. §§ 3-416(a)(1) & 4-207(a)(1). The depositary bank could further recover from the transferee for breach of transfer warranty. *Id.*

17. Actually, that scenario is rather unlikely, because most non-bank check cashing agencies will not cash "three party" checks.

signature scenario, the particular bank that bears the loss is the payor bank rather than the depositary bank. Again, however, the question of which bank bears the loss is a secondary point. The significant point is that the loss is borne by one of the providers of the payment system rather than by a user of the system.

Now, consider what would happen if the rule of *Price v. Neal* were reversed. The way that the U.C.C. currently expresses the rule of *Price v. Neal* is by saying that the only warranty concerning the drawer's signature that is given on presentment of an item is a warranty that the presenting bank has "no knowledge" of forgery of the drawer's signature. In the ordinary case, the presenting bank would have no way of knowing whether the drawer's signature was genuine, so the payor bank cannot recover for breach of warranty. The usual way that people have suggested that the rule of *Price v. Neal* be reversed would be to change the warranties given on presentment of an item from a warranty of "no knowledge" of forgery of the drawer's signature to a flat warranty that the drawer's signature was genuine. Thus, the payor bank could recover from the presenting bank for breach of warranty even though the presenting bank had no reason to suspect that the drawer's signature was forged. In turn, the presenting bank could recover from the depositary bank, and the depositary bank could recover from the payee, for breach of the transfer warranty of the genuineness of the drawer's signature. The result would be that the loss rests with the payee. From the standpoint of potential ability to prevent the loss, that seems to make sense. However, if the question is properly framed—not as a question of ability to prevent avoidable losses but as a matter of allocating the risk of unpreventable forgeries—it becomes far from clear that it makes sense to eliminate the *Price v. Neal* rule.

It is worth remembering that in the real world there is no such thing as a "drawer" or a "payee." There are only people who use the check system. Thus, our diagrams might be further recast as follows:

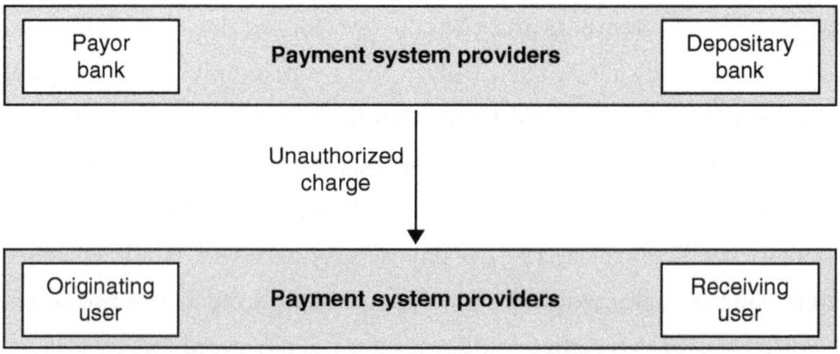

Figure 6 Unauthorized Charge in General.

Sometimes a user plays the role of drawer and sometimes the role of payee. But that is a matter of detail. The important distinction is that one is either a user of the payment system or a provider of the payment system. The combination of the rules of forged indorsements and forged drawers signatures produces a simple result. The providers of the payment system bear the risk of unavoidable loss. By contrast, if the rule of *Price v. Neal* were rejected, there would be no uniform general principle. Whether the loss would be borne by providers or users would depend on the quirk of where and how the fraudster intervened in the payment transaction. If the fraudster intervened at the originator end, the risk of unpreventable losses would be borne by a user. If the fraudster intervened at the beneficiary end, the risk of unpreventable losses would be borne by a provider.

Thus, correctly viewed, the rule of *Price v. Neal* is not at all anomalous. Quite the contrary, the rule of *Price v. Neal* is entirely consistent with the rules on forged indorsements. The anomalous situation is the one that would prevail if the rule of *Price v. Neal* were eliminated.

If such a change were made, the result would be that the burden of some unpreventable losses would not be borne by the providers of the payment system but by the users of the system.[18] Thus, the rules on forged indorsements and the rules on forged drawers' signatures together embody a very basic but important principle: The burden of unpreventable losses should rest with the providers of the payment system rather than with the users of the payment system. That result makes perfect sense. The providers are the ones who design whatever security systems are used by the payment system and decide whether increasing security would be cost effective. So long as the providers bear the risk of losses that could not have been preventable by a user's care, the providers will have the incentive to implement an appropriate level of security.

18. The *Price v. Neal* principle has been changed in a relatively minor respect by the most recent revisions of Articles 3 and 4. The change involves the recently developed practice of consumers agreeing with utility companies and others to whom they make routine payments that the payee, rather than drawer, can create an item that will be collected through the check system for the amount of the consumer's monthly bill. As applied to such an item, the ordinary rule of *Price v. Neal* that would impose the loss from unauthorized items on the payor bank can well be considered inappropriate. Instead, it seems appropriate to impose on the entity that created the item the burden of assuring itself that the customer has genuinely consented. That change is effected by the 2002 amendments to Articles 3 and 4. The amendments define a "remotely-created consumer item" as "an item drawn on a consumer account, which is not created by the payor bank and does not bear a handwritten signature purporting to be the signature of the drawer." U.C.C. § 3-103(a)(16). The revision then creates a warranty by the transferor or presenter that the item has been authorized by the consumer. U.C.C. §§ 3-416(a)(6), 3-417(a)(4), 4-207(a)(6), 4-208(a)(4). The effect of the changes is that a user does bear the risk of loss, but the limitation of the change to remotely created consumer items assures that that change applies only in cases where the user who will bear the risk of loss is the party that submitted the item for collection. So limited, the change does not significantly deviate from the basic principal that the providers of the payment system bear the risk of loss for unpreventable losses.

II. HISTORY OF CHECK COLLECTION LAW

So how does it happen that so many modern lawyers and law professors assume that the Code rule is that the bank always wins? Here, as in so many places, the answer may be found in history. This chapter began with the stirring quote from Frederick K. Beutel describing Article 4 of the U.C.C. as a "vicious piece of class legislation." What was he talking about?

Let us go back to the first half of the twentieth century and consider what the law of check collection looked like. In the first place, the law of negotiable instruments, as codified in the Uniform Negotiable Instruments Law, had very little to say about the process of collection of checks. Today, books on the law of payment systems have extensive discussion of the process of check collection. That was not the case in former times. For example, Britton's 1943 treatise—the pre-eminent pre-U.C.C. law book on negotiable instruments law—had no chapter on the check collection system and that topic does not even appear in the index.[19] That is not to say that check collection was an uncontroversial subject. Quite the contrary. Disputes about check collection law raged in the early part of the twentieth century, and those disputes are the origins of the modern assumption that the U.C.C. is profoundly pro-bank.

To understand the pre-U.C.C. disputes about the law of check collection, consider the facts of a once well-known case, the 1924 U.S. Supreme Court decision in *Federal Reserve Bank of Richmond v. Malloy*.[20] Malloy Brothers in Florida received a check drawn on the Lumber Bridge Bank of North Carolina. Malloy Brothers deposited

19. William Everett Britton, Handbook of the Law of Law of Bills and Notes (1943).

20. 264 U.S. 160 (1924). The fact that the U.S. Supreme Court used to hear cases about check collections is, in itself, a testament to how different the world was then.

the check in their account at the Perry Bank in Florida. The check was forwarded for collection through several intermediary banks until it reached the Federal Reserve Bank of Richmond. The Richmond FRB sent the check to the Lumber Bridge Bank for collection. The Lumber Bridge Bank, the payor bank, stamped the check paid and charged the amount of the check to the drawer's account. The Lumber Bridge Bank made payment to the presenting bank, the Richmond FRB, by delivering a bank draft drawn by the Lumber Bridge Bank on an account that it maintained at the Atlantic Banking & Trust Co. in Greensboro, North Carolina. The Richmond FRB sent that draft to the Atlantic Bank for payment, but was notified that the draft was being dishonored because the Lumber Bridge Bank did not have sufficient funds on deposit to cover it. The Richmond FRB again demanded payment from the Lumber Bridge Bank, but, after tiring of the Lumber Bridge Bank's excuses, the Richmond FRB gave up and returned the check unpaid through the various collecting banks to the payee, Malloy Brothers. Malloy Brothers brought suit against the Richmond FRB, contending that the Richmond FRB had acted improperly in its efforts to collect the check.

The case presented at least three issues in the law of check collections: whether the Richmond FRB should be regarded as an agent of the depositor or of the depositary bank, whether the Richmond FRB acted improperly in sending the check directly to the drawee rather than presenting it through another bank in the same location as the drawee, and whether the Richmond Bank acted improperly in accepting payment for the check in the form of a bank draft rather than cash. All of these were hotly disputed issues at the time.[21] But for our purposes, we need not delve into the complexities of these

21. For discussion of these and other issues in check collections, see John Edson Brady, The Law of Bank Checks 275–344 (1915); 2 Thomas B. Paton, Paton's Digest of Legal Opinions 1298–1303 (1942); Hal S. Scott, *The Risk Fixers*, 91 Harv. L. Rev. 737 (1978).

matters. Rather, we need only note how different the facts were from anything that we would encounter in check collections today.

Under modern methods of check collection, a problem of the sort involved in the *Malloy* case would not arise. In particular, there would be no need to examine separately the process of transmission of the check from the depositary bank to the payor bank and the process of transmission of the funds from the payor bank to the depositary bank. Each step in the forward collection process would be matched by a simultaneous settlement. That is, when a depositary bank forwards checks for collection to the next bank in the chain, the depositary bank will receive settlement for the checks in the form of a credit to an account maintained by the depositary bank with some other bank, typically a Federal Reserve Bank. So too, when the last collecting bank presents checks to the payor bank for payment, the presenting bank will receive a settlement for all of the checks presented for payment, typically by a credit in favor of the presenting bank and corresponding debit to the payor bank's account at a Federal Reserve Bank. In other words, at each stage in the process, the transmission of the check for collection and settlement for the check occur simultaneously. By contrast, in the *Malloy* case, the Lumber Bridge Bank had not made any settlement with the presenting bank, the Richmond FRB, at the time that the check was presented. Moreover, when the Lumber Bridge Bank did make what we would today call a settlement, it did so by sending the Richmond FRB a draft on another bank where the Lumber Bridge Bank purportedly had funds on deposit.

There is another significant difference between modern conditions and those that prevailed at the time of the *Malloy* case. The problem in *Malloy* was that the payor bank, the Lumber Bridge Bank, wasn't good for the money that it was obliged to pay on presentment of the check. The problem was not that the drawer had written a bad check, but that the bank itself was unable to pay good checks. The opinion does not reveal whether the Lumber Bridge Bank actually failed, but it was certainly close to that, inasmuch as it made payment for a check presented to it by giving a bank draft drawn on insufficient funds. Therein lies the heart of the problem of check collections in the nineteenth and early twentieth centuries. In past times, bank failure was an everyday occurrence, and that mattered to ordinary people. In the era before the evolution of modern methods of check collection, to say nothing of deposit insurance and comprehensive bank regulation, the failure of a bank would routinely have an impact on the process of check collection. As a commentator remarked in opening a 1930 article on questions of collection law, "The frequency of bank failures within the past decade has given rise to many cases . . . and the efforts of the courts to apply the rules to the rapidly changing methods of banks have increased the confusion."[22]

Let us note only one of these disputed issues. Suppose that in a scenario akin to the *Malloy* case, the payor bank fails to make payment of a check and the check is returned to the customer who deposited it. Suppose that it turns out that the presenting bank made some error in handling the check so that it was presented a day or so later than would ordinarily have been the case. Suppose further that if the check had been presented in a more timely fashion, it would have been paid. Now consider the dispute between the customer and the depositary bank. The customer would point out that if the presenting bank had acted in a more timely fashion, the problem would never have arisen, because the transaction would have been settled just before the calamity occurred. So, who bears the risk of

22. M.G. Wallace, *Comments on the Proposed Uniform Check Collection Code,* 16 Va. L. Rev. 792 (1930).

sloppy conduct by the presenting bank? Is it the customer or the customer's bank?

In the nineteenth and early twentieth centuries, the case law on this issue point was terribly messy. In simplified form, the dispute could be described as a choice between the "Massachusetts rule" and the "New York rule." Under the Massachusetts rule, all collecting banks would be regarded as agents, or sub-agents, of the depositor. Thus the depositary bank would not be liable to the depositor for the acts of another collecting bank, assuming that the depositary bank exercised due care in the selection of its collection agents. Under the New York rule, the depositor would succeed in his dispute with the depositary bank, on the theory that if the depositary bank wanted to carry out its functions by engaging other banks to act for it, it did so at its peril. As the Michigan Supreme Court put it, "as long as banks and bankers or other persons hold themselves out to collect such bills or drafts for a compensation, or their advantage, they ought to be governed by the same rules of law that apply to other persons, and, if they wish to avoid such responsibility, it is very easy for them to accept such business only upon a special agreement as to their duties and liabilities. Failing to do this, I think they must, in taking such bills or drafts, be responsible, as other business men are, for the misconduct of their selected agents at home or abroad."[23]

This presents only a simplified version of the dispute. Complexities abounded. For example, even in jurisdictions that generally held that a depositary bank was not liable to its customer for the negligence of other collecting banks, the customer might still prevail. Suppose that the dispute between the customer and the depositary bank was governed by the Massachusetts rule. If the customer

23. Simpson v. Waldby, 30 N.W. 199, 206 (Mich. 1886).

appointed the depositary bank as his agent for purposes of collection, then he would lose under the Massachusetts Rule. Suppose, however, that he could characterize his transaction with the depositary bank in an entirely different way: he did not ask the bank to try to collect the check for him as his agent, he sold it to the bank. If so, then what happened thereafter was the bank's problem not the customer's problem. As one might expect, the case law was terribly messy on the question whether a transaction between a customer and his bank was a sale or not. As one authority put it, "While a check is in circulation it is usually a simple matter to determine its ownership, but the moment it is deposited in a bank confusion reigns, and there is nothing, apparently, more elusive or difficult to locate than the title to a bank check in the process of collection."[24]

In 1928, a proposed statute known as the Bank Collection Code was issued by the American Bankers Association.[25] Unsurprisingly given its sponsorship, the statute adopted a pro-bank approach to essentially all of the issues that were so controversial in the cases. The basic principle of the Bank Collection Code was that any collecting bank was the agent of the depositor, not the agent of the depositary bank.[26] Thus the depositary bank was not liable for acts of other collecting banks. In other words, the Massachusetts rule prevailed. Similarly, the Bank Collection Code resolved all other disputed issues of check collections in favor of the bank. For example, the Bank Collection Code authorized any collecting bank to make direct presentment to the payor bank, reversing the result of the case law that had generally ruled that a collecting bank acted

24. Brady, *supra* note 21, at 310.
25. Wayne L. Townsend, *The Bank Collection Code of the American Bankers' Association*, 8 Tul. L. Rev. 21, 236 (1933).
26. *Id.*, at 24–34.

improperly if it sent a check directly to the payor bank.[27] Moreover, the Code explicitly authorized a presenting bank to accept a bank draft, rather than cash, as payment of a check presented to the payor bank.[28]

Although the American Bankers Association succeeded in quickly and quietly obtaining enactment of the Bank Collection Code in almost twenty states, adverse commentary soon emerged.[29] One of the leaders in the effort to stop the Bank Collection Code was Frederick K. Beutel. In 1935, he published an article in the Tulane Law Review harshly criticizing the Bank Collection Code.[30] Evidently the efforts of Beutel and others were successful and the Bank Collection Code was not passed by any other legislatures. Then, several decades after the Bank Collection Code controversy, the Uniform Commercial Code was proposed. Although a relatively pro-customer version of the materials on bank collections was included in early drafts, that approach came under attack by bankers. In response, the proponents of the U.C.C. relented and included in Article 4 provisions largely patterned on the Bank Collection Code.[31] Beutel apparently became livid. In 1952, he published his famous article in the *Yale Law Journal* excoriating the proposed Article 4.[32] In the years since, a citation to Beutel's piece has become almost mandatory in any article on the politics of the U.C.C.

27. *Id.*, at 46–48. The theory of the cases was that since the interests of the payor bank and payee were adverse, a bank could not be both the agent for collection and the bank that was to pay.
28. *Id.*, at 236–243.
29. *Id.*; Roscoe T. Steffen, *The Check Collection Muddle*, 10 Tul. L. Rev. 537 (1936); Robert T. Donley, *Some Problems in the Collection of Checks*, 38 W. Va. L. Q. 195 (1932).
30. Frederick K. Beutel, *The Proposed Uniform Bank Collections Act and the Possibility of Recodification of the Law on Negotiable Instruments*, 9 Tul. L. Rev. 378 (1935).
31. The story of Article 4 is told in detail in Allen R. Kamp, *Downtown Code: A History of the Uniform Commercial Code 1949–1954*, 49 Buff. L. Rev. 359 (2001).
32. Beutel, *supra* note 1, at 335, 362–63. Beutel's discussion of Article 4 was largely a reworking, with increased vitriol, of his *Tulane Law Review* article.

What is striking about the Beutel story is that in recent decades no one has actually stopped to think about the substance of Beutel's criticism. Beutel is commonly cited these days for the proposition that the U.C.C., or at least the provisions dealing with checks, were a sell-out to bankers.[33] In fact, Beutel's concern was far narrower. He was upset that Article 4 adopted the approach of the American Bankers Association Bank Collection Code to disputes between a depositor and a depositary bank concerning problems in the collection process.[34] That dispute has been essentially irrelevant for decades.[35]

The basic idea of the Bank Collection Code was that a depositary bank should not be liable to its depositor if collection of a check was not completed as a result of some defect in the performance of another collecting bank. In the early twentieth century that was a serious problem because uninsured bank failure was an everyday occurrence, and because settlement for check collections commonly took the form of remittance drafts. It was quite common that an

33. Perhaps because Beutel's words seem so stirring, or because the title of his article was broader than its actual scope, the fact that he was talking about a rather obscure set of issues within Article 4 is often overlooked. His article is commonly cited as asserting that the "sell-out" to the bankers involved the payment systems articles, Articles 3 and 4, as a whole. Edward L. Rubin, *The Code, The Consumer, and the Institutional Structure of the Common Law*, 75 Wash. U. L.Q. 11, 12 n.3 (1997); Mark E. Budnitz, *The Revision of U.C.C. Articles Three and Four: A Process Which Excluded Consumer Protection Requires Federal Action*, 43 Mercer L. Rev. 827, 831 n.28 (1992); James Stuart Bailey, *Allocation of Loss for Forged Checks Under Articles 3 and 4 of the U.C.C. and the Proposed Revisions Thereto*, 22 Pac. L.J. 1263, 1273 n.55 (1991). Indeed, the article is sometimes cited as asserting that the entire U.C.C. was a sell-out to bankers. Robert E. Scott, *The Politics of Article 9*, 80 Va. L. Rev. 1783, 1823 n. 116 (1994); Kevin M. Teevan, *A History of Legislative Reform of the Common Law of Contract*, 26 U. Tol. L. Rev. 35, 75 n.259 (1994).

34. To be sure, Beutel objected to various provisions in Article 4, such as the rules on stop payment and variation by agreement. The main subjects of his attack, however, were the rules on check collection.

35. Indeed, the issue was dead by the time that Beutel wrote in 1952, inasmuch as bank failure affecting check collections was by then a phenomenon of the past. Such is the fate of legal academics. We always fight battles from the past—the present book for example.

intermediary or payor bank would have finished processing the check on forward collection without having made a final settlement. So controversy raged over the question whether the depositor or the depositary bank took the risk of the insolvency of another bank involved in the collection process. That is no longer a live issue. Modern methods of check collection make the problem unlikely to arise. Even if it did, we have essentially universal deposit insurance. Moreover, under modern methods of dealing with the failure of a bank, the routine mechanism is that the governmental authority with responsibility for supervision of the failed bank arranges for a transfer of the ordinary business, including check collections, to some other bank.

If you look at modern treatments of the law of check collections, you find nothing about the disputes that were the main focus of this body of law in the early part of the twentieth century.[36] Section 4-201 says that all collecting banks are acting as agents or sub-agents of the depositor and Section 4-202 says that collecting banks need only exercise ordinary care in selecting other collecting banks. For Beutel,

36. The discussion of the Massachusetts rule and New York rule occupied a prominent place in the two editions of Brady on Bank Checks prepared by John Brady himself in 1915 and 1926. That discussion was dropped in the 1962 third edition, prepared by Henry Bailey. In his preface, Bailey noted that his revision "eliminate[ed] considerable obsolete material." The issue is not discussed in any modern treatise on negotiable instruments and checks. The last casebook that discussed the issue in any detail seems to have been Farnsworth's casebook on negotiable instruments, first published in 1968. As late as the fourth and final edition published in 1993, Farnsworth retained an extensive textual note on the history of bank collections in the era of widespread bank failure. E. Allan Farnsworth, Cases and Materials on Negotiable Instruments 186–91 (4th ed. 1993). The only modern casebook that contains any mention of the issue is Edward L. Rubin & Robert Cooter, The Payment System: Cases, Materials and Issues (2nd ed. 1994), which has a very brief discussion of the Massachusetts and New York rules, *id.* at 445–446. Given how prominent a role Dean Rubin has played in suggesting the illicit role of banks in the evolution of the U.C.C., see Edward L. Rubin, *Thinking Like a Lawyer, Acting Like a Lobbyist: Some Notes on the Process of Revising UCC Articles 3 and 4*, 26 Loy. L.A. L. Rev. 743 (1993), it is striking that even he presents the issue with only the laconic statement that "The UCC adopts the Massachusetts rule." Rubin & Cooter, The Payment System 446.

those would have been fighting words. But bank failure is no longer a matter of concern to the ordinary user of the check system. Accordingly, Section 4-201 and related provisions are presented in modern books as fairly routine matters. Certainly there is nothing of the sense one gets from earlier works that there are important policy issues in such matters as the choice between the Massachusetts rule and the New York rule.

With uninsured bank failure no longer a serious concern, there is really only one scenario where the status of collecting banks as agents makes any difference. Suppose that a check that has been processed for forward collection is not paid by the payor bank. Today, that would typically occur because the check was drawn on insufficient funds. Under current law, if that happens, then any settlements given for the item on forward collection can be revoked. Thus, the bounced check will be returned to the depositor. In the routine case, no one seems to think that is an unjust outcome. Certainly one will not find anyone today suggesting that the rather obscure rule of Section 4-201 amounts to a "sell-out" by the code sponsors to the greedy bankers. Indeed, if there is one word that comes to mind in presentations of such issues in the law of check collections it would be "boring."

III. THE COST OF CONFUSION

The usual misperception that the U.C.C. adopts a profoundly pro-bank orientation does, however, have consequences in modern law. Consider the approach that courts should take to agreements between banks and bank customers concerning checking accounts. As we have seen, it is a fundamental principle of payment systems law that banks, as providers of the payment system, bear the risk of unpreventable losses. Suppose that an agreement drafted by the bank has the effect of shifting some portion of that risk to the customers. If one looked at such an agreement as a reversal of basic principles of payment systems law, then one would be suspicious of the agreement. One the other hand, suppose that one had been misled by the "bank always wins" quip into thinking that the basic principle is that the bank is not liable for unauthorized payments, at least if the bank has not acted carelessly. From that orientation, an agreement disclaiming a bank's responsibility for unauthorized payment would not seem at all odd. Cases involving agreements governing facsimile signatures on checks reveal that this is not merely an academic issue.

Suppose that a checking account is maintained by a corporation or other organization. Given the volume of checks drawn by the organization, it will not be feasible for the organization to have manual signatures placed on its checks. Accordingly, the routine practice is that a check drawn by an organization will bear a facsimile signature. The customer and bank will enter into an agreement authorizing the bank to honor checks bearing the facsimile signature. A well-known case, *Jefferson Parish School Board v. First Commerce Corp.*,[37] raises issues about the enforceability of such agreement. In *Jefferson Parish*, a drawer sued the drawee bank for paying checks over a forgery of the drawer's signature. The action failed because the drawer had signed a resolution concerning the use of facsimile signatures. According to the resolution, the bank was authorized to honor any checks which bore or purported to bear the facsimile signature of the authorized parties "regardless of by whom or by what means the actual or purported facsimile signature or signatures thereon may have been affixed thereto, if such facsimile signature or signatures

37. 669 So. 2d 1298 (La. Ct. App. 1996).

resemble the facsimile specimens" on file with the bank.[38] The appellate court affirmed the grant of summary judgment in favor of the bank, on the grounds that the resolution was effective and, under the resolution, there was no factual issue concerning the bank's authority to charge the customer's account.

According to the *Jefferson Parish* opinion, the only issue posed was whether the resolution was effective. The court treated this issue under Section 4–103(a), which provides that "[t]he effect of the provisions of this Article may be varied by agreement, but the parties to the agreement cannot disclaim a bank's responsibility for its lack of good faith or failure to exercise ordinary care or limit the measure of damages for the lack or failure. However, the parties may determine by agreement the standards by which the bank's responsibility is to be measured if those standards are not manifestly unreasonable." Though the court did not discuss the point in any detail, its conclusion seems to have been that the agreement either did not disclaim the bank's responsibility to exercise ordinary care or that it established a standard of care which was not manifestly unreasonable, to wit, that the bank was authorized to pay checks that bore a signature which "resembled" the authorized signature.

The *Jefferson Parish* case does not state explicitly how the malefactor produced the checks. One can imagine two versions of the forged facsimile check scenario. In the first category are cases in which the malefactor produces the bogus checks by getting access to the machine used to produce genuine checks. In the second category are cases in which the malefactor produces bogus checks without getting access to the facsimile signature machine or any other facilities under the control of the actual drawer. Such cases are probably increasingly common because modern desktop publishing

38. *Id.*, at 1300.

technology makes it a fairly simple matter for a malefactor to produce a bogus check, using a genuine check as a model. It appears that *Jefferson Parish* was a case of the second sort, for the report indicates that the customer contended that the bank would be unable to produce any evidence of negligence on the drawer's part in safeguarding blank checks or the facsimile signature machine. Of course, under the court's view of the law, that fact made no difference. However the checks were produced, the bank was authorized by the resolution to honor them, so long as, in the language of the resolution, the signature "resembled" an authorized facsimile signature.

In some of the cases upholding agreements absolving the drawee bank from responsibility for paying a check bearing a facsimile, it seems clear from the facts that the wrongdoer produced the checks by unauthorized use of the actual facsimile machine.[39] In those insider fraud cases, the result would presumably be the same even if there were no resolution absolving the bank from liability for honoring checks bearing facsimile signatures. Section 3–406 provides that "[a] person whose failure to exercise ordinary care substantially contributes to . . . the making of a forged signature on an instrument is precluded from asserting . . . the forgery against a person who, in good faith, pays the instrument." In a forged facsimile signature case not involving a specific facsimile signature agreement, the drawer would contend that the signature was unauthorized. The drawee bank would respond that because the customer's own conduct had substantially contributed to the making of the unauthorized signature, the customer is precluded from denying the authenticity of the signature under the basic rule of Section 3–406. Indeed, the comments to

39. Arkwright Mutual Ins. Co. v. NationsBank, 212 F.3d 1224 (11th Cir. 2000); Wilmington Trust Co. v. Phoenix Steel Corp., 273 A.2d 266 (Del. 1971); Wall v. Hamilton County Bank, 276 So. 2d 182 (Fla. Dist. Ct. App. 1973); Phoenix Die Casting Co. v. Mfgs. & Traders Trust Co., 289 N.Y.S.2d 254 (N.Y. App. Div. 1968) (applying pre-Code law).

Section 3–406 refer to a drawer's failure to exercise care with a signature stamp as a prime example of negligent conduct.[40] Thus, the effect of an agreement that the drawee bank is permitted to pay checks bearing facsimile signatures is only to resolve, in advance, what would be a fairly straightforward issue of negligence.

Thus, the significant cases are the outsider fraud cases such as *Jefferson Parish,* in which the wrongdoing is not attributable to any lapse of security within the organization of the drawer. Suppose we take seriously the approach taken in *Jefferson Parish.* The only limit on the enforceability of an agreement shifting to the customer the loss resulting from payment over a forgery of a drawer's facsimile signature would be the Section 4-103 rule on variation by agreement. That rule prohibits only disclaimers of the statutory obligations of good faith or ordinary care.

It is far from clear that this provision imposes any significant limits on facsimile signature agreements. The issue is not who bears the loss of unauthorized signatures where someone was at fault. Rather the issue is who bears the loss if no one was at fault, that is, in cases where the loss could not have been prevented by ordinary check processing operations. It is also far from clear whether the requirement of good faith imposes any significant limitations on facsimile signature agreements. The Code defines "good faith" as "honesty in fact and the observance of reasonable commercial standards of fair dealing."[41] It would be hard to argue that an agreement in

40. U.C.C. § 3-406 cmt. 3. The comments to the predecessor section were even clearer on the point, noting that "[t]he most obvious case" of negligence triggering the preclusion rule "is that of the drawer who makes use of a signature stamp or other automatic signing device and is negligent in looking after it." Former U.C.C. § 3-406 cmt. 7.

41. U.C.C. § 1-201(20). Prior to the 1990 revisions, the more limited definition of "good faith" as only "honesty in fact" applied to Articles 3 and 4. The 1990 revision made the more expansive definition of "honesty in fact and the observance of reasonable commercial standards of fair dealing' applicable in Articles 3 and 4. U.C.C. §§ 3-103(a)(6), 4-104(c) (1990). The most recent revision of Article 1 changes the general definition in Article 1 to include

which a bank disclaims responsibility for forged facsimile signatures violated the requirement of "honesty in fact." The second aspect of the good faith definition—observance of reasonable commercial standards of fair dealing—does not impose a general requirement of conduct consistent with ordinary practice of others in a similar situation.[42] The requirement is not a general requirement of "observance of reasonable commercial standards," it is only a requirement of observance of reasonable commercial standards "of fair dealing."[43] Standing alone, it is not immediately obvious that a disclaimer of liability is a violation of concepts of "fair dealing." Indeed, the many cases upholding exculpatory provisions in facsimile signature agreements seem to suggest that no substantial issue of "fair dealing" is presented.

Jefferson Parish and similar cases involve only facsimile signature agreements, and those agreements absolved the bank of responsibility only if the forged check bore a facsimile signature that appeared to be genuine. But the approach illustrated by the *Jefferson Parish* case may have far more serious consequences. Taken seriously, *Jefferson Parish* would seem to lead to the conclusion that a facsimile signature agreement would be enforceable even if the forgery were crude. Nor is it obvious why the *Jefferson Parish* approach would be limited to facsimile signatures. Taken seriously, the *Jefferson Parish* approach would seem to lead to the result that an agreement could say that a bank can charge a customer's account for any check that appeared to have been drawn on the account, even though the customer had absolutely no involvement with the creation of that check.

the broader concept; hence the specific definitions in Articles 3 and 4 have been dropped as unnecessary.

42. U.C.C § 3-103 cmt. 4.

43. U.C.C. §§ 1-201(20), 3-103 cmt. 4.

To see the steps in that argument, let us begin with the usual form of facsimile signature agreement. Such agreements commonly absolve the bank of responsibility for paying a check bearing a forgery of an authorized facsimile signature, so long as the signature on the check "resembles" a genuine signature on file with the bank.[44] Suppose that the agreement did not require that the signature "resemble" an authorized signature. Would it still be enforceable? If one assumes that it is the routine practice of payor banks to conduct a manual examination of checks before making final payment, the requirement of "resemblance" might make some sense. If a bogus facsimile signature were so poorly produced that any ordinary physical examination would have raised questions about its authenticity, and the routine practice of payor banks were to conduct such an examination, then it might make sense to say that a bank's payment of a check bearing an easily detectable forgery of the facsimile signature was not a payment made in the exercise of ordinary care. Yet it is by now widely known that payor banks do not regularly conduct a manual examination of checks in the payment process. Some degree of sampling may be routine, but it is certainly not the case that all checks are subject to individual examination. Thus, it is hard to see why it should be essential to the effectiveness of a facsimile signature agreement that it be limited to cases in which the signature "resembles" the genuine facsimile signature.

If one concludes that the common limitation of "resemblance" in facsimile signature agreements is not necessary to effectiveness of the agreement, what of the requirement that the check bear any facsimile signature at all? Suppose a facsimile signature agreement provided that the bank could pay any check, whether signed or not,

44. Perini Corp. v. First Nat'l Bank, 553 F.2d 398, 400 (5th Cir. 1977); Cumis Ins. Soc'y, Inc. v. Girard Bank, 522 F. Supp. 414, 416 (E.D. Penn. 1981); Jefferson Parish Sch. Bd. v. First Commerce Corp., 669 So. 2d 1298, 1300 (La. Ct. App. 1996).

provided that the MICR encoding correctly identified the payor bank and the account.[45] Could one say that the agreement violated Section 4–103(a) by disclaiming the bank's obligation of good faith and ordinary care? It is a bit hard to see why. To be sure, the payor bank could still conduct whatever degree of random manual examination it felt prudent. If the bank examined the check, found no signature, but went ahead and paid the check, it would not be difficult to conclude that that bank had failed to exercise ordinary care. But that is a trivial case.[46] The real issue is whether the bank would be liable in the case where no manual examination of the particular check was conducted. If the agreement provides that the bank is not liable in such a case, and if the bank's conduct in paying that check did not "vary unreasonably from general banking usage,"[47] it is not immediately obvious why the fact that the particular check lacked a signature should make any difference.

Let us assume that the enforceability of a facsimile signature agreement does not depend on the inclusion of the common provision that the item bears a signature that "resembles" an authorized facsimile signature. The next question is whether the use of a facsimile signature makes any difference. Suppose that the customer has not authorized facsimile signatures. Consider, for example, an ordinary personal checking account. Suppose that the agreement provided that the bank would not be liable for paying any check bearing the correct MICR code for the payor bank and the account.

45. The MICR line on a check routinely identifies the amount of the check as well as the payor bank and the account; however, it has long been clear that a check can be properly payable even though the account balance is not sufficient to cover the amount of the check. U.C.C. § 4-401(a).

46. Moreover, the agreement could easily be modified to deal with this case. The agreement could provide that the bank will not be liable for paying any check with the correct MICR encoding, unless the check was paid as a result of a failure by the bank to exercise ordinary care.

47. U.C.C. § 3-103(a)(9).

Would that agreement be enforceable, at least in the case in which the particular check was one of the many that was not subject to random manual inspection under the bank's customary practice? If we take the approach of the facsimile check cases seriously, it is hard to see why the agreement should not be enforceable. If the only limitation on the enforceability of facsimile signature agreements is the weak requirement of Section 4–103 that an agreement cannot disclaim responsibility for a lack of good faith and ordinary care, then it is hard to see why the principle of those cases is not equally applicable to cases that do not involve facsimile signatures, or to cases where the check in question bears no signature at all.

Jefferson Parish also raises concerns about the rules on responsibility for checks bearing forged indorsements, as opposed to forgeries of the drawer's signature. Suppose that the drawer draws a genuine check and sends it off toward the payee, but the check is stolen before arriving at the payee. The scalawag forges the indorsement of the payee and initiates collection. Since the payee is not a customer of the payor bank, that bank would have no way of knowing anything about the signature of the payee, and so would be expected to pay the check. Under Section 4–401, the payor bank can charge the item to the customer's account if it is "properly payable." It is perfectly well settled that if a payor bank pays a check bearing a forged indorsement, it has not followed its customer's instruction, and the amount of the check cannot be charged to the customer's account.[48] Suppose, however, that an agreement between a payor bank and its customer were to provide that the bank would not be liable for payment of checks bearing forged indorsement. Would such an agreement be enforceable? If, as the

48. U.C.C. § 4-401 cmt. 1 ("An item containing a forged drawer's signature or forged indorsement is not properly payable."); White & Summers, *supra* note 4, § 15-3, at 553–555.

Jefferson Parish case suggests, the only limit on agreements between banks and their customers is the Section 4–103 principle that an agreement cannot disclaim the obligations of good faith and ordinary care, it is hard to see why such an agreement would be not be enforceable. After all, there is at least some theoretical basis, however weak it may be in modern practice, for a contention that a payor bank should be aware of its own customer's signature. By contrast, there is no way that a payor bank could determine whether the indorsement of a payee of its customer's check was forged.

One hopes that the approach of facsimile signature cases such as *Jefferson Parish* would not be extended to the point of permitting payor banks to completely reverse the basic rules of check fraud. Perhaps courts would find a way of reading Section 4-103 or the obligation of good faith in a fashion that would preclude a payor bank from fundamentally shifting the basic rules on liability for improper payments. But it is not easy to see how courts would reach that result given the way that the Article 4 provision on variation by agreement is drafted.

The heart of the problem may be that Article 4 deals both with the responsibilities of payor banks and collecting banks. Article 4 had its origins in disputes over the liabilities of banks acting as collecting banks, such as the controversy over the ABA Bank Collection Code described earlier in this chapter. In that setting, the wording of Section 4-103 makes some sense, because the basic obligation of a collecting bank is to exercise ordinary care in processing a check for forward collection. But, the question in cases like *Jefferson Parish* is very different. The question is not the obligation of a collecting bank, but whether a payor bank may charge its customer's account for a payment that was not completed in accordance with the customer's actual instructions. The provisions dealing with the responsibilities of a payor bank to its customer seem to have been added to Article 4 without careful thought about the differences between the roles of a payor banks and collecting banks. The obligation of a payor bank to its customer has nothing to do with negligence. The payor bank owes money to its customer. It can reduce that liability only if it makes a payment that was actually directed by the customer. Suppose that Creditor owes money to Debtor, and Debtor sues to collect the debt. It is obviously not a defense to Creditor's action that Debtor paid money to someone else. It makes no difference that Creditor was tricked into making the payment to someone else, or that Creditor acted in an entirely understandable, non-negligent fashion. You can only satisfy your debts by paying your actual creditor. The Section 4-103 rule on variation by agreement, and the similar general provision in Section 1-302, simply do not speak to settings in which the obligation in question is not an obligation to exercise care, but is a flat obligation to pay a debt.

But, even on the specific issue involved in the facsimile signature cases, it is worth wondering why courts seem so willing to accept agreements that absolve banks from liability. In particular, one wonders whether the approach in cases like *Jefferson Parish* is a product of the common assumption that the basic rule in the law of the check system is that "the bank always wins." Suppose it were well understood that the basic rule of the check collection system is, as was explained earlier in this chapter, that the burden of unpreventable losses should rest with the providers of the payment system rather than with the users of the payment system. It would then be immediately obvious that a broad interpretation of facsimile signature agreements would be fundamentally inconsistent with that general principal. Accordingly one would expect courts to react to facsimile signature agreements in about the same way they would react to a fine print legend in some other agreement that is fundamentally inconsistent with the arrangement. Suppose, for example, that fine print on a bank certificate of deposit said that the bank is not obligated to pay the designated amount if, through no fault of the bank, it has encountered financial difficulties. No one would think that that provision is enforceable. By contrast, if courts approach facsimile signature agreements with the thought, even if unarticulated, that the usual rule of the check system is that the bank always wins, then there seems nothing at all odd about the fact that a facsimile signature agreement absolves the bank from liability.

So the irony becomes apparent. Law professors' scoffing remarks that the rule of the U.C.C. is that "the bank always wins," may have led to a world in which there is a danger that courts will reach results that absolve banks of liability, despite the fact that the Code embodies precisely the opposite rule.

7

Are Checks Ever Transferred?

The fundamental concept of negotiable instruments law is that negotiable instruments are intended to be freely transferrable and are, in fact, frequently transferred. The law of checks, found in U.C.C. Articles 3 and 4 is based on the idea that it is useful to treat checks as a species of negotiable instrument. That would make sense only if checks are routinely transferred. To be sure, the physical piece of paper on which a check is written passes through a number of hands on its way from the payee to the drawer's bank. But, there is no need to regard the passage of the check through the banking system as a "transfer" of an item of property. Rather, as will be discussed in Chapter 9, it would make more sense to treat the check as a payment instruction communicated to the banking system rather than as an item of property. For the negotiable instruments orientation to make sense, it would have to be the case that checks are routinely transferred from person to person outside of the banking system. Let us consider whether that is plausible by looking first at teaching materials routinely used in courses on payment systems and then by looking at the cases.[1]

1. The subject of this chapter may seem odd to lawyers familiar with practices involving checks in the England where, as a result of the "crossed check" device, checks are not transferred from the payee to another person outside the banking system but are simply deposited in a bank by the payee. As this chapter explains, the reality is the same in the United States,

I. CHECK TRANSFER IN PAYMENT SYSTEMS COURSEBOOKS

In modern teaching materials on checks one routinely finds discussion of the transfer of checks from one person to another outside the banking system. Virtually all works on the law of the check system include some version of a story of check fraud along the lines of the one presented by White and Summers.[2] In their story, a buyer of goods drew a check payable to the seller. The check was stolen by the wrongdoer and indorsed to "Gullible Grocer." Grocer deposited the check for collection and it was paid by the payor bank. The key to the story is that the wrongdoer transferred the check to someone else, forging the indorsement of the actual payee. White and Summers make no effort to explain why Gullible Grocer was willing to take the check from the wrongdoer. Did Grocer do so in payment of goods sold by Grocer to the wrongdoer? Was Grocer operating a check cashing service? Did the thief impersonate the payee? Curiously, in teaching materials on checks, there is rarely any effort to explain how these assumed transfers of checks take place.

although the crossed check device is unknown here. As was noted in the preceding chapter, under English law a payor bank might not be liable for paying a check over a forged indorsement. Users of checks in England could, however, protect themselves against forged indorsement loss by the device of "crossing" the check, that is, drawing two parallel lines across the face of the check and adding language indicating that the check is to be deposited either at any bank, or at a specified bank. A payor bank that paid a check inconsistently with the crossing could be liable to its customer under the Crossed Checks Act of 1876, 39 & 40 Vict., c. 81, latter included in the Bills of Exchange Act, 45 & 46 Vict., c. 61, § 79. Moreover, if the check is crossed with the legend "not negotiable," any subsequent holder has no better title than his transferor. Bills of Exchange Act, 45 & 46 Vict., c. 61, § 81. Confusion over the effect of crossings with the words "account payee only" led to further legislation in 1992. *Legislative Comment, The Cheques Act 1992*, J. Bus. L. 270–271 (1993).

2. James J. White & Robert S. Summers, Uniform Commercial Code 548–49 (5th ed. 2000).

Consider the following stories from several modern books on the law of checks:

> Drawer drew a check to the order of Payee. The check was stolen from Payee by Thief who signed Payee's name to the check as a blank indorsement. Thief then delivered the check to Jennifer, who purchased for value, in good faith and without notice that the indorsement was forged. Jennifer indorsed and deposited the check with Depositary Bank which presented the check and recovered payment from Payor Bank.[3]
>
> Drawer issues a check "to the order of payee" for $1,000. Forger steals the check from Payee, forges Payee's name on the check and sells the check to Adams who deposits it in his or her account with Depositary Bank. The check goes through collection channels when it is paid by Drawee.[4]
>
> Fred forges Julia's indorsement on a check made payable to Julia. Fred then transfers the check to Raoul. Raoul is not the holder of the check. . . . If Payor Bank pays Raoul, the drawer of the check is not discharged. Payor Bank may not debit Drawer's account. Drawer is still liable to Julia.[5]

Suppose I go to a department store to buy shirt. If I try to pay for the shirt with a check that I draw payable to the store, chances are that I'll actually have a somewhat difficult time persuading the store to allow me to pay for the shirt by check. At the very least, the salesclerk will look at me like I'm some kind of Neanderthal because I'm not paying with a credit card or debit card. But, suppose that I try to

3. William D. Warren & Steven D. Walt, Payments and Credits 287 (7th ed. 2007).
4. Bradford Stone, Uniform Commercial Code in a Nutshell 315 (6th ed. 2002).
5. Lary Lawrence, An Introduction to Payment Systems 227 (1997).

pay for the shirt by transferring to the department store a check drawn by Jones, payable to Smith, bearing what purports to be Smith's indorsement to me. One thing we can be very sure of—the department store clerk isn't going to let me take the shirt. Indeed, what I would be trying to do is likely to seem so weird that the clerk might well call the security people—if not the men in white coats.

Occasionally, there is at least some recognition that one would have to strain to imagine how such transfers could take place. For example, in a hypothetical in Prof. Mann's payment systems casebook, a patient writes a check to her doctor. The scalawag, Will Ladislaw, also a patient of that doctor, steals the check and forges the doctor's indorsement. Ladislaw transfers the check to another person, Edward Casaubon, in partial payment of an unrelated debt.[6] Presumably the thought is that Casaubon might be willing to try anything to get payment from his debtor.

Some of the examples make a bit more effort at realism by having the scalawag cash the check—usually at a grocery store or check cashing agency—rather than buying something with it or transferring it to a creditor. Here are some typical examples:

> Kingman worked as a nurse in Duffy's medical office. One morning, Kingman found a check lying on the floor next to the

6. Ronald J. Mann, Payment Systems and Other Financial Transactions 90–91 (3rd ed. 2006). In other respects, however, Prof. Mann's hypothetical is as implausible as the others. The problem does not state explicitly what the drawer did, but the implication is that when the doctor called to ask why the bill had not been paid, the patient accepted the doctor's contention that he never got the original check and issued a replacement check. It is pretty hard to image that happening. If the patient told the doctor that she had paid the bill, it seems highly unlikely that the doctor would continue to press her for payment, particularly since she would have the cancelled check from the payor bank. Moreover, to get to the warranty issues that the problem is designed to address, it must be assumed that the payor bank recredited the drawer's account. Prof. Mann seemingly recognizes the unreality of this assumption by the tongue-in-cheek statement that that the payor bank "promptly agreed to recredit" the drawer's account.

> receptionist's desk. The check had been drawn on First Bank and made payable to Duffy's order by Blanchard, one of Duffy's patients. After determining that no one was looking, Kingman pocketed the check. Kingman subsequently forged Duffy's signature on the back of the check, and cashed it at the MidgetMart Grocery Store. MidgetMart deposited the check for collection in Merchants Bank.[7]
>
> Sam has a checking account at State Bank. Sam wrote a check for $100 payable to Jane. Jane lost the check. Harry found the check, forged Jane's signature and sold the check to Check Cashing Inc. for $90. Check Cashing Inc. sent the check to State Bank.[8]

Such examples are a tad more realistic since they do not require us to assume that a check is being indorsed from one person to another as a form of payment. Rather, the check with the forged indorsement is cashed at a check cashing agency or a grocery store. These are not really examples of the transfer of checks from person to person outside the banking system. A check cashing agency is simply a provider of payment services that does not happen to be organized as a bank. A grocery store that cashes checks has, in essence, chosen to operate an auxiliary business of cashing checks.

Moreover, if we look at the check cashing examples a bit more closely, we see that they still have an air of unreality. In the scenarios commonly found in the teaching materials, someone goes to a check cashing agency and gets that agency to cash a check payable to someone else, purportedly indorsed to the person who appears at the

7. Clayton P. Gillette, Robert E. Scott & Alan Schwartz, Payment Systems and Credit Instruments 289–90 (2nd ed. 2007).

8. Linda J. Rusch, Payment Systems Problems, Materials, and Cases 250 (3rd ed. 2007).

agency. Suppose that Kingman goes to a grocery store seeking to cash a check drawn by Blanchard payable to Duffy, bearing what purports to be Duffy's indorsement to Kingman. Chances are that MidgetMart Grocery Store will not cash the check for Duffy. Grocery stores typically have signs posted saying something along the lines of "No Third Party Checks." That is, they will cash checks for the customer who draws the check, or perhaps will cash payroll checks payable to the customer, but they will certainly not cash checks payable to someone else and purportedly indorsed to the customer. Indeed, cases presenting fact patterns like this tend to be criminal actions. What Kingman is trying to do is so obviously suspicious that MidgetMart is likely to call the police and Kingman will end up in jail.[9]

For many law students, the law school courses on commercial law are their first introduction to the operations of the business and financial system. A student whose undergraduate major was philosophy, and who has been using credit and debit cards almost exclusively in his personal financial affairs, is unlikely to have any significant degree of experience with checks, let alone indorsement of checks for any purpose other than deposit at a bank. It is only natural to assume that the people who wrote the books and teach the classes are discussing problems that actually occur in the real world. The student is likely to suppose that the transactions described do occur and that it is just his lack of familiarity with business that makes them seem so odd. So, the fact that professors teach Articles 3 and 4 through unrealistic hypotheticals may well be a significant reason that the profession in general has failed to realize how anachronistic this whole body of law is.

9. *E.g.*, State v. Kirkpatrick, 480 S.E.2d 400 (N.C. 1997).

II. CHECK TRANSFER IN CASES

How might we confirm the suspicion that indorsement of checks from one party to another in a transaction unrelated to the issuance of the check is a phenomenon that occurs in the classroom, not the world? One method is a brute force examination of cases. If checks really were indorsed from person to person, that phenomenon should be reflected in cases involving forgery of indorsements. So one can look at cases involving forged indorsements to see what transaction patterns they reveal. In essence, the method is testing whether there is a needle in the haystack by looking at the pieces of hay one by one to discover, not surprisingly, that they are hay straws not needles.

A search for cases in the past two decades that in some way involved forged indorsement of checks or other instruments produced about 500 cases.[10] The forged indorsement cases fall into fairly predictable patterns. Probably the most common are cases where an employee or other agent of the payee of checks embezzles by diverting checks from the payee. In the sample, about 120 cases fit into this pattern. To obtain the value from the stolen checks, the employees must either transfer them to someone else or deposit them for collection. The scalawag employees are evidently not as silly as is assumed in the negotiable instruments literature, for they never try to transfer the checks to unrelated parties.

10. Two searches were performed in 2007. First, the "allcases" library in Westlaw was searched for "forged indorsement." That yielded over 700 cases, of which about 450 actually involved a transfer of an instrument. This included a large number of criminal prosecutions for forgery. Those cases give a particularly useful depiction of the actual practices of people who forge indorsements, who are, after all, criminals. The "allcases" search was supplemented by a search in the UCC-CS library on Westlaw for cases that cited sections 3-204, 3-205, or 3-206. That yielded about 125 cases, of which about 40 or so were not found in the "forged indorsement" search and actually involved transfer of an instrument.

In some cases, the dishonest employees simply deposit the checks into their own accounts. Sometimes they are fairly clever about it. In *Maryland Industrial Finishing Co., Inc. v. Citizens Bank,*[11] a company's bookkeeper deposited checks payable to the company after placing the company's indorsement stamp on them. The employee deposited the checks at a drive-through window along with a deposit slip that she had filled out with the name of the company but her own personal account number.[12] Or, the employee's cleverness might involve evading detection by the employer, as in *American Fuji Seal, Inc. v. U.S.,*[13] where the IRS erroneously issued tax refund checks to a company. The accounting manager who received the checks realized that nothing in the company's records would show that any funds were expected from the IRS. Accordingly, he forged the employer's indorsement and deposited the checks in his personal account. Sometimes the employee is at least a bit cautious, as by using a remote ATM machine to deposit checks payable to the employer into the employee's personal account.[14] But in a surprisingly large number of cases, the employee simply forges the employer's indorsement and deposits the check in the employee's personal account.[15] Indeed,

11. 642 A.2d 317 (Md. Ct. Spec. App. 1994).
12. For similar schemes, see In re Lou Levy & Sons Fashions, Inc., 988 F.2d 311 (2d Cir. 1993); Flavor-Inn, Inc. v. NCNB Nat'l Bank, 424 S.E.2d 534 (S.C. Ct. App. 1992).
13. 34 Fed.Cl. 274 (1995).
14. Menichini v. Grant, 995 F.2d 1224 (3rd Cir. 1993).
15. Schrier Brothers v. Golub, 123 F.App'x 484 (3d Cir. 2005); John Hancock Fin. Servs., Inc. v. Old Kent Bank, 346 F.3d 727 (6th Cir. 2003); Guardian Life Ins. Co. v. Weisman, 223 F.3d 229 (3d Cir. 2000); U.S. Fid. & Guar. Co. v. Bank of Bentonville, 29 F. Supp. 2d 553 (W.D. Ark. 1998); Continental Cas. Co. v. Fifth/Third Bank, 418 F. Supp. 2d 964 (N.D. Ohio 2006); In re World Metals, Inc., 313 B.R. 720 (Bankr. N.D. Ohio 2004); San Tan Irr. Dist. v. Wells Fargo Bank, 3 P.3d 1113 (Ariz. Ct. App. 2000); Lee Newman, M.D., Inc. v. Wells Fargo Bank, 104 Cal. Rptr. 2d 310 (Cal. Ct. App. 2001); Interior Crafts, Inc. v. Leparski, 853 N.E.2d 1244 (Ill. App. Ct. 2006); Haddad's of Ill., Inc. v. Credit Union 1 Credit Union, 678 N.E.2d 322 (Ill. App. Ct. 1997); UNR-Rohn, Inc. v. Summit Bank, 687 N.E.2d 235 (Ind. Ct. App. 1997); Med Data Serv. Bureau, L.L.C. v. Bank of La., 898 So. 2d 482 (La. Ct. App. 2004); Quality Gas Prods., Inc. v. Bank One Corp., 885 So. 2d 1179

in some of the cases, the employee takes the check to a bank and obtains cash for it.[16]

The more careful scalawags employ a slightly different strategy. Rather than depositing the checks in the employee's own personal bank account, the dishonest employee opens an account in the name of the employer, purporting to be authorized to do so. Then the employee can withdraw funds from the account for personal use. For example, in *Oswald Machine & Equipment, Inc. v. Yip*,[17] the dishonest employee obtained a job running the bookkeeping function of an engine repair and sales company called "Oswald Machine & Equipment, Inc." As part of his job, Yip had charge of processing deposits to the company's accounts at Wells Fargo and Bank of America. Shortly after being hired, Yip opened an account at another bank in the name of an entity that he identified as "Oswalds Machine Equipment Co." of which he purported to be the sole proprietor. Until his imprisonment when his activities were discovered nearly four years later, Yip diverted nearly one million dollars into the bogus account. The story is a typical example of a common pattern of employee embezzlement,[18] right down to the fact that,

(La. Ct. App. 2004); Cable Cast Magazine v. Premier Bank, 729 So. 2d 1165 (La. Ct. App. 1999); Arkwright Mut. Ins. Co. v. State Street Bank & Trust Co., 703 N.E.2d 217 (Mass. 1998); Halla v. Norwest Bank Minn., 601 N.W.2d 449 (Minn. Ct. App. 1999); Yarbro, Ltd v. Missoula Fed. Credit Union, 50 P.3d 158 (Mont. 2002); Springfield Twp. v. Mellon PSFS Bank, 889 A.2d 1184 (Pa. 2005); Bank/First Citizens Bank v. Citizens & Assocs., 82 S.W.3d 259 (Tenn. 2002); Southwest Bank v. Info. Support Concepts, Inc., 149 S.W.3d 104 (Tex. 2004); Pub. Citizen, Inc. v. First Nat'l Bank, 480 S.E.2d 538 (W. Va. 1996); Allied Ins. Ctr., Inc. v. Wauwatosa Sav. & Loan Ass'n, 546 N.W.2d 544 (Wis. Ct. App. 1996).

16. Stenseth v. Wells Fargo Bank, 48 Cal. Rptr. 2d 192 (Cal. Ct. App. 1995); Glazer v. First Amer. Nat'l Bank, 930 S.W.2d 546 (Tenn. 1996).

17. 13 Cal. Rptr. 2d 193 (Cal. Ct. App. 1992).

18. For similar facts, see Rodrigue v. Olin Employees Credit Union, 406 F.3d 434 (7th Cir. 2005); Northwestern Nat'l Life Ins. Co. v. Laurel Fed. Sav. Bank, 133 F.3d 916 (4th Cir. 1997); Fed. Ins. Co. v. Pueblo Int'l Ins., 5 F.3d 428 (9th Cir. 1993); U.S. Small Bus. Admin. v. Citibank, 31 UCC Rep. Serv. 2d 795 (S.D.N.Y. 1997); Wisper Corp. v. Cal. Commerce Bank, 57 Cal. Rptr. 2d 141 (Cal. Ct. App. 1996); Auto-Owners Ins. Co. v. Bank One, 852

in retrospect, it seems astonishing the employer did not discover the theft earlier.[19]

There are also many cases in which checks are issued to two or more parties jointly, such as insurance payments for damage to a house payable to the insured and its mortgagee.[20] The insured doesn't bother to tell the mortgagee, but simply forges the mortgagee's indorsement and deposits the check. Similar, and distressingly common, are cases in which lawyers receive checks on behalf

N.E.2d 604 (Ind. Ct. App. 2006); Delta Chem. & Petroleum, Inc. v. Citizens Bank, 790 So. 2d 862 (Miss. Ct. App. 2001); Martin Glennon, Inc. v. First Fidelity Bank, 652 A.2d 199 (N.J. Super. Ct. App. Div. 1995).

19. Indeed, after Yip's embezzlement was discovered, the employer learned that Yip had several previous rubs with the criminal justice system for similar offenses. All the more ironic, the employer hired Yip after it discovered that its previous bookkeeper had embezzled over one million dollars in earlier years. 13 Cal. Rptr. 2d at 195.

20. Bank of Am. v. Allstate Ins. Co., 29 F. Supp. 2d 1129 (C.D. Cal. 1998); A.C.E., Inc. v. Inland Mortgage Co., 969 S.W.2d 176 (Ark. 1998); Chapital v. Guar. Sav. & Homestead Ass'n, 681 So. 2d 1307 (La. Ct. App. 1996); Pamar Enters. v. Huntington Banks, 580 N.W.2d 11 (Mich. Ct. App. 1998); Stromberg v. Moore, 170 S.W.3d 26 (Mo. Ct. App. 2005); Sovereign Bank v. United Nat'l Bank, 821 A.2d 87 (N.J. Super. Ct. App. Div. 2003); Mouradian v. Astoria Fed. Sav. & Loan, 689 N.E.2d 1385 (N.Y. 1997); State ex rel. N.D. Hous. Fin. Agency v. Ctr. Mut. Ins. Co., 720 N.W.2d 425 (N.D. 2006).There are also numerous similar cases of checks payable to joint payees for other reasons where one of the payees forges the indorsement of the other. Elliott v. United States, 332 F.3d 753 (4th Cir. 2003) (checks payable to family members deposited by one over forgery of other's indorsement); Am. State Bank v. Union Planters Bank, 332 F.3d 533 (8th Cir. 2003) (checks payable to farmer and crop lender deposited by farmer alone); Stefano v. First Union Nat'l Bank, 981 F. Supp. 417 (E.D. Va. 1997) (checks payable to family members deposited by one over forgery of other's indorsement); Md. Nat'l. Bank v. Resolution Trust Corp., 895 F. Supp. 762 (D. Md., 1995) (check payable to individual and boat seller deposited over forgery of boat seller's indorsement); Crystaplex Plastics, Ltd v. Redevelopment Agency, 92 Cal. Rptr. 2d 197 (Cal. Ct. App. 2000) (check payable to supplier and subcontractor deposited over forgery of supplier's indorsement); Aprile v. Suncoast Sch. Fed. Credit Union, 596 So. 2d 1290 (Fla. Dist. Ct. App. 1992) (check payable to husband and wife deposited by husband over forgery of wife's indorsement); E.S.P., Inc. v. Midway Nat'l Bank, 466 N.W.2d 417 (Minn. Ct. App. 1991) (check payable to contractor and subcontractor deposited over forgery of contractor's indorsement); Bursey v. CFX Bank, 756 A.2d 1001 (N.H. 2000) (check payable to husband and wife deposited by husband alone).

of clients and forge the client's indorsement when depositing the check in accounts controlled by the lawyers.[21]

None of these routine cases involve any actual transfer of the check outside the banking system. Of course, in some of the cases the check did appear to bear the indorsement of the payee to a person other than a bank. But the purported indorsee was the scalawag. In the model assumed in so many discussions of negotiable instruments law, the payee's indorsement is forged by the thief, the thief transfers the check to a third party, and the third party initiates bank collection. So, to fit the assumed model, a case would have to involve a check that appears to bear an indorsement from the payee to an indorsee, and the scalawag would have to be someone other than the person who initiates bank collection. In the actual cases, there are no genuine non-bank indorsees. Rather, the scalawag is the purported indorsee who initiates bank collection. For example, in *Morrow v. Apple Bank for Savings*,[22] the perpetrator of a fraudulent investment scheme persuaded the victim to issue a check payable to a certain entity. The perpetrator then forged that entity's indorsement and deposited the check in an account he controlled. So the check did seem to bear an indorsement for a transfer outside the banking system, but that was simply part of the means by which the scalawag induced the victim to issue the check and hand it to him.[23] Similarly,

21. There were over forty such cases in the sample, e.g. Advocate Health & Hosps. Corp. v. Bank One, 810 N.E.2d 500 (Ill. App. Ct. 2004); In re Hollembeak, 807 P.2d 1292 (Kan. 1990); In re Lewis, 728 So. 2d 846 (La. 1999); Williams v. Liberty Bank & Trust Co., 746 So. 2d 275 (La. Ct. App. 1999); Hoppe v. First Midwest Bank, 899 S.W.2d 879 (Mo. Ct. App. 1995); Leeds v. Chase Manhattan Bank, 752 A.2d 332 (N.J. Super. Ct. App. Div. 2000); N.J. Lawyers' Fund v. First Fidelity Bank, 696 A.2d 728 (N.J. Super. Ct. App. Div. 1997); Lawyers' Fund for Client Prot. v. Bank Leumi Trust Co., 727 N.E.2d 563 (N.Y. 2000); In re Disciplinary Proceedings Against Konnor, 602 N.W.2d 534 (Wis. 1999).

22. 599 N.Y.S.2d 31 (N.Y. App. Div. 1993).

23. The check was made payable to Depository Trust Company ("DTC") and the scalawag forged DTC"s indorsement. DTC is the clearing corporation for securities holding in the

in *Olympic Title Ins. Co. v. Fifth Third Bank,*[24] a dishonest representative of the owner of real estate obtained a check intended to pay off a mortgage on the real estate as part of a refinancing arrangement. Rather than turn the check over to the mortgagee, the scalawag forged the indorsement of the mortgagee and deposited the check in an account controlled by the scalawag. So too, in *Stella v. Dean Witter Reynolds, Inc.,*[25] a dishonest employee of a brokerage obtained checks drawn by the firm payable to one of its customers, forged the indorsement of the customer, and succeeded in cashing the checks at a bank.[26]

One does encounter some cases where a check appears to have been indorsed by one person to another, but that is just part of the fraudulent scheme. For example, *State v. Hill*[27] was a criminal prosecution of a person involved in misappropriation of the proceeds of a social security check. The $829 check had been sent to a recently deceased man. The decedent's girlfriend was persuaded by a dishonest friend to forge the decedent's indorsement on the check. The dishonest friend then cashed the check at a bank, keeping $250 of the proceeds for her "services." The case is certainly not one where the check had been indorsed from one person to another in payment of an unrelated obligation. The only reason for the indorsement seems to have been that the friend, unlike the decedent's

United States. It is far from clear why the scalawag thought it useful to induce the victim to issue a check payable to DTC, since it is hard to imagine any circumstance in which an investor would issue a check to DTC. The fact that the depositary bank took the check for deposit even though it bore such an odd indorsement is simply another instance of the phenomenon that a depositary bank will rarely have any occasion to examine the indorsements on deposited checks.

24. 54 UCC Rep. Serv. 569 (Ohio Ct. App. 2004).
25. 574 A.2d 468 (N.J. Super. Ct. App. Div. 1990).
26. Why the bank cashed the checks for the scalawag is unclear. The opinion reports that bank "employees testified that cashing third-party checks, checks payable to corporations and checks payable to pension funds at [the scalawag]'s request became a regular routine, although they knew that the practice was in direct violation of stated bank policy." *Id.* 472.
27. 97 P.3d 1014 (Idaho Ct. App. 2004).

girlfriend, was willing to try to cash the check.[28] In *Sun Bank, N. A. v. Merrill Lynch, Pierce, Fenner and Smith, Inc.*,[29] a bank lent money to Buyer for the purchase of goods from Seller. The bank made the loan by issuing a check payable to Seller and delivering it directly to Seller. However, a dishonest former employee of Seller got hold of the check and indorsed it on behalf of Seller back to Buyer. Buyer then deposited the check in an account it maintained with a brokerage firm. On its face, it appears that the check had been indorsed from one party to another, but that appears to have been simply part of the scam by which Buyer diverted to itself the proceeds of the loan that the bank thought were going to Seller.[30]

Indeed, the possibility that a check was indorsed from one party to another outside the banking system is, in fact, so odd that it is likely to set off red flags if noticed. For example, in *State v. Kirkpatrick*,[31] a person attempted to cash at a convenience store a check purportedly indorsed by the payee. As it happened, the clerk at the convenience store knew the payee, and, thinking it odd that she would have indorsed the check to someone else, called the payee to see

28. Curiously, the bank actually handed over cash rather than simply accepting the check for deposit.

29. 637 So. 2d 279 (Fla. Dist. Ct. App. 1994).

30. As to the subsequent party, the brokerage firm, the case is just yet another instance of the common phenomenon that a depository, whether bank or other, rarely has any occasion to look at indorsements on checks deposited by its customers.For similar cases of indorsement to a participant in the scheme, see United States v. Rosario, 118 F.3d 160 (3d Cir. 1997) (tax refund check stolen by tax preparer who forged payee's indorsement and persuaded her nephew to cash the check; nephew deposited it in bank for collection); United States v. Stone, 987 F.2d 469 (7th Cir. 1993) (person who stole $368 social security check forged payee's indorsement to an acquaintance to whom she paid $100 for cashing the check for her at a bank); United States v. Davis, 918 F.2d 174, No. 90-5009, 1990 WL 175648 (4th Cir. 1990) (person who stole a social security check and forged payee's indorsement persuaded her uncle to cash it for her at a bank); Johnson v. Thrift Savs. & Loan Co., No. C-920115, 1993 WL 323380 (Ohio Ct. App. 1993) (government check payable to discharged service member was deposited for collection by his mother-in-law over forgery of his indorsement).

31. 470 S.E.2d 54 (N.C. 1996).

whether she actually had done that. Not surprisingly, she had not, and the person who appeared with the check was convicted for uttering a check with a forged indorsement. Or, there is *United States v. Gonzalez*,[32] where a newly employed bank teller permitted a person to deposit stolen Treasury checks over forged indorsements. The teller's assertion that she did not realize there was anything wrong apparently did not convince the jury who convicted her of knowingly receiving stolen Treasury checks. In a similar vein, one can find some amusement in *SEC v. Cook*,[33] where a check cashing service took a check purporting to bear the payee's indorsement from a person having no apparent connection with the payee. The person who transferred the check to the check cashing agency explained that it "belonged to a friend of his who needed to cash it quickly because he was going through a divorce and was worried that someone would try to 'grab the money.'" The person who presented the check refused to answer any questions about the transaction, invoking his Fifth Amendment privilege against self-incrimination. The person at the check cashing agency who conducted the transaction "pled guilty to money laundering for alleged members of the South Florida crew of the La Cosa Nostra crime family."

Sometimes the mechanics of the mass processing of checks make collection over a forged indorsement possible even though there is no plausible story that could explain why the check was purportedly indorsed. For example, in *Getty Petroleum Corp. v. American Express Travel Related Services Co.*,[34] an employee of Getty Petroleum purloined checks drawn by Getty to its dealers and used them to pay

32. 131 F.3d 149, No. 97-301137, 1997 WL 723054 (9th Cir. 1997).
33. 45 UCC Rep. Serv. 2d 1131 (N.D. Tex. 2001).
34. 683 N.E.2d 311 (N.Y. 1997).

her own credit card bills, forging the indorsement of the payees.[35] If anyone at the credit card company had looked at the checks, it would have been obvious that something was wrong. Why would an individual be paying her credit card bill with a check drawn by an oil company payable to a service station and purportedly indorsed by the service station to an unrelated individual? But it is easy to see how the credit card company might set up its accounts receivable function in a way that it simply applied to the cardholder's account whatever check was sent in payment, without bothering to examine the parties to the check.[36]

In some cases, the assumption that checks are routinely transferred complicates what would otherwise be a simple matter. For example, in *Brentar v. Rupert*,[37] the drawer of a check alleged that he had drawn the check payable to one person but given it to another for transmission to the payee. The person to whom the check was given deposited it in her own account, indorsing it in her name beneath what appeared to be the blank indorsement of the original payee. To any normal person, the assertion that the original payee actually indorsed in blank would be wildly implausible. However, in the case itself, the drawer was unable to prove that the payee's indorsement was a forgery, in part because the indorsee could make

35. *Id.*, at 313.

36. The court held that the case was governed by the fictitious payee rule of U.C.C. 3-405, because Getty had issued the checks as a matter of its own internal accounting procedures, never intending them to be sent to the designated payees, who were to be credited for the amount by adjustment to their running accounts with Getty. Moreover, because the fictitious payee rule of U.C.C. 3-405 places the loss on the drawer without an exception for cases where the person who takes through the forged indorsement failed to act carefully, the court ruled that the credit card company was protected even though its conduct struck the court as quite sloppy.

37. No. 73903, 1998 WL 895285 (Ohio Ct. App. 1998).

a plausible argument that the original payee had, for some reason, indorsed it to her.[38]

Then there are the cases that stand for little other than the proposition that chutzpah has no limits. For example, in *Harris v. Resolution Trust Co.*,[39] a person had apparently stolen seven checks, forged indorsements on them, and deposited them in his account. The crook himself brought an action complaining that the depository bank had charged back credit given for some of the checks upon discovery of the forgery. The fraudster's theory was not exactly clear, even though he must have had plenty of time to puzzle over the matter since he seems to have brought the suit while in prison as a result of the matter. Aside from that, the case shows only that banks' internal procedures for processing deposits typically would not detect even fairly obvious forged indorsements.

In short, it is extremely difficult to find in the reported decisions any cases that clearly present the fact pattern routinely assumed in casebooks and secondary sources. My survey of over five hundred cases involving forged indorsement yielded only a handful that seem to involve indorsement of checks to third parties in transactions unrelated to the issuance of the checks, though the facts generally do not clearly indicate the nature of the relationship between the payee and indorsee. In *Intelogic Trace Texcom Group, Inc. v. Merchants National Bank*,[40] a lender issued a check to a payee, and then the payee indorsed it to another entity in payment of pre-existing debts.

38. The plaintiff faced other problems as well. The case was dismissed as untimely under the statute of limitations. No one seems to have noticed that the drawer would probably not have been a proper plaintiff in conversion action in any event. *See* Stone & Webster Eng'g Corp. v. First Nat'l Bank & Trust Co., 184 N.E.2d 358 (Mass. 1962).

39. 15 F.3d 1085 (9th Cir. 1994).

40. 626 N.E.2d 839 (Ind. Ct. App. 1993).

That entity deposited the check for collection.[41] There is no explanation of the relationship between the payee and the indorsee. Similarly, in *Community National Bank v. Channelview Bank*,[42] Community Bank issued a cashier's check payable to Foster, receiving payment from an account maintained by Brink. Brink testified that "Foster" was a fictitious name that he sometimes used. Brink went to Woods and asked if Woods would cash the check for him. Woods gave Brink cash for the check, requiring that Brink indorse it both in the name of Foster and in the name of Brink. Woods deposited the check in his account at Channelview Bank, and Community Bank paid it. Several months later, Community Bank sought return of the funds from Channelview Bank, though the opinion does not indicate why. Perhaps some problem arose in the relationship between Community Bank and Brink. Community Bank based its claim on an allegation that the signature of Foster was forged, but the court rejected that contention, ruling that Foster was merely a name used by Brink, who had indorsed. So the case is essentially one where a cashier's check payable to one person, Brink, was indorsed to another person, Woods, and then deposited for collection. But, there is nothing in the opinion to explain who Woods was, or what his relationship to Brink may have been.[43]

About the closest one can come to the assumed model is *Ohio Citizens Bank v. Venture Metal Products Co.*,[44] where Ford Motor

41. The issue in the case was whether the impostor/fictitious payee rule applied to the indorsement of the payee where the person who negotiated for the loan misrepresented his authority to act for the payee.

42. 814 S.W.2d 424 (Tex. App. 1991).

43. Perhaps the facts were a variant of the fairly common scenario where the purchaser of expensive property, such as an automobile, obtains a bank check from the bank where the purchaser maintains an account and then makes payment by indorsing the check over to the seller. *E.g.*, Patriot Bank v. Navy Fed. Credit Union, 47 UCC Rep. Serv. 2d 662 (Va. Cir. Ct. 2002).

44. 622 N.E.2d 758 (Ohio Ct. Com. Pl. 1993).

Company drew a check payable to City Fire Apparatus. The check was deposited for collection by Venture Metal Products Co., after a handwritten indorsement in the name of City Fire Apparatus that was apparently forged. The opinion presents no facts explaining how Venture Metal products came into possession of the check or what its relationship with the payee may have been.[45]

So, what are we to conclude from a survey of recent cases about how likely it is for a check to be indorsed from the payee to an unrelated party? To be sure, that may happen from time to time. But it is hardly common—three or four possible cases out of over five hundred in the case survey. It seems quite clear that it makes little sense to design or teach the law of the check collection system from the perspective of these few oddball cases, rather than from the perspective of the routine cases where checks are simply used as instructions to banks for the transfer of funds from drawer to payee.

III. CONSEQUENCES OF CONFUSION ABOUT CHECK TRANSFER

So, the picture of check practice that one gets from the casebooks and treatises is, as one might well suspect, not at all borne out by the

45. One might also note Lund v. Chemical Bank, 665 F. Supp. 218 (S.D.N.Y. 1987), rev'd 870 F.2d 840 (2d Cir. 1989), where an enterprise engaged in aircraft operations made a public offering, the proceeds of which were to be used to purchase aircraft. Checks representing the proceeds of the offering were issued to the entity, and then were indorsed to the aircraft sellers. While the case involved checks that were indorsed by the payee to another before deposit, that transaction was hardly a transfer of the check to an unrelated party as payment for some other transaction.Finally, there is Franzese v. Fidelity N.Y. FSB, 625 N.Y.S.2d 275 (N.Y. App. Div. 1995), where a check payable to Maria Franzese was indorsed by her in blank and delivered to one Howard Finger who deposited it at the defendant bank. The opinion reveals nothing about the transaction between Franzese and Finger, but it seems unlikely that Finger was an innocent indorsee since Franzese had also sued him for fraud.

litigated cases. In theory, checks are negotiable instruments that might be transferred from party to party in transactions outside the banking system. In reality, that almost never happens. All right, one might say, the picture of practice that one gets from the books is a bit unrealistic, but there is no other way to teach this material. And, so what if students spend some time with somewhat implausible hypotheticals?

The problem, however, is far more severe. The lesson commonly drawn from unrealistic examples of the sort described above is that the fundamental principle of loss allocation for the check system is a principle of negligence. Consider, for example, the common hypothetical in which the drawer issues a check to the payee, a scalawag steals it from the payee, forges the payee's indorsement, and transfers the check to an indorsee, who deposits it for collection at a depositary bank. In that hypothetical, the loss rests with the indorsee. The ordinary explanation is that indorsee was the person who dealt with the scalawag. Thus, the indorsee was in the best position to detect or prevent the wrongdoing, and so should bear the loss.

In the previous chapter it was shown that it is a mistake to regard negligence as the basic loss allocation rule for checks. Rather, the fundamental principle is that the providers of the check system, not the users, should bear the risk of unpreventable check frauds. The forged indorsement examples that appear in so many of the casebooks and other legal sources seem to provide a counter-example to the contention that the risk of loss is borne by providers rather than users. In Mann's example, Casaubon, a user not a bank, bears the loss. In Warren and Walt's example, Jennifer, a user not a bank, bears the loss. In Lawrence's example, Raoul, a user not a bank, bears the loss. Each of these folks—Casaubon, Jennifer, and Raoul—share the characteristic that they were the ones who took the check bearing the forged indorsement from the scalawag. So each of them might have prevented the loss by exercising greater care in their dealings with the scalawag. If one's thinking about the basic principles of the check collection system is founded on hypotheticals such as these, one is likely to conclude that negligence is the fundamental principle of loss allocation for the check system. That is the conclusion invariably drawn by commentators of the law of the check system. As Speidel, Summers, and White put it in one of the leading law school casebooks:

> In general, the Uniform Commercial Code and the law that preceded it allocate the loss occasioned by the passage of an instrument with a forged indorsement or the passage of an altered instrument to the person who took it from the thief. In modern economic parlance that person normally can be regarded as the least cost risk avoider. Because this person dealt with the thief, use of more careful identification procedures might have averted the loss. Thus this person should bear the cost.[46]

But, consider another attribute shared by all of these characters who could have prevented the loss by more careful dealings with the forger. Either they are a bank or they are a figment of the imagination. As both common sense and the exhaustive case survey reported in this chapter make clear, there are no Casaubons, Jennifers, or Raouls. No one, other than a depositary bank, or someone else such as a check cashing agency engaged in essentially the same economic activity, ever takes a check from a person over a forged indorsement. The Casaubons, Jennifers, and Raouls are the only people who receive payment from a person by accepting a

46. Richard E. Speidel, Robert S. Summers & James J. White, Payment Systems Teaching Materials 165 (5th ed. 1993).

check payable to someone else and purportedly indorsed by the payee to the person with whom they were dealing. But none of them exist. No one who does exist would ever do anything like what each of them did.

The consequence is actually quite severe. If students learn the law of the check system from such wildly unrealistic hypotheticals, and if professors teaching the law have gotten so used to using such hypotheticals that they forget how unrealistic they are, then the law is likely to be formulated in terms that would only make sense if any of these people actually existed. The common perception that negligence is the fundamental principle of loss allocation for the check system rests on nothing more than this confusion. If one examined loss allocation through realistic scenarios, it would be apparent that the fundamental principle of loss allocation is not negligence. Rather, it is that the risk of unavoidable loss should be borne by the providers of the payment system not by the users of the system.

8

What Would a Modern Law of Promissory Notes Look Like?

People commonly use promissory notes as a simple way of evidencing loans or other monetary obligations. It seems only natural that there might be a body of law governing such transactions. This chapter examines Article 3 of the U.C.C. from that perspective. Does Article 3 contain a sensible body of law for notes used in simple lending transactions?[1] Or, to state the question in another way, suppose that instead of being wedded to history, we started afresh to draft a modern statute concerning promissory notes. Would we end up with anything like the material that we now find in Article 3 of the U.C.C.?

I. ACTIONS ON NOTES: ELEMENTS AND DEFENSES

Viewed as a law of simple debt contracts, Article 3 begins by stating the obligation of the parties and the requirements for recovery in an action on a note. The Article 3 rules on these matters, however, are quite inconsequential. Section 3-412 says that the issuer of a

1. For a generally skeptical assessment of the contribution of Article 3 to the law of promissory notes, see Neil B. Cohen, *The Calamitous Law of Notes*, 68 Ohio St. L.J. 161 (2007).

note "is obliged to pay the instrument . . . according to its tenor." That is hardly surprising. Do we really need a statute to tell us that?

On the requirements for recovery, there does appear to be a slight difference between negotiable instruments law and general contract law. Section 3-308 provides that one can make out a prima facie case simply by production of an instrument. In other words, in an action on a negotiable note, consideration is presumed. Of course, if the debtor denies that there was consideration for the note, the creditor must prove consideration.[2] Moreover, the authenticity of the signature of the maker is presumed, though if specifically denied in the answer, the burden is on the plaintiff to prove the signature. Thus, a creditor with a negotiable note can establish a prima facie case merely by production of the note, while one with a non-negotiable note would have to plead and prove the fact of the debt. That is hardly a major difference. As a matter of pleading, it is only the difference between "defendant signed a note" and "plaintiff lent defendant money and defendant signed a note."[3]

Next consider whether the fact that a debt is or is not represented by a negotiable instrument makes any difference in the matters that might be raised in defense of an action to recover the debt. In teaching this subject, I commonly write out and sign two notes, each in the amount of $1,000,000 and hand them to two students. I make one payable to the order of the first student and the other

2. U.C.C. § 3-303(b) ("The drawer or maker of an instrument has a defense if the instrument is issued without consideration.").

3. Under the Federal Rules of Evidence, an item of "commercial paper"—which presumably means an instrument that qualifies as an Article 3 "negotiable instrument"—is self-authenticating. Fed. R. Evid. 902; United States v. Pang, 362 F.3d 1187, 1192–93 (9th Cir. 2004). If the note does not qualify as "commercial paper," then the creditor would have to establish the authenticity of the maker's signature. That, however, is not a significant difference. A creditor suing on a note that does not qualify as "commercial paper" need only submit a discovery request for admission of the authenticity of the signature. Fed. R. Civ. P. 36.

payable to the second student. We go through the usual analysis, concluding that the first student is the holder of a negotiable instrument, while the second merely has a simple written contract. But, nothing of any significance turns on that distinction. Section 3-305 uses many words to say a fairly simple point—in an action by the original creditor, the maker of a negotiable note can raise "any defense . . . that would be available if the person entitled to enforce the instrument were enforcing a right to payment under a simple contract." If I were sued on either note, I would have a complete defense of professorial histrionics, or lack of consideration if one prefers legalistic language. So, aside from the holder in due course rules, there is really nothing of any content on Article 3 on the enforcement of notes.

So, what about the holder in due course rules? To those already familiar with negotiable instruments law, it would be apparent that the holder in due course rules have nothing to do with a simple two-party case in which the note has never been transferred. But, that is not so obvious to students confronting Article 3 for the first time. From the instrumentalist orientation that underlies so much of our teaching and thought about law, it is only natural that if a student encounters a certain legal rule, she will assume that it represents a resolution of some genuine real-world problem. Students know that promissory notes are routinely used to evidence simple lending transactions, they see that Article 3 contains the law of promissory notes, and they see that most of Article 3 is about the rights of holders in due course. It is only natural for them to assume that these rules must be significant in routine cases. So, returning to my classroom play, it always takes some time to get students to see that the holder in due course rules would be relevant only if the student who has the negotiable note manages to find someone who is willing to pay real money for an assignment of it. The students have enough common sense to realize that no one would be so silly as to pay real money for an assignment of my classroom note.

Under the pre-1990 version of Article 3, it was even harder for students to see that the holder in due course rules have nothing to do with a simple two-party case. Section 3-302(2) of the old version of Article 3 contained the statement that "a payee may be a holder in due course."[4] Under that version, virtually all students began their analysis of the simple two-party case by considering the possible effect of the rule that a payee could be a holder in due course. It took nearly a half-hour of explanation to get back to the simple point where we would be without Article 3—the note is just a piece of paper with an agreement written on it.[5]

II. PRESENTMENT, NOTICE OF DISHONOR, AND PROTEST

Part 5 of Article 3 sets out the rules on presentment, notice of dishonor, and protest. These were simplified somewhat from the pre-1990 version of Article 3, but they are still quite complex and detailed. What significance do these rules have in the modern world?

4. Former U.C.C. § 3-302(2).

5. The current version of Article 3 is a bit less likely to confuse students into thinking that the holder in due course rules have anything to do with a simple two-party scenario. The statement in former Article 3 that a payee can be a holder in due course has been deleted and replaced with an excellent detailed comment explaining the issue under the revision as well as former Article 3 and the N.I.L. U.C.C. § 3-302 cmt. 4. But, the revision also deleted the statement in former Section 3-305 that a holder in due course takes free from defenses "of any party to the instrument with whom the holder has not dealt." The comment to the current version has an entirely accurate explanation of why that phrase was never really needed and might be misconstrued. U.C.C. § 3-305 cmt. 2. On the other hand, that phrase in former Section 3-305 was very useful in explaining why the holder in due course rules were irrelevant in the typical simple two party case. The debtor had obviously dealt with the creditor. Accordingly, the debtor was not someone "with whom the [creditor] has not dealt." Now, one must go through the detailed explanation instead of being able to point to a simple statement in the text.

The answer is simple: None. Any promissory note copied out of any formbook, or any promissory note drafted by a lawyer not committing malpractice, will explicitly state that the maker and any other obligor waive presentment, notice of dishonor, and protest. Why does Article 3 have rules whose only function is to be waived?

As usual, the answer is to be found in history. In the era when negotiable instruments did circulate as a form of private currency, these were important matters. In the seventeenth and eighteenth centuries, people would regularly have to take bills and notes as a form of payment, since there frequently was no other available payment medium. At the time the instruments were taken, there would be no way of knowing for sure whether they would be paid. A bill or note might have been transferred from hand to hand in a long chain of payment transactions on the assumption that it would be paid by the drawee or maker. If the instrument were dishonored, some or all of those transactions might be unsettled as holders of the bill sought to shift the loss to prior parties. A very large part of the law of bills and notes in the eighteenth century arose out of this phenomenon.

Suppose that a person made payment by transferring an instrument. To do so, he would commonly have to indorse the instrument and thereby incur a secondary liability on it.[6] Suppose that by the time that the instrument came due, the maker had become insolvent. The holder of the instrument might pursue the indorser. The indorser would be likely to search for any possible basis for resisting liability.

6. In theory, one transferring such an instrument might have avoided liability on it, either by transferring it without indorsement if it had already been indorsed in blank, or by indorsing without recourse. In practice, however, it was unlikely that a creditor would accept the bill that way, because a refusal to indorse would suggest that the debtor himself was suspicious about the soundness of the bill. One of the main reasons that bills were an acceptable medium of exchange was that the accumulation of indorsements added security to the bill. *See* Heylyn v. Adamson, 97 Eng. Rep. 503, 507 (K.B. 1759) (Mansfield, C.J.) ("In common experience, every body knows that the more indorsements a bill has, the greater credit it bears.").

After all, it is not as though he had gotten something for nothing. He would have received value at the time he indorsed, but he would have done so only because he had given value at the time he received the instrument. So far as he was concerned, the transaction was closed long ago. Yet if the maker became insolvent, the instrument might come back to haunt the indorser.

The problem is nicely illustrated by a late eighteenth-century English case, *Tindal v. Brown*.[7] Tindal was the holder of a note made by Donaldson and indorsed by Brown. On the day the note came due, Tindal sent his clerk to Donaldson to demand payment. Donaldson was not home, so the clerk left word, and returned the following morning. That day the clerk did find Donaldson home, and Donaldson said that he would pay the note later that day when his bank was open. At that point, Tindal faced a problem: should he immediately give notice of dishonor and proceed against prior parties, thereby incurring the inconvenience and expense of protests, notary fees, and lawsuits, or should he hold off for a short while in the hopes that the maker would pay. Tindal chose to wait, but that proved costly. The note was not paid that day, and the following morning Donaldson admitted that he could not pay it. At that point, Tindal turned to the indorser, Brown, and demanded that he pay. Brown resisted on the ground that Tindal should have notified him immediately when he could not obtain payment from Donaldson, and that his delay in doing so, even if only a day or so, discharged Brown's secondary liability.

Cases like this gave rise to a major dispute about the proper role of the judge and jury. The jury in *Tindal* evidently felt that the holder had given notice within a reasonable time and gave a verdict against the indorser. The judges took a different view. As Lord Mansfield

7. 99 Eng. Rep. 1033 (K.B. 1786).

observed "what is reasonable notice is partly a question of fact, and partly a question of law . . . wherever a rule can be laid down with respect to this reasonableness, that should be decided by the Court, and adhered to by every one for the sake of certainty."[8] The other judges felt at least as strongly. As Judge Buller put it, "the numerous cases on this subject reflect great discredit on the Courts of Westminster. They do infinite mischief in the mercantile world; and this evil can only be remedied by . . . considering the reasonableness of time as a question of law and not of fact."[9]

Taking the issue from the jury was one thing; deciding what to do with it was another. Problems of specifying the precise obligations of a holder upon dishonor did not go away after *Tindal*. Rather, the problems came to occupy a larger and larger portion of the courts' time, for the judges had taken it upon themselves to resolve these matters by general rules rather than leaving them to the jury. From the end of the eighteenth century through the early nineteenth century, innumerable cases posed fine points about the diligence required of the holder of a dishonored instrument.[10] As Theophilus Parsons put it in the introductory remarks to the chapter of his mid-nineteenth-century treatise dealing with the subject:

> It may be doubted whether any branch of commercial law, somewhat narrow in itself, exhibits so large a number of cases, and so

8. *Id.*, at 1034.
9. *Id.*, at 1035.
10. Haynes v. Birks, 127 Eng. Rep. 323 (C.P. 1804) (if bill has been left with banker for collection, does this extend time for giving notice?); Smith v. Mullett, 170 Eng. Rep. 1131 (Ellenborough at nisi prius 1809) (is it sufficient if holder puts notice in post at end of day following receipt but too late for last post?); Williams v. Smith, 106 Eng. Rep. 447 (K.B. 1819) (if party to be notified is in different city, must notice be sent by the next practical post, or is it sufficient to send by post the following day?); Geill v. Jeremy, 170 Eng. Rep. 1081 (Tenterden at nisi prius 1827) (if no post will go out the next day, must holder give notice by the last post of day of receipt?).

> boundless a variety in their facts and the conclusions from them, as those which relate to the subject of this chapter. It is not easy to imagine any circumstance attending non-notice which in some form or other is not urged as an excuse for it. And the decisions of the courts permit authorities to be cited on both sides of almost every question.[11]

By the twentieth century, all this had been forgotten. The author of one twentieth-century treatise all but suggests that readers skip the chapter covering these subjects.[12] White and Summers introduce their treatment with the remark that "Article Three, Part 5 defines 'dishonor,' 'presentment,' and related terms, specifies when presentment is necessary, and tells when one must give notice of dishonor—all in boring and incessant detail."[13] It is hard to imagine any twentieth-century lawyer remarking, as Judge Kenyon did in the late-eighteenth century, that such issues are "of infinite importance in every hour's transactions in the commercial world."[14]

So, what do we see in the current case law? A search revealed about one hundred cases in the last two decades citing some provision of the Article 3, Part 5 rules on dishonor. In most of them, the court simply happened to have cited a rule about which there was no dispute in the case. A few cases involve the puckish efforts of non-customers of banks who tried to cash checks and objected to

11. 1 Theophilus Parsons, A Treatise on the Law of Promissory Notes and Bills of Exchange 521 (1863). The chapter on excuse of notice runs over 110 pages.
12. Roy A. Redfield, The Law of Commercial Paper 262 (1929). ("Some readers may prefer to treat this chapter and the two immediately following as a reference matter. These chapters are occupied with consideration of detailed rules laid down by the Act for guidance through the formalities observable at maturity. . . . [T]he reader . . . may tread lightly over the ground in front of us.").
13. 2 James J. White & Robert A. Summers, Uniform Commercial Code §16–8 (practitioner's ed. 1995).
14. Brown v. Harradan, 100 Eng. Rep. 943, 945 (K.B. 1791).

fees or identification requirements.[15] But, by far the largest category consists of cases that surprised even the present author, who is all too familiar with the oddities produced by the anachronism of negotiable instruments law.

About one-third of the cases involve anarchists, tax protestors, and the like. When they get a tax assessment, summons, or any other government document that they would prefer to ignore, they write on it "refused for cause without dishonor U.C.C. § 3-501." Somehow they have persuaded themselves that they can ignore the document by citing this provision of the U.C.C. Judges confronted with these arguments generally have absolutely no idea what the gadflies are talking about. Section 3-501 provides that a person to whom an instrument is presented for payment may request additional documentation to assure itself that the person is entitled to payment. It further states that the obligor may decline to pay if that documentation is not provided or if the person making presentment is otherwise not entitled to payment, and that doing so is not a "dishonor." At a time when instruments actually did circulate, these rules were entirely understandable, since the maker of a note would have no way of knowing the identity of the person who was entitled to receive payment. Today, of course, no one (with the possible exception of the present author) would have any reason to know anything about that problem. So, it is not surprising that no one would have any idea what Section 3-501 is talking about. No doubt the folks who think that they can make the government go away by writing magic words on a summons would do something else equally absurd if there were no Section 3-501. But, the cases are instructive as a lesson about the odd things that happen if we

15. Messing v. Bank of Am., 821 A.2d 22 (Md. 2003); Moorehouse v. Chase Manhattan Bank, 76 S.W.3d 608 (Tex. App. 2002); Sexton v. PNC Bank, 792 A.2d 602 (Pa. Super. Ct. 2002).

leave a rule on the statute books that has not been relevant for several centuries.

III. RENEWAL NOTES

Now, let us consider whether Article 3 provides any useful guidance on issues that actually *do* arise in modern actions on promissory notes. In the cases, one commonly encounters the scenario where several people sign a note for an original loan, and, when the loan comes due, the most active of the borrowers negotiates a renewal of the loan. All too commonly, the active borrower tells the others nothing about the renewal, simply forging their signature on the renewal note. When the loan goes into default, the lender proceeds against all who signed the original note, only then discovering that some of the signatures on the renewal note were forgeries. Those whose signatures were forged defend on the grounds that although they were liable on the original note, the creditor accepted the renewal note in full satisfaction of the obligation on the original note. Since their genuine signatures did not appear on the renewal note, they are discharged if the creditor accepted the renewal note as full satisfaction of the obligation on the original note.[16]

In theory, Article 3 states a rule to resolve this question. Section 3-604 provides that the holder can discharge the obligation of a party to an instrument "by an intentional voluntary act, such as surrender of the instrument . . . ." But, that rule really says very little, since the result turns on the intention of the parties in implementing

16. Cases are collected in Gary D. Spivey, Annotation, *Renewal Note Signed by One Comaker as Discharge of Nonsigning Comakers*, 43 A.L.R. 3d 246 (1972).

the renewal.[17] When the issue is considered a bit more carefully, it becomes apparent that the concept of intention is virtually useless. Suppose that Jones and Smith signed the original note, and that Jones obtained a renewal, signing the renewal note and forging the signature of Smith. Suppose that the creditor is asked "Did you intend that Jones and Smith would be liable for the debt; or did you intend that the parties who signed the new note would be liable for the debt?" What is the creditor supposed to say? The problem arises precisely because the creditor was not aware of the fact that the parties who signed the renewal note were not the same as the parties who signed the original note. Yet under the test of "intention," the outcome rests on whether the creditor intended one thing or another, where the creditor was unaware of the difference between the two.

There is another situation where the delivery of a renewal note may have significant consequences. Suppose that Supplier has been selling goods to Buyer on 90 days open account credit. Suppose that Buyer has fallen behind in its payments. It would hardly be surprising if Supplier becomes less careful about the quality of the goods it shipped to someone who was not paying on time. Buyer would realize that it owed money, but would believe that it could resist payment for at least part of the debt by raising a defense of breach of warranty. Suppose that Buyer then gets a lucrative contract for which it needs additional supplies from Supplier. Suppose that Supplier says that it will not sell any more goods unless Buyer signs a note for the balance then due and agrees to pay for any new sales 30 days after the date of invoice. Suppose that Buyer agrees and orders new goods. Suppose that shortly thereafter, before making any payment on the note, Buyer finds another supplier who offers

17. Hubbard Realty Co. v. First Nat'l Bank, 704 F.2d 733, 735–36 (4th Cir. 1983); Peoples Bank of S.C. v. Robinson, 249 S.E.2d 784 (S.C. 1978).

better prices. Buyer then stops ordering from Supplier. Suppose that Supplier sues for the amount of the note as well as any additional credit sales. Buyer seeks to defend the action on the note by raising its breach of warranty contentions.

If one looks at Article 3, or at any legal sources organized by the categories in Article 3, it would appear that Buyer can raise the breach of warranty contention in defense of Supplier's action on the note. Supplier is not a holder in due course, so under Section 3-305(a)(2) Supplier's right to enforce the note "is subject to . . . a defense of the obligor that would be available if [Supplier] were enforcing a right to payment under a simple contract." Buyer could obviously have raised the breach of warranty defense if Supplier had sued on the original open account debt, and Section 3-305(a)(2) seems to say that the situation is no different by virtue of the fact that Buyer gave Supplier a note for the amount of the open account.

Suppose, though, that one had never seen Article 3. How would one approach the issue? One might well wonder whether Buyer's opportunity to contest the amount of the debt might be affected by the fact that, after Buyer was aware of the possible defenses, Buyer did sign a piece of paper in which Buyer agreed to pay the full amount. After all, when Buyer signed the note Buyer said nothing about the possible breach of warranty defense. Consider how Supplier's lawyer might have researched the question in the era before Article 3 or its ancestor, the Uniform Negotiable Instruments Law. He presumably would have gone to the library to look at one of the large treatises on the law of bills and notes. In the early twentieth century, there was a two-volume work entitled "Defenses to Commercial Paper."[18] That would have been a plausible place to

18. Joseph A. Joyce & Howard C. Joyce, A Treatise on the Law of Defenses in Actions on Commercial Paper (Daniel W. Crockett, ed., 2nd ed. 1924).

begin the research. There, in the chapter on Waiver and Estoppel, our lawyer would have found a section on "Waiver and Estoppel by bill or note." In that section, our lawyer would have found the very helpful statement that "one who gives a note for the payment of a debt after the same has been contracted waives all defenses of which he had full knowledge at the time such settlement was made," along with extensive case annotations on the point.[19] Or, the lawyer might have approached the issue simply as a common law accord and satisfaction issue, and, through conventional case law research techniques, come upon an A.L.R. Annotation on the subject.[20]

So, there are genuine issues about the effect of the execution of a promissory note on the rights of creditors and debtors. But, many of these issues have nothing to do with the transfer issues that are the focus of Article 3. As a result, a lawyer who uses sources organized around Article 3 to research promissory note issues will come up empty-handed. By contrast, a lawyer who realizes that a note is just a form of written agreement would research the issue through ordinary search methods and would be far more likely to come upon the relevant authorities than if she used Article 3 sources.

IV. THE CURIOUS HISTORY OF THE ACCOMMODATION PARTY PROVISIONS

Perhaps the harm produced by Article 3 is nowhere more apparent than in the provisions concerning "accommodation parties," the Article 3 term for guarantor or surety. There is, of course, a general law of suretyship, so if Article 3 had no special rules about

19. *Id.*, at 1275-76.

20. Annotation, *Renewal Note as Discharging Original Obligation or Indebtedness* 52 A.L.R. 1416 (1928).

accommodation parties, that would mean only that suretyship questions concerning Article 3 instruments would be determined by the general law of suretyship. So, what is the function of the Article 3 accommodation party rules?

One possible role for special Article 3 rules would be to make it clear whether a party to an instrument was a surety or principal obligor. In one situation, the Article 3 rules do that. Suppose that Don signs as maker a note payable to Charles, and Irving adds his indorsement. Irving is described by Section 3-205(d) as an "anomalous indorser," that is an indorser who is not in the chain of title. The fact that a party has signed as an anomalous indorser gives notice that he is an accommodation party.[21] Perhaps the only odd thing here is the language of Article 3. Irving is called an anomalous indorser even though in modern practice, his indorsement is the most routine thing in the world and everyone knows what it means. The real anomalous cases would be those in which notes were actually transferred from one holder to another by indorsement.

But, aside from that case, Article 3 does not attempt to provide clarity on whether someone is a principal or a surety. Indeed, it goes out of its way to say the opposite, providing that "an accommodation party may sign the instrument as maker, drawer, acceptor, or indorser."[22] One of the most common situations in the cases is that of two parties, each of whom signed as maker. One of the makers contends that he or she signed only as surety for the other maker. Article 3 might have a simple rule for such cases. It might, for example, provide that unless a maker adds language explicitly indicating suretyship status, the maker is to be treated as a principal obligor.

21. U.C.C. § 3-419(b).
22. *Id.*

But, that is not what the statute does. Rather, any maker can litigate whether he or she was an accommodation party.

Other parts of the rule that an accommodation party can sign in any capacity are truly odd. Suppose that Maker signs a note payable to Payee. Payee indorses the note to Holder. Presumably one would assume that Maker borrowed from Payee and then Payee assigned the debt to Holder. Under Article 3, however, it is open to Maker to argue that she was really an accommodation party, and that Payee was the actual principal obligor on a loan made to Payee by Holder. If one were starting afresh, it is hard to see why one would adopt such a counterintuitive rule. It is a bit like saying that if one person signs as maker a note payable to another person, it is open to the maker to argue that he was really the creditor and the payee was the debtor; they just happened to have signed a note that made it look like the opposite.[23]

So, why have a statutory rule saying, in essence, "it's OK for people to sign instruments in a misleading fashion?" As usual, the answer probably lies in long forgotten history. Suppose that a bank is in financial difficulties and fears that the bank examiners will discover its problems. An officer of the bank goes to a friend or associate and asks if the friend will sign a note payable to the bank.

23. Article 3's refusal to adopt clear rules on who is a principal and who is a surety is also presumably the reason for the odd provision that "an accommodated party that pays the instrument has no right of recourse against, and is not entitled to contribution from, an accommodation party." U.C.C. § 3-419(f). All that says is that if the principal debtor pays, the principal debtor cannot recover from the guarantor. That would seem to be such an obvious point that not even Article 3 would need to say it. The rule might, however, be useful if the parties implemented the arrangement in one of the fashions permitted by the other Article 3 rules. Suppose, for example, that the guarantor signed as maker a note payable to the principal debtor, and the principal debtor then indorsed to the actual creditor. In the non-accommodation setting, an indorser who is called upon to pay has a right to recover from a maker. But, that does not make sense if the parties have implemented the arrangement in the convoluted fashion permitted by Article 3 of having the principal debtor appear as payee-indorser.

The banker promises that the bank will not sue on the note, rather it needs it only to hold off the bank examiners. As a matter of ordinary language, one might say that if the friend agrees, he has done so as an "accommodation," that is "favor," to the bank. Then, if the note happens to end up in someone else's hands, perhaps the friend should be able to show that he was actually an "accommodation party," at least if the issue is whether the friend has a right of recourse against bank if the friend is called upon to pay the note. But, if the friend is sued on the note, chances are that bank has long ago failed. So, the only case in which one can imagine the friend asserting his status as accommodation party is if the friend is sued on the note and seeks to raise suretyship defenses. The setting in which that is most likely is that the bank has failed and its receiver is seeking to collect on the note from the friend. Oddly, the effect of the Article 3 rule is that it makes it possible for the friend to defend by saying, in essence, "I only signed in that confusing way in order to help the bank pull the wool over the eyes of the bank examiners." In former times, one did actually encounter such cases. Today, any such contention would generally fail as a result of non-U.C.C principles that preclude a party from relying on alleged side deals when sued by the receiver of a failed bank.[24]

Actually, the origins of the notion that one can sign an instrument in a counterintuitive fashion probably lie further back in history. Let us cast our minds back several centuries, to the era predating modern banking and payment facilities. Suppose that a cotton manufacturer in Lancashire routinely sells its goods through merchants in London. Suppose that the manufacturer ordinarily either ships the goods to the merchants on consignment, or sells

24. Alfred M. Pollard, Keith H. Ellis & Joseph P. Daly, Banking Law in the United States § 20.03 (1999).

them to the merchants on credit. Once the merchants have sold the goods or promised to pay for them, the manufacturer would have a right to money from the merchants arising out of its shipment of the cloth. The manufacturer might make use of that credit by drawing a bill of exchange on the merchant, asking the merchant to accept it, and then discounting the bill with another merchant or financer. To a person discounting the bill, it would appear that the bill had arisen out of a genuine mercantile transaction, that is, the manufacturer had shipped goods to the merchant and the merchant had agreed to pay for them. In the banking theory of the late eighteenth century, that was really the only prudent form of investment for a banker. The banker would be discounting a "real bill" that arose out of an ordinary mercantile transaction, and the source of payment of the bill would have been the funds that the merchant received when the cotton was sold.[25]

Now, suppose that our manufacturer is unable to find merchants interested in either buying its goods or taking them on consignment. As a result, the manufacturer will have no "real bills" that it could discount with banks or other financers, and the manufacturer might well face financial ruin. In desperation, the manufacturer turns to a friend or business associate. The manufacturer says, "Suppose I draw a bill of exchange on you and you accept it. Then, I'll be able to discount the bill because it will appear to the bankers as though I have sold you that amount of goods. Of course, my financial difficulties are only temporary, so by the time that the bill comes due, I'll be able to pay it and you won't have to. Please, please, please . . . and, if the tables are turned, I'll do the same for you if you

25. The classic articulation of the real bills theory of banking is found in 2 Adam Smith, The Wealth of Nations, c. II (1776). For modern criticism, see Lloyd W. Mints, A History of Banking Theory (1945).

need help." Friend agrees and accepts the bill. Manufacturer fails and friend is sued as acceptor.

In the late eighteenth century a bill of the sort we are imagining would have been called an "accommodation bill," as distinguished from a "real bill." Calling something an "accommodation bill" was not merely a term of description, it was an epithet. The term had a connotation akin to such modern terms as "junk bonds" or "subprime mortgages." People who issued "accommodation bills" were engaged in a form of transaction that was regarded as highly inappropriate in the financial theory and mores of the time. In the late eighteenth and early nineteenth centuries, controversy swirled over the legal treatment of accommodation bills.[26] Courts struggled to find some way of using the rules of private law to discourage the disreputable practice of financing through accommodation bills, but often found that such efforts would backfire by giving the fraudsters a basis for asserting that they were not liable because the instruments on which they were sued were not real bills but were merely accommodation paper. By the early part of the nineteenth century, however, the courts had largely given up the effort to use the rules of private law in an effort to stamp out accommodation bills.

As we have repeatedly seen, however, the hand of history lies heavy on Article 3. At the time of the controversy over accommodation bills, the suggestion that a person on whom a bill was drawn might have accepted it solely for accommodation of the drawer and so be entitled to raise suretyship defenses sometimes produced outraged judicial response. In one such case in the early nineteenth century, the judge remarked that "if the Defendant can succeed in establishing the principle, that we must so subvert and pervert the situation of the

26. For a more detailed discussion of accommodation bills issues in the eighteenth century, see James Steven Rogers, The Early History of the Law of Bills and Notes 223–49 (1995).

parties as to make the acceptor merely a surety, and the drawer the principal, the consequence contended for must follow."[27] By the end of the nineteenth century, that sense of horror had died out, and, indeed, the controversy had been long forgotten. One sees the change in the use of language. In the late eighteenth century, one spoke of "accommodation bills" or "accommodation paper." By the end of the century, one spoke of an "accommodation party," and it was perfectly permissible to speak that phrase in polite company.

Section 28 of English Bills of Exchange Act of 1882 acknowledged the rejection of the old sense of horror at accommodation paper:

> An accommodation party to a bill is a person who has signed a bill as drawer, acceptor, or indorser, without receiving value therefore, and for the purpose of lending his name to some other person. An accommodation party is liable on the bill to a holder for value and it is immaterial whether, when such holder took the bill, he knew such party to be an accommodation party or not.

With only changes in the form of expression, that rule remains in Section 3-419 of the current version of Article 3:

> If an instrument is issued for value given for the benefit of a party to the instrument ("accommodated party") and another party to the instrument ("accommodation party") signs the instrument for the purpose of incurring liability on the instrument without being a direct beneficiary of the value given for the instrument, the instrument is signed by the accommodation party "for accommodation." An accommodation party may sign the instrument as maker, drawer, acceptor, or indorser and . . . is obliged to

27. Fentum v. Pocock, 128 Eng. Rep. 660, 662 (C.P. 1813).

> pay the instrument in the capacity in which the accommodation party signs.

What has been completely forgotten is why there is any need to have such a rule.

If a bill or note is signed for the accommodation of another person, then the accommodation party may have the benefit of special suretyship defenses. That is a matter that we shall turn to next. The rules in Section 3-419 deal with a different question: does the mere fact that an instrument was signed for accommodation mean that it is not enforceable. Today it is hard to imagine why anyone would think there was any real issue on that score. People sign guaranties and "co-sign" notes all the time. It seems obvious that such undertakings are enforceable, though there may be special suretyship defenses. In the eighteenth century, however, there were real issues about whether courts should simply refuse to enforce accommodation bills. By the time that Chalmers codified the law of bills and notes in the late nineteenth century, the point had largely been forgotten. But, it was perhaps understandable that he included Section 28 to drive home the point that the old notion that there was something suspicious about accommodation bills had become a dead letter. It is, however, a bit odd to continue to have a statute that, in essence says "we gave up on the effort to stamp out accommodation bills nearly two hundred years ago." After all, all that the quoted passage of Section 3-419 says is that it doesn't matter that a party signed for accommodation. All kinds of things don't matter. We generally do not have a statute saying so.[28]

28. Section 3-419 really has no more content than a statute saying that if a person signs an instrument to obtain a trombone, the party shall be known as a "trombone party," but a trombone party is obliged to pay the instrument in the capacity in which he signed.

V. ACCOMMODATION PARTIES AND GUARANTORS

Let us consider other Article 3 provisions on accommodation parties. Many of these seem quite odd. For example, Section 3-419(b) says that an accommodation party's obligation "may be enforced notwithstanding any statute of frauds." At first glance that seems peculiar since, by definition, a party to a negotiable instrument has signed a writing stating the promise to pay. Where do such odd provisions come from? As usual, the answer is history. If you look at nineteenth-century treatises on bills and notes, you do find chapters on guaranty of bills and notes. Here is how Theophilus Parsons began his discussion:

> "Guaranty" . . . is an undertaking by some one that another shall perform his contract or fulfill his obligation, or that if he does not, the guarantor will do this for him. Now it is plain that this is in effect the contract of every indorser and of every surety. But the law merchant, which creates and defines the law of indorsement, applies this law only to the indorser strictly so called. The contract of guaranty is left to the general law of contracts. . . . We cannot, therefore, define a guarantor of a bill or note any better, than by saying that he is one who engages that the note shall be paid, but is not an indorser nor a surety. . . .
>
> It must be remembered that, while a surety of a note is generally a maker, a guarantor is never a maker. The surety's promise is to pay a debt, which becomes his own debt when the principal fails to pay it; and the surety may therefore be sued at once as soon as the note is due and dishonored. But the guarantor's promise is always to pay the debt of another. The distinction between the two is slight, as the words are commonly used.

> But as a matter of law, and in its legal consequences, the distinction is important, and it may be regretted that it has not always been carefully observed by courts.
>
> This engagement or contract of guaranty may be, and often is, written on the back of the note or bill; but may as well, so far as the guaranty is concerned, be written on a separate piece of paper, if it refers to the bill or note in a way which is sufficient to identify it. And this is held to constitute a guaranty of the note, although a part of the description is obviously inaccurate and inapplicable.[29]

It seems fairly unlikely that any modern lawyer, even one with as antiquarian a bent as I, could figure out what Parsons was saying in that passage. If, however, one looks a bit deeper at the discussion in the nineteenth-century treatises and cases, one begins to get a sense of what is going on.

Most of the problems addressed in the nineteenth-century treatises and cases are more or less what one would expect in the setting of actions against guarantors. Uncompensated sureties are trying to get off the hook by technical arguments. The key to understanding the origins of the Article 3 provisions on accommodation parties is to see how those arguments were framed. Consider a common form of nineteenth-century legal argument. One starts with the notion that there are several legally distinct categories of transactions, albeit having similar economic effect. Then one says that your client's deal was really a Category A deal, although the creditor treated it as a Category B deal. The legal formalities are different for the two categories. Since the creditor treated the case as a Category B deal, he failed to follow the proper Category A formalities, and therefore the client is not liable.

29. 2 Parsons, *supra* note 11, at 117–18.

In the nineteenth-century cases that seem to have given rise to some of the Article 3 rules on accommodation parties, the two categories were: (1) a party to the instrument, that is, one who undertook an obligation on the instrument as maker, drawer, acceptor, or indorser, versus (2) a guarantor of the obligation of someone who was a party to the instrument. Suppose that the guaranty contract had been written on the same paper as the note. Depending on where the tactical advantage lay, the person who signed in that form would argue either that he really was an indorser not a guarantor, or that he really was a guarantor not an indorser. An indorser could argue for discharge if the holder had failed to make proper presentment and give proper notice of dishonor, while that argument would not be available if one were considered a guarantor.[30] We saw earlier in this chapter how arcane the law of dishonor had become by the nineteenth century. No wonder it sometimes seemed appealing to uncompensated sureties.

It appears, though, that the tactical advantage usually ran the other way. A guarantor did not have the benefit of negotiable instruments law defenses such as improper presentment or notice, since he was not thought of as a party to the instrument. On the other hand, there were a host of trick arguments that could be spun out of the theory that the guarantor's liability was an independent obligation. Thus, someone might contend that he was a guarantor of the instrument, not an indorser, and therefore his obligation could not be enforced by a transferee of the instrument, as opposed to the person who held it when he gave his guaranty.[31] Or, he might contend that because his contract was that of a guarantor, rather

30. Warrington v. Furbor, 103 Eng. Rep. 334 (K.B. 1807).

31. True v. Fuller, 38 Mass. (21 Pick.) 140 (1838); Lamourieux v. Hewit, 5 Wend. 307 (N.Y. Sup. Ct. 1830). The point was commonly discussed under the heading of whether a guaranty was negotiable.

than a party to the instrument, it fell within the particularly rigorous provision of the statute of frauds requiring that an undertaking to answer for the debt of another was enforceable only if it recited the specific consideration given for that separate undertaking.[32]

Now, consider what to do about all these sorts of trick arguments when codifying the law of bills and notes. If we are doing so in the early twenty-first century, we would probably do best not to say anything at all. Indeed, many of the rules on guarantors or accommodation parties that we find in Article 3 seem like "beans in your ears" law. Recall the old saying that it's not a good idea to tell children not to put beans in their ears, because they would otherwise never have thought of trying.

Consider, for example, the Article 3 rules that specify in detail the difference between one who guarantees "collection" versus one who guarantees "payment."[33] The difference is that a guarantor of collection can be sued only if the creditor has first tried unsuccessfully to collect from the principal debtor. Of course creditors are usually going to try to collect from the principal debtor first. But there is a big difference between what one is likely to do in practice and what one is legally obligated to do. It is inconceivable that any creditor would actually want to undertake a legally enforceable duty to try to collect from the principal before she had a right to pursue a guarantor. A creditor who did so would be giving the already litigious guarantor another basis for arguing against liability. Indeed, other than as a result of legal malpractice, it is hard to see how one could end up with something that really was intended as merely a "guaranty of collection." But, so long as Article 3 has in it an explicit rule about this odd category of "guaranty of collection,"

32. Brewster v. Silence, 8 N.Y. 207 (1853).
33. U.C.C. § 3-419 (d) & (e).

uncompensated sureties are going to say "That's me" and courts are going to have to say "No it's not."[34]

In general, the conclusion that may be drawn from the pre-codification law is that the principal objective of statutory provisions governing guarantors of negotiable instruments was to forestall arguments of the general form of "I'm a guarantor, not an indorser, and therefore . . . ." That seems to the point of most of the rules of present Section 3-419, as well as some other rules on guaranty, such as the Section 3-202(4) rule that words of guaranty and the like added to an indorsement do not prevent negotiation.

Even if there is still any need for rules intended only to reject hyper-technical arguments by sureties, it is hard to see why there is a special need for such rules in Article 3. For example, Section 3-419(b) says that an accommodation party is liable "whether or not the accommodation party receives consideration." That is largely a response to an oddity of suretyship law. Uncompensated sureties still routinely argue that "I didn't get anything" should be a defense.[35] But, they never succeed, since "somebody else got the money" is simply definition of what it means to be a surety.[36] The simple contract analysis is that the uncompensated surety did receive consideration, in that the creditor did what the surety asked,

34. Cusimano v. First Md. Sav. & Loan, Inc., 639 A.2d 553 (D.C. 1994); Nogg Bros. Paper Co. v. Bickels, 446 N.W.2d 729 (Neb. 1989); Ford v. Darwin, 767 S.W.2d 851 (Tex. App. 1989). Sometimes courts get confused by this too, as in Evergreen Bank v. Sullivan, 980 F. Supp. 747 (D. Vt. 1997), where the court seems to have treated a party who had signed a guaranty agreement, not an Article 3 instrument, under the Article 3 rule on guaranty of collection, but, fortunately, concluded that the creditor had sufficiently pursued the principal debtor.

35. Gen. Motors Acceptance Corp. v. Jackson, 614 So. 2d 302 (La. Ct. App. 1993); Dalo v. Thalmann, 878 A.2d 194 (R.I. 2005).

36. First City Bank v. Cooper, No. 89-320-11, 1990 WL 27326 at *7 (Tenn. Ct. App.1990) ("At the outset one should understand that an accommodation party's failure to receive dollars in his pocket from the creditor is not a defense. Time and again sureties respond to a holder's suit by arguing, 'I am a surety and I did not receive consideration for my contract.' This is a losing argument.").

that is, make the loan to the principal debtor. Sureties have had some success with a lack of consideration argument when they became sureties well after the time that the creditor made the loan to the principal debtor. But even this "after-acquired surety" argument is generally disfavored by general suretyship law. For example, the Restatement of Contracts provides that the after-acquired surety argument will not work if the suretyship obligation is undertaken by a writing that "recites a nominal or purported consideration" or if the creditor reasonably relies on the surety's promise.[37] In any event, it is hard to see any reason why this question should be treated differently in Article 3 than in general suretyship law.

VI. SURETYSHIP DEFENSES

The most elaborate, and least defensible, rules in the present Article 3 on accommodation parties are the rules in Section 3-605 on suretyship defenses. It is not clear why we have such rules. The English Bills of Exchange Act has no provisions on suretyship defenses. It does have a brief section on accommodation parties, but the point of that section is only to provide that the fact that a party signed for accommodation does not affect the party's liability. At the time the Act was adopted, it was perhaps understandable that people felt it useful to have such a provision, simply to confirm rejection of the late eighteenth-century cases suggesting that there was something particularly suspicious about accommodation bills.

The Uniform Negotiable Instruments Law went beyond the Bills of Exchange Act and added several provisions reciting principles of general suretyship law on defenses, such as that release of the

37. Restatement (Second) of Contracts § 88 (1981).

principal debtor or extension of time releases the guarantor, unless the creditor makes a reservation of rights.[38] It is not clear why the drafters thought it necessary to include these rules of general suretyship law. Ames was puzzled by the matter, noting that "There seems to be no sufficient reason, on the one hand, for inserting these doctrines of suretyship in a negotiable instruments code, or, on the other hand, if they are to be inserted, for omitting other doctrines of suretyship of equal importance."[39] Britton's well-regarded treatise on the N.I.L. also recognized that this statutory rule was unnecessary, since it merely restated general suretyship law.[40]

A review of recent cases suggests that there is little reason to have any special statutory rules on suretyship defenses in Article 3. A search for cases in the past two decades produced about two hundred Article 3 cases on suretyship defenses. For the most part, they are simply routine suretyship defense disputes, where there is no reason to suppose that the outcome or analysis would have been any different if the cases had been treated under general suretyship law. The best of the cases recognize that most of the Article 3 accommodation party defense rules simply restate the general law of suretyship.[41] More commonly, however, having special Article 3 rules on suretyship seems to increase the confusion of an already difficult

38. N.I.L. § 120(5)-(6).

39. James Barr Ames, *The Negotiable Instruments Law*, 14 Harv. L. Rev. 241, 254 (1900). The discussion of the accommodation party rules was only part of Ames' highly critical assessment of the N.I.L. The President of the National Conference of Commissioners on Uniform Laws wrote a defense of the act in response to Ames' criticism, but did not offer any explanation of why it was thought useful to include these principles of general suretyship law. Lyman D. Brewster, *A Defense of the Negotiable Instruments Law*, 10 Yale L. J. 84, 96 (1900).

40. William Everett Britton, Handbook of the Law of Bills and Notes 1094 (1943).

41. United States v. Am. Nat'l Bank and Trust Co, No. 89 C 1754, 1989 WL 58279 (N.D. Ill. 1989); Venaglia v. Kropinak, 956 P.2d 824 (N.M. 1998); ESL Fed. Credit Union v. Bovee, 801 N.Y.S.2d 482 (N.Y. Sup. Ct. 2005).

subject, as in the numerous cases involving the question whether someone was a surety or a principal debtor. Courts commonly confuse the matter further by phrasing the issue as whether a party was an "accommodation party" or a "co-maker."[42]

The only points on which the Article 3 rules might actually differ from general suretyship law are matters involving the special rights of holders in due course. Even there, it is far from clear that there is any need for special Article 3 rules on accommodation parties. Suretyship defenses could simply be treated in the same fashion as any other defense that is cut off by a holder in due course. Not surprisingly, however, cases that actually involve holders in due course are as rare in this setting as in any other. Of about two hundred recent cases surveyed, only three seem to have involved someone who might actually have been a holder in due course.[43]

In many cases, courts seem to use a misunderstanding of the relationship between general suretyship law and Article 3 as a convenient way of disposing of arguments that could have been rejected on sounder grounds. For example, suppose that a surety who is sued

42. In re Flamingo 55, Inc., 378 B.R. 893, 909 (Bankr. D. Nev. 2007); Currie State Bank v. Schmitz, 628 N.W.2d 205, 208 (Minn. Ct. App. 2001); Kaufman v. Fairchild, 810 P.2d 1145, 1147 (Idaho Ct. App. 1991); Narans v. Paulsen, 803 P.2d 358, 360 (Wyo. 1990). Sometimes the Article 3 rules manage to leave everyone confused. In McCarthy v. Sessions, 572 N.Y.S.2d 749 (N.Y. App. Div. 1991), the litigant seems to have thought that if he were an accommodation party then he would not be liable. The court looked to the holder in due course rules to reject that contention, even though the plaintiff was the original creditor.

43. J & B Schoenfeld Fur Merchs., Inc. v. Kilbourne & Donohue, Inc., 704 F. Supp. 466 (S.D.N.Y. 1989) Ashland State Bank v. Elkhorn Racquetball, Inc., 520 N.W.2d 189 (Neb. 1994); First Westroads Bank v. Opstein, No. A-92–136, 1994 WL 380290 (Neb. Ct. App. 1994). Moreover, neither the *Ashland State Bank* nor *First Westroads Bank* cases fits the classic model of the holder in due course who takes the instrument as a form of currency. In both cases, the payees of the notes had pledged the notes to a bank. There are also cases in which federal receivers of failed banks are permitted to sue free from defenses that might have been asserted against the original payee bank. *E.g.*, FDIC v. Wrapwell Corp., 922 F. Supp. 913 (S.D.N.Y. 1996); First City, Texas-Beaumont, N.A. v. Treece, 848 F. Supp. 727 (E.D. Tex. 1994). These cases, however, would have been resolved in the same way under federal law regardless of what Article 3 said.

on a note contends that he is not liable because the creditor took action that gave rise to a suretyship defense. Suppose that the court intuits, probably correctly, that the argument should lose. To reach that result properly, the court should consider whether the facts give rise to the defense. Suppose, however, that the defendant has relied solely on the articulation of suretyship defense rules in Article 3. Suppose, further, that either the instrument is not actually a negotiable instrument, or that the defendant did not incur suretyship status by signing the note. A simple, though bogus, way of disposing of the case is for the court to say that the defendant's argument loses because Article 3 does not apply. In fact, all that follows from that observation is that the case is governed by general suretyship law, which undoubtedly contains a substantive rule essentially identical to the Article 3 rule. But, in many cases, the court does not get to that point, either because the court does not realize it, or hopes no one else will notice.[44]

Finally, there is the question of whether the suretyship defenses should be available to a non-accommodation co-maker. Suppose two people sign a note as makers, both being principal debtors. As a matter of general contribution law, if one pays the full amount, she would be entitled to contribution from the other. That relationship can be described in suretyship terms. It is as if each of the obligors is liable for half the debt as a principal obligor and is liable for the other half of the debt as a surety for the other obligor. That would mean any co-maker, not just an accommodation party, might be able to assert suretyship defenses to the extent of her right of contribution.

44. First City Bank v. Air Capitol Aircraft Sales, Inc., 820 F.2d 1127, 1134 (10th Cir. 1987); Heller Financial, Inc. v. Papachristou, No. 93 C 363, 1993 WL 169677 (N.D. Ill. 1993); FDIC v. Henry, 818 F. Supp. 452, 456 (D. Mass 1993); City Nat'l Bank v. Reiman, 601 N.E.2d 316, 322–23 (Ill. App. Ct. 1992); Pemstein v. Stimpson, 630 N.E.2d 608, 612 (Mass. App. Ct. 1994); Mgfs. & Traders Trust Co. v. Int'l Packaging, Inc., 617 N.Y.S.2d 91 (N.Y. App. Div. 1994); Citizens & So. Nat'l Bank v. Lanford, 443 S.E.2d 549, 551 (S.C. 1994).

Imagine, for example, the routine case of a husband and wife who co-sign a note for a business venture. The creditor deals with the husband, and allows him an extension of time. After default (and, commonly, after the divorce), the creditor pursues the wife. Even if the wife is a principal obligor, she would have a right of contribution from the husband if she is forced to pay the full amount of the debt. In other words, she can be thought of as principal obligor for half the debt and surety for the other half. If so, then she might argue that she is entitled to assert suretyship defenses to the extent of one-half of her liability on the note. The cases under the former version of Article 3 were in considerable disarray on this issue. In some of the cases, one has the sense that the court believed that the asserted defense would ultimately be without merit, and just disposed of the case in a quick and dirty fashion by saying the defendant was not an accommodation party.[45] But, even where the point was more explicitly raised, there was considerable disagreement in the cases.[46]

The 1990 revision of revised Article 3 may well have made the problem worse.[47] In its original form, the 1990 version of Section 6-605(f) expressly gave a principal co-maker the defense of impairment of collateral, to the extent of her right of contribution. By contrast, the defenses of release, extension, or other modification were stated as applicable to "an indorser or accommodation party."[48] That suggested that a principal co-maker did not have the defenses; though one might well wonder if the non-accommodation

45. *See* United States v. Unum, Inc. 658 F.2d 300 (5th Cir. 1981); Campo v. Maloney, 442 A.2d 997 (N.H. 1982); Fed. Fin. Co. v. Landers, 740 A.2d 345 (Vt. 1999).

46. John S. Herbrand, Annotation, *Who is "Party" Discharged on Negotiable Instrument to Extent of Holder's Unjustifiable Impairment of Collateral*, 93 A.L.R.3d 1283 (1979).

47. Neil B. Cohen, *Suretyship Principles in the New Article 3: Clarifications and Substantive Changes*, 42 Ala. L. Rev. 595, 616–619 (1991).

48. U.C.C. § 3-605(b), (c) & (d) (1990).

co-maker could still resort to general suretyship law.[49] After the American Law Institute completed the *Restatement (Third) of Suretyship and Guaranty* project in 1995, the sponsors of the U.C.C. recommended a revision of Section 3-605 to bring it into conformity with the rules articulated in the Restatement. The current (2002) version seems to resolve the issue. Section 3-605 now gives the suretyship defenses to a "secondary obligor" rather than using the "indorser or accommodation party" language of the 1990 version. The definition of "secondary obligor" makes clear that it includes a principal co-maker, to the extent of her right of contribution.[50] So the statute now seems to say explicitly that a principal co-maker has, to the extent of her right of contribution, all the same suretyship defenses as an accommodation party.[51] Another question is whether courts will get it right or will continue to apply their old case law.

To be sure, the 1990 revision of Article 3 did some good. In general, it sought to base suretyship defense law on the question whether the surety was likely to have suffered any real harm from the creditor's action, rejecting some of the convoluted arguments that had formed the basis of much earlier law. That change made it possible for the *Restatement (Third) of Suretyship and Guaranty* to look to the Article 3 revision as support for making similar changes in general suretyship law. But, now that that change has been made, there is

49. U.C.C. § 1-103 ("Unless displaced by the particular provisions of the Uniform Commercial Code, the principles of law and equity, including the law merchant and the law relative to capacity to contract, principal and agent, estoppel, fraud, misrepresentation, duress, coercion, mistake, bankruptcy, and other validating or invalidating cause supplement its provisions.").

50. U.C.C. §§ 3-103(a)(17) & 3-116(b).

51. The Official Comments state explicitly that "this section also deals with the rights of co-makers of instruments, even when those co-makers do not qualify as accommodation parties. The co-makers" rights of contribution under Section 3-116 make each co-maker a secondary obligor to the extent of that right of contribution." U.C.C. § 3-605 cmt. 3.

really no good reason to have a separate body of law for suretyship arrangements implemented through signatures on Article 3 instruments. After all, the coverage of the Article 3 rules is really quite limited. All of the suretyship defenses can be waived. Indeed, the main function of a guaranty agreement is to waive all potential suretyship defenses. That is such a significant concern in lending arrangements that any carefully implemented transaction will invariably make use of a separate guaranty agreement, simply for the purpose of providing a carefully drafted comprehensive waiver of suretyship defenses. Even if the parties fail to do that and rely on the "quick and dirty" method of having the guarantor sign a note, they will invariably include a waiver of suretyship defenses.[52] Accordingly, the likelihood of the Article 3 substantive rules coming into play is so small that it hardly justifies having a separate set of rules. The matter would be far better left to the general law of suretyship.[53]

VII. PROMISSORY NOTES ARE JUST CONTRACTS

So, what would the law of promissory notes look like if it were drafted for the post-negotiability era? The answer is actually quite simple. It would look like general contract law. Indeed, it would be general contract law. There really is no need or justification for having a separate body of statutory law to govern those debt

52. Neil Cohen, who served as Reporter for the RESTATEMENT (THIRD) OF SURETYSHIP AND GUARANTY, relates an anecdote from his early legal practice of being asked whether he had waived suretyship defenses in a note he had drafted. When Neil asked the partner what they were, the response was "I don't know either, but I know that you're supposed to waive them." Neil B. Cohen, *Striking the Balance: The Evolving Nature of Suretyship Defenses*, 34 WM. & MARY L. REV. 1025 (1993).

53. Cohen, *supra* note 1, at 170–74.

contracts that happen to be implemented by signing promissory notes, as distinguished from those debt contracts not governed by Article 3. As we have seen in this chapter, having a separate body of statutory law for promissory notes only adds confusion, largely by preserving remnants of historical oddities that otherwise would have long ago been forgotten.

In fact, it is not really accurate to describe Article 3 as providing the law governing *notes* as debt contracts. Rather, Article 3 is a law about *transfer* of notes. As we have seen, the whole point of Article 3 is to articulate the rules that were thought necessary in the era when notes and other instruments were commonly transferred from party to party as a mechanism of payment. Now that such transfers never or rarely occur, there really is no reason to have an Article 3. To see the point more clearly, suppose that works on general contract law were written in the style of Article 3. We would start by saying that the most important thing about contracts is that they can be assigned. When we discussed any specific issue, whether it be consideration, contract formation, defenses, or whatever, the analysis would consist primarily, if not exclusively, of a discussion of the impact of the particular issue on the rights of assignees of contract rights. Any modern lawyer reading such a work would immediately be struck by how odd it is. Of course there are issues and rules on assignment of contracts, but those are hardly the most important aspect of the law of contracts. Indeed, the subject of assignment is usually a prime candidate for omission when time runs short at the end of a contracts course.

9

What Would a Modern Law of Checks Look Like?

In the previous chapter, it was argued that there is no modern role for negotiable instruments law in the setting of promissory notes. This chapter considers the analogous question in the setting of checks.

To begin, consider the old chestnut that still provides the fodder for classroom games: "Can you write a check on a cow?" Although urban legend sometimes presents this as an actual event, the story actually comes from the British humorist A. P. Herbert. One of Herbert's series of anecdotes published in Punch Magazine in the early twentieth century tells of a disgruntled taxpayer who presented the collector of taxes with a check written on the side of a cow. Herbert's story tells of the discussion before the court about whether the item really was a negotiable instrument.[1]

It is not entirely clear what the point of the story is supposed to be. The legal analysis is that if the taxpayer used the correct wording, the fact that the check was written on a cow rather than the conventional piece of paper does not disqualify it from classification

1. A. P. Herbert, Uncommon Law 201–06 (1935, reprint 1991). In other versions encountered in law school classrooms, the taxpayer presents the shirt off his back, on which he has written a check for the amount of his tax debt.

as a negotiable instrument. But the further point, rarely explored in the classrooms, is that absolutely nothing turns on that conclusion. Presentation of a negotiable instrument to one's creditor does not result in satisfaction of the debt. The debt is discharged only if the instrument is paid. If the payee took the cow to the payor bank, the payor bank could—for good reason, bad reason, or no reason at all—refuse to pay it to the payee. The payee would have no right against the payor bank.[2] In an ordinary case where a payor bank refuses to pay a check, the drawer might have an action for damages against the payor bank.[3] The drawer's wrongful dishonor action is akin to the tort action of defamation in that the payor bank's refusal to pay an ordinary check might be construed by the payee as an indication that the drawer was writing bad checks. But, it is pretty obvious that the payor bank is not acting wrongfully against the drawer if it refuses to pay a check written on the side of a cow. That is a matter of the agreement between the drawer and the payor bank. It has nothing to do with the abstract legal question whether the item is or is not a negotiable instrument.

So the lesson to be drawn from the bovine check story is that absolutely nothing follows from the conclusion that a thing that looks like a check is, or is not, a negotiable instrument. Why then have a law of checks that is based on the notion that checks are a species of negotiable instrument? We can see how twisted the law of checks has become by looking at a variety of issues involving checks that have been approached through the concepts of negotiable instruments law.

2. U.C.C. § 3-408.
3. U.C.C. § 4-402.

I. INDORSEMENT OF CHECKS

Consider how the Article 3 rules on transfer of negotiable instruments apply to checks. Since checks are generally issued in order form, the Article 3 mechanism for their transfer is indorsement. Article 3 divides the concept of indorsement into the subcategories of special and blank. A special indorsement specifies the person to whom the instrument is payable, as where a check payable to the order of Jones is indorsed by Jones with the words "pay to the order of Smith /s/ Jones." A blank indorsement specifies no particular indorsee, as where a check payable to the order of Jones is indorsed by Jones with merely his signature. There is a further distinction between restrictive and non-restrictive indorsements. Although other forms are theoretically possible, the only significant example of a restrictive indorsement is one "for deposit only." The text and comments to the relevant sections of Article 3 explain these concepts in extensive detail, as do most treatises and casebooks.[4] The question is why.

As was shown in Chapter 7, the only thing that ever really happens to a check is that it is deposited for collection by the payee. In that setting, the concept of indorsement plays essentially no role. Theoretically, if a depositary bank gives its customer credit for a check that is returned unpaid, the depositary bank could recover the amount of the check from its depositor on the ground that by indorsing the check the depositor incurred liability on it in the event of dishonor. But, it is hard to see why a depositary bank would resort to that bills and notes concept, since it has a far simpler basis for recovery. Under Section 4-214, if a depositary bank fails to receive

4. U.C.C. §§ 3-204, 3-205, 3-206; James J. White & Robert A. Summers, Uniform Commercial Code 479–85 (5th ed. 2000).

a final settlement for a check, it can revoke any provisional settlement given to its customer. If the customer has already withdrawn any provisional credit, the depositary bank can recover the amount of the check from the depositor. Given that rule, there is really no need for indorser's liability.[5]

Indeed, indorsement seems to play absolutely no role in the modern check system. Under the rigid rules of negotiable instruments law, it was necessary for a customer to indorse checks when depositing them. Otherwise the depository bank would not qualify as a holder, because the check would have been payable to the order of the customer but not indorsed by the customer. In practice, however, depositary banks frequently do not obtain the indorsement of their depositors. If a single check is deposited over the counter at a bank, the teller will ordinarily ask the customer to indorse, but if the checks are deposited at a night depositary or under a lock box arrangement, the depositary bank will have no occasion to determine whether the checks are or are not indorsed. Article 4 has always had a provision allowing a depositary bank to supply a missing indorsement of its depositor,[6] but under the pre-1990 version there was some dispute in the cases about whether a bank that had not done so could qualify as the holder of a check.[7] The 1990 revision eliminates that problem by providing that a depositary bank is the holder of any check received for collection from a customer who was a holder, whether or not the bank goes through the silly

5. In some cases, a check may pass through the hands of a party, such as a check cashing agency or grocery store, which is not actually a depositary bank, though it is acting in essentially the same fashion. Even there, indorsement liability is not needed. The right of a check cashing agency to recover the amount paid to someone for a check which is dishonored could easily be based on restitution concepts.

6. U.C.C. § 4-205 (1990).

7. Barkley Clark & Barbara Clark, The Law of Bank Deposits, Collections and Credit Cards ¶ 5.03 (2009).

step of adding the customer's indorsement.[8] So, if absolutely nothing turns on the presence or absence of the customer's indorsement, why have the concept at all?

One purported explanation found in the books runs along the following lines: Suppose that a check is payable to the order of Joe Jones. Joe Jones indorses it in blank, with no restrictive legend. The check is stolen from Jones by Scalawag. Scalawag deposits it for collection in his own bank account. The analysis is that because Jones indorsed in blank, the check became payable to bearer. Consequently, even Scalawag was the "holder" because he was in possession of an instrument payable to bearer.[9] Although the Scalawag could be a holder, he would not be a holder in due course, since he stole the check rather than taking it for value. So Jones could have asserted his claim of ownership against the thief. But, when the depository bank received the check from Scalawag, the depository bank could qualify as a holder, because the check had been indorsed in blank by Jones. Moreover, the depository bank would ordinarily have no reason to know of the theft and so could qualify as a holder in due course. Accordingly, the depositary bank did not act improperly when it collected the check for Scalawag. The moral invariably drawn is that it is very risky to indorse a check in blank without the restrictive legend "for deposit only."[10] The corollary is that someone like our fellow Joe Jones who was so foolish as to indorse in blank has only himself to blame for his loss.

But let us stop and think. In the routine case, indorsement plays no role in the check collection system. The only situation in which

8. U.C.C. § 4-205.

9. U.C.C. § 3-201 cmt 1.

10. Ellen A. Peters, A Negotiable Instruments Primer 27 (2nd ed. 1974); Robert Braucher & Robert A. Riegert, Introduction to Commercial Transactions 69 (1977); Lary Lawrence, An Introduction to Payment Systems 60 (1997).

the rules on indorsement matter is where a payee indorses in blank without the restrictive legend. Commercial law cognoscenti all make fun of that person. But why should we have a set of rules whose only consequence is to impose a loss on someone whose only error was a failure to understand the arcana of negotiable instruments law? It is hardly a justification for the odd rule to say that people should know about it and if they did they could avoid the harsh consequence. That would be like having a rule saying that contracts are unenforceable if they are signed in green ink, and then justifying that rule by saying that anyone who is so foolish as to sign in green ink deserves to lose.

The entire problem, and any need for rules on indorsement, could be eliminated if the statute were rewritten to say simply that if a depositary bank receives a check for collection it is obligated to credit any value received for the check to the account of the payee. There would be no need for the payee to indorse, no need for rules about the significance of the "for deposit only" legend, and no occasion for imposing loss on someone who happens to have indorsed a check in blank.[11]

II. LOST OR STOLEN BANK CHECKS

The persistence of the view that checks are appropriately treated as negotiable instruments can produce genuine adverse consequences. Consider the plight of a person who loses a bank check. For example, suppose that a person who is moving from one part of the country to another closes his old bank account and receives

11. The result would be similar to the treatment of "crossed checks" under English law, discussed in chapter 7, note 1.

his money in the form of a bank check. The person plans to use the bank check to open a new account in his new home. Upon arriving in his new locale, the person is horrified to discover that he has lost the bank check. The person contacts the bank that issued the check, anticipating that the problem can be resolved with, at most, some nuisance. Little does he realize how problematic his situation may be.

Under the pre-1990 version of Article 3, the owner of a lost instrument could recover from the person obligated on the instrument, but only if he provided security to protect the obligated person from loss that it might suffer in the event that the lost instrument turned up and was presented for payment. Suppose that the bank check was payable to the order of the person who purchased it. If he had not indorsed it, then neither someone who found it nor any subsequent transferee could qualify as a holder, because the instrument could not bear the genuine indorsement of the payee. In that case, the bank could safely provide the owner with a refund. Suppose, however, that the payee had foolishly indorsed the check in blank before losing it. Suppose further that someone found the check and transferred it for value to someone else. The hypothetical transferee could qualify as a holder and hence could have a right to enforce the instrument as a holder in due course. In that case, the bank that issued the check might end up paying twice if it refunded the money to the owner and then a holder in due course showed up with the check. Though that scenario may be unlikely, Article 3 provided that as a condition to getting a refund, the owner could be required to post security to protect the obligated bank against that risk.[12] The expense of getting such a security bond

12. The problem was particularly severe in New York which had a non-uniform version of Section 3-804 that made it mandatory, not discretionary, for the court to require indemnity. *See* Diaz v. Manufacturers Hanover Trust Co., 401 N.Y.S.2d 952 (N.Y. Sup. Ct. 1977).

might well be prohibitive. Thus, the person who lost the check would be out of luck.

The revised version of Article 3 adds a rather complicated provision directed to this problem. Under Section 3-312, the person who lost the check can submit to the obligated bank a "declaration of loss" explaining that the check has been lost and has not been transferred. The declaration of loss has no effect for ninety days, that is, if someone who qualifies as a holder in due course shows up with the check within that period, the obligated bank is free to pay the check. After the ninety-day period, however, the obligated bank is required to pay the amount of the check to the claimant and is relieved of any liability on the instrument. At the time this provision was drafted, there was some concern that it had the effect of making it unsafe for anyone to take a bank check more than ninety days after its date, but the thought seems to have been that the potential harm to the owner of the lost instrument outweighed any such concerns.

The problem that this provision deals with is entirely a product of treating checks as negotiable instruments. Suppose that a bank check were treated simply as an instruction to make payment to the payee. A person who got a bank check as a way of moving his bank account from one place to another would be the only person entitled to receive payment. We would never talk about "transfer" of the check, and would never have occasion to ask whether there might be a transferee who qualified as a holder in due course. The obligated bank could simply issue a refund to the person who lost the check. There would be no need for security, or for the elaborate provision in revised Article 3 about a "declaration of loss," because the check would be treated simply as an instruction to pay money to the person who bought it, not to any potential transferee.

One might object that there might be situations where it does make sense for a person to buy a bank check intending to transfer it to another party. The author's recollection is that at the time that Section 3-312 was drafted some concern was expressed that people might buy bank checks payable to themselves and keep them for awhile intending to use them to make payment to others. The example posed was that a person who attends various property auctions might want to carry a bank check so that he would be able to make a deposit on a property that he bid for. Under Section 3-312, such bank checks are, in effect, only good for ninety days. The problem illustrates not that it makes sense to treat all checks, or all bank checks, as negotiable instruments, but that there might be relatively unusual circumstances in which that treatment makes sense. We might have a system in which bank checks come in two versions. The ordinary version—the one that would be provided to the usual customer—would be a check that is payable only to the original payee, that is, it would not be "negotiable" in the sense that it could be transferred to someone who could qualify as a holder in due course. We could also have a different version—for people who need a transferrable instrument—that is governed by rules akin to the holder in due course rules. The problem with current law is that it insists on treating the ordinary case under rules appropriate only for the unusual case. Some people need vehicles that can travel on land or in water; but that is no reason for saying that all cars must be amphibious.

The complexity of the rules of revised Article 3 on lost or stolen bank checks may also be an illustration of the increasing irrelevance of Article 3. In sources on the law of checks, one can find elaborate discussion of the details and complexities of revised Section 3-312.[13]

13. Henry J. Bailey & Richard B. Hagedorn, Brady on Bank Checks ¶ 4.16 (rev. ed. 2009); Fred H. Miller & Alvin C. Harrell, The Law of Modern Payment Systems 399–400 (2003); William D. Warren & Steven D. Walt, Payments and Credits 91–95 (7th ed. 2007).

On the other hand, if one looks for litigated cases, one finds nothing other than a few cases that refer to Section 3-312 but involve other issues. One suspects that the whole problem may be a remnant of the past. Today, people seeking to move funds from one bank account to another are likely to do so by means of a wire transfer rather than a bank check. With no paper bank check, there is no problem of loss or theft. That may be the reason that we do not see decisions dealing with the complex new provisions of Section 3-312. The provision may well be a clever solution to a problem that is no longer of any practical significance. But, like so much else in Article 3, it remains in the statute and therefore remains a subject that law students learning the statute are expected to master.

III. THE UNNECESSARY COMPLEXITY OF THE CHECK COLLECTION RULES

Treating checks as negotiable instruments rather than as payment instructions makes the law of the check system needlessly complex. Consider the explanation needed of the process of collection and payment of checks. When payees deposit checks, depositary banks make a provisional settlement for them. That settlement can be revoked if the depositary bank does not itself receive a settlement that becomes final. As the bundles of checks proceed toward the payor banks in the forward collection process, similar provisional settlements are made between the collecting banks. Ultimately, the checks are presented to the payor bank for payment. The payor bank makes a provisional settlement when the checks are presented, and that settlement becomes final if not revoked in a timely fashion. When the settlement made by the payor bank becomes final, all prior settlements made in forward collection become final.

Sorting through the relevant U.C.C. provisions to find the law governing that process is by no means an easy task. Consider only the stage of payment by the payor bank. Section 4-215(1) provides that the check is finally paid by the payor bank when the payor bank has (1) paid the check in cash, (2) settled for the check without having a right to revoke the settlement, or (3) made a provisional settlement and failed to revoke that settlement in a timely fashion. The first of these—payment in cash—seems to be fairly straightforward, though relatively rare.[14] Let us consider the other two.

One possibility listed in the statute is that the payor bank settles for the check without having a right to revoke that settlement. Though this appears on its face to be a rule describing situations where a payor bank might be held to have made final payment, the reality is the opposite. In practice, the payor bank will always have a right to revoke any provisional settlement given for the item on presentment.

14. In the routine check processing system, when checks are presented to the payor bank, the payor bank settles for them by making a provisional settlement, not by paying cash. Occasionally, the holder of a check brings it to the payor bank and asks the bank to cash the check. Even in such cases, it is not really clear what is meant by the colloquial phrase "cash a check." Suppose that the payee of a check takes it to her bank and asks if the bank will "cash" the check. The bank might well hand over cash, but ordinarily it will do so only if the payee's account has sufficient funds to cover the amount of the withdrawal. The bank is simply doing two things at once: taking the check for deposit and allowing its account holder to withdraw an equivalent amount from her account. Now, suppose that the check happens to be drawn on an account at the same bank where the payee maintains her account. Again the bank may hand over cash when it takes the check, but the analysis is presumably the same: the bank takes the check for deposit, and the bank withdraws an equivalent sum from the payee's account. We would have a situation that could aptly be described as "paying" the check in the Section 4-215 sense only if the payor bank was willing to "cash" it either for a person who did not also keep an account at that bank or for a person who had an account with a balance less than the amount of the check. Banks are commonly reluctant to do that, and often impose fees to discourage the practice. There are a number of cases in which persons attempting to cash checks at payor banks have, on a variety of implausible bases, argued unsuccessfully that they should not be obligated to pay fees or provide identification. Messing v. Bank of Am., 821 A.2d 22 (Md. 2003); Moorehouse v. Chase Manhattan Bank, 76 S.W.3d 608 (Tex. App. 2002); Sexton v. PNC Bank, 792 A.2d 602 (Pa. Super. Ct. 2002).

So why have the statutory rule? The comments to the equivalent provision of former Article 4 provide a clue. They indicate that the main point of this provision was to permit banks to include a provision in their deposit agreements avoiding the effect of pre-Code cases that had held that a payor bank had made final payment.[15] In all of the cases cited, a bank that was both payor and depositary had done something that could be described as paying the check to the depositor before discovering that the drawer's account did not have sufficient funds to cover the check.[16] In those cases the banks were unsuccessful in their efforts to recover the money from the depositor, because the courts ruled that the bank had made final payment. The effect of the rule now in Section 4-215(b) is that banks can avoid any such risk by simply adding a provision to their deposit agreement stating that they have a right to revoke any money paid to a depositor for a check drawn by another customer so long as they act in a timely fashion.

The only part of Section 4-215(a) that really matters is the rule in Section 4-215(a)(3) that a check is finally paid if the payor bank makes a provisional settlement and fails to revoke it in a timely fashion. Moreover, that rule is primarily a cross-reference to other bodies of law, since the time requirements for revocation of settlement are typically specified by rules of clearinghouses or the Federal Reserve System for checks collected through the Fed. It is also a bit difficult to see what the relationship is between Section 4-215, which speaks of settlement by a payor bank becoming final, and Section 4-302, which

15. Former U.C.C. § 4-213, cmt 4.

16. Cohen v. First Nat'l Bank, 198 P. 122 (Ariz. 1921); Briviesca v. Coronado, 120 P.2d 649 (Cal. 1941); W.A. White Brokerage Co. v. Cooperman, 290 N.W. 790 (Minn. 1940); Scotts Bluff County v. First Nat'l Bank, 212 N.W. 617 (Neb. 1927); Provident Sav. Bank & Trust Co. v. Hildebrand, 196 N.E. 790 (Ohio Ct. App. 1934); Schaer v. First Nat'l Bank, 124 S.W.2d 108 (Tex. Comm'n App. 1939); Union State Bank v. People's State Bank, 211 N.W. 931 (Wis. 1927).

speaks of a payor bank becoming "accountable" for a check. Section 4-302 says that if a check is presented to payor bank, but the payor bank does not even make a provisional settlement at the time of presentment, then the payor bank becomes accountable for the amount of the check if it does not return the item or give notice of dishonor in a timely fashion. The puzzlement here is how it would happen that a check would be presented to a payor bank without the payor bank making a provisional settlement for it. In the modern check collection system, that never happens. The answer, of course, is that the statute is not stating a rule for modern check processing. Rather, the statute is telling us what the rule should be for situations of the sort that were common in the past. As was explained in more detail in Chapter 6, in former times payor banks did not routinely make a provisional settlement at the time of presentment. Rather they might receive a check on presentment and sometime later figure out how to transfer funds to the presenting bank. That never happens anymore. But, as should by now hardly seem surprising, the U.C.C. still dutifully states the rule for such cases, by providing that a payor bank becomes accountable for an item if it retains it without settling.

So the only situation that has continuing modern significance is where the payor bank makes a provisional settlement at the time of presentment and makes final payment simply by failing to revoke that settlement. Except where a shorter rule is established by a clearinghouse rule or Federal Reserve rule—which, by the way, is almost always the case—the relevant time for the payor bank to revoke is midnight of the banking day following the banking day of presentment. Section 4-301 explains that this rule reflects the practice of "deferred posting." A modern reader might well ask "Deferred from what?" Again, the answer is history.

Suppose we looked at the processing of checks by the payor bank through the lens of old negotiable instruments law. The check is a draft, and the payor bank is the drawee. The process of payment of the check would be a matter of presentment and either payment or dishonor. It would seem to be a simple matter to decide whether the payor bank paid the check or not, but, recall another concept of negotiable instruments law—acceptance. Aside from certification of checks, the concept of acceptance plays no role in modern check processing. Payor banks do not accept checks thereby promising to pay them, they either do or do not pay them. Suppose, however, that a check is presented for payment to a payor bank, a period of several days goes by, and then the payor bank gives notice that it is dishonoring the check. Might the payor bank's delay in deciding to dishonor be taken to show that it had actually accepted the check and so became liable as a party to it? In the nineteenth century, that question would have been viewed not as a matter of the law of check collections, but as part of the law of bills and notes. Specifically, the issue was part of the complex law on what constituted acceptance of a bill of exchange. Not surprisingly, the nineteenth-century case law was in some disarray, but there was plenty of authority for the proposition that undue delay could constitute acceptance.[17]

The Negotiable Instruments Law tried to bring some order to this field, but still treated the question as a matter of the law of bills of exchange rather than as a question specific to the check system. Section 136 of the N.I.L. provided that the drawee had twenty-four hours to decide whether to accept a bill or not. Section 150 provided that if a bill was presented for acceptance and not accepted

17. The cases are discussed in 2 Joseph F. Randolph, A Treatise on the Law of Commercial Paper 246–47 (1888).

within the prescribed twenty-four hour period, it was to be treated as dishonored. Section 137, however, provided that if the drawee destroys the bill or "refuses within twenty-four hours . . . to return the bill accepted or non-accepted, he will be deemed to have accepted the same." Unfortunately, since the N.I.L. treated check collections merely as an instance of broader principles of bills and notes, it did not clearly address the process of payment or dishonor by payor banks. Nor did it state clearly whether the rules on acceptance applied to check processing by payor banks. The result was hardly surprising. In a somewhat notorious decision, *Wisner v. First National Bank*,[18] the Pennsylvania Supreme Court ruled that Sections 136 and 137 of the N.I.L. did apply to check processing by payor banks, though they spoke in terms of acceptance. The result was that the failure of a payor bank to return a check within twenty-four hours of presentment constituted acceptance. That decision was fairly controversial. The case was followed in many other jurisdictions, although leading works on negotiable instruments law disagreed on its soundness and the Pennsylvania legislature overruled it by statute shortly after it was decided.[19]

As a result, a payor bank could not confidently assume that it had any more than twenty-four hours after a check was presented to decide whether it should be paid. By the middle of the twentieth century, that time pressure became particularly problematic, particularly given labor shortages during World War II. As Fairfax Leary pointed out, the notion that undue delay would preclude the payor bank from returning the check was not itself problematic. Rather the problem was that the twenty-four hour period

18. 68 A. 955 (Pa. 1908).

19. Compare Frederick K. Beutel, Beutel's Brannan Negotiable Instruments Law 1249–54 (7th ed. 1948) (approving *Wisner* case) with William E. Britton, Handbook of the Law of Bills and Notes 829–32 (1943) (criticizing *Wisner* case).

for timely action established by these interpretations of the N.I.L. was too short.[20] Accordingly, in the mid-twentieth century, virtually all jurisdictions adopted "deferred posting" statutes which permitted a payor bank an extra day to decide whether or not to pay. When the U.C.C. was drafted, the deferred posting notion was carried forward in Section 4-301. There is nothing wrong with the rule. The oddity is only that it is explained as a matter of "deferred posting"—a concept which makes no sense unless one happens to be familiar with the pre-Code controversy.

So, let us summarize. We have rules on payment of checks in cash, but that rarely happens. We have rules on what would happen if a payor bank fails to make a provisional settlement when checks are presented, but that rarely, if ever, happens. Assuming a real world case in which the payor bank does make a provisional settlement, the time for revocation of the settlement is typically specified not by the statute, but by a clearinghouse rule or Federal Reserve regulations. If a shorter time is not specified elsewhere, the payor bank can draw comfort from the fact that the "deferred posting" rule of Section 4-301 rejects the strained interpretation that some courts had placed on the rules for dishonor contained in the Uniform Negotiable Instruments Law. Can't we simply forget about the past? Why not write the rules in light of how check collection is actually conducted today, instead of burying those rules in elaborate provisions that would prove quite useful if the nineteenth century should happen to return? When we come to the matters that are actually significant, it is really not necessary to write rules in the form of "Do not apply results that were reached in odd cases over a century ago, which, by the way, no one remembers anymore."

20. Fairfax Leary, *Deferred Posting and Delayed Returns—The Current Check Collection Problem*, 62 Harv. L. Rev. 905, 918 (1949).

IV. THE UNNECESSARY COMPLEXITY OF THE CHECK FRAUD RULES

The problem of the allocation of forgery and fraud losses in the check collection system provides a perfect illustration of the unnecessarily byzantine complexities introduced into payment systems law by the negotiable instruments law approach.

Consider, for example, the rights of a payee from whom a check is stolen: Drawer draws a check on his account at Payor Bank payable to the order of Payee and delivers it to Payee. Scalawag steals it from Payee, forges Payee's indorsement and deposits it in his account at Depositary Bank. Depositary Bank presents it to Payor Bank and Payor Bank pays it. Payee, being in possession of an instrument drawn to his order was the holder of the check. Scalawag did not become the holder of the check, because he was not in possession of an instrument drawn or indorsed to him or his order or to bearer or in blank. Moreover, Scalawag did not acquire the instrument by negotiation, which requires a voluntary delivery of the check and, in the case of order paper, an indorsement. Scalawag did write on the back of the check words that appeared to be the signature of Payee, but this was not really an "indorsement" of the check. That is because an indorsement must be written by or on behalf of the holder of the check and Scalawag was not himself the holder of the check. Since Scalawag could not indorse the check when he deposited it at Depositary Bank, Depositary Bank could not become the holder of the check. Accordingly, Depositary Bank could not become a holder in due course of the check. Since Depositary Bank was not a holder in due course of the check, it took the check subject to Payee's claim of rightful ownership of the check. Having dealt with the check in a fashion inconsistent with Payee's claim of ownership, Depositary Bank is liable to Payee for conversion of the check.

Alternatively, Payee might decide to sue Payor Bank rather than Depositary Bank, in which case we will have to consider whether paying a check over a forged indorsement amounts to a conversion of the check. That is an intriguing puzzlement in this property language world, but it is resolved by the statement in Section 3-420(a) that "[a]n instrument is . . . converted if . . . a bank makes payment . . . with respect to the instrument for a person not entitled to enforce the instrument or receive payment." Of course, if Payee does proceed against Payor Bank, Payor Bank will not be without recourse. Section 4-208 provides that upon presentment Depositary Bank warranted that it was a person entitled to enforce the instrument. As was noted above, Depositary Bank was not a holder of the check, and therefore was not a person entitled to enforce it. Accordingly, Depositary Bank is liable to Payor Bank for breach of warranty.

The most striking thing about the standard analysis, as set out above, is that it proceeds entirely in terms of concepts of ownership and the like directed at the check. The analysis consists of a detailed examination and characterization of the peregrination of the check, and every step in the analysis consists of the assertion or denial of a claim of a property interest in the check. Curiously absent is any focus on, and nearly any mention of, the payment. The point of the check system is, after all, to direct the transfer of funds. The scenario of the collection and payment of a stolen check, with or without a forged indorsement, is simply an instance of a misdirected funds transfer. Why not approach the problem from the perspective of transfer of funds rather than focusing on the piece of paper that happens to embody the instruction to transfer the funds? Consider analogous problems in connection with wire transfers governed by Article 4A of the U.C.C. That article has comprehensive rules on the allocation of loss resulting from fraud in connection with wire transfers. The Article 4A rules, however, do not proceed by asking whether someone did or did not have "good title" to the electronic messages that were involved in the funds transfer.

Even for checks, there is no conceptual obstacle, nor lack of common-law precedent, for an approach that focuses directly on the real problem—the misdirected funds transfer—rather than a roundabout approach focused on claims of title to the check. The situation is simply that Drawer instructed the banks to transfer funds to Payee and, instead, the banks transferred funds to Scalawag. The law of restitution provides a simple alternative to the complex property concept-based analysis of negotiable instruments law. Drawer issued an instruction directing that funds be transferred from him to Payee. Instead, Payor Bank inadvertently transferred funds to Depositary Bank, which permitted Scalawag to make off with the funds. In a variety of situations, the law of restitution has evolved remedies for mistaken payment of money that not only permit the party who made the mistaken payment to recover it from the recipient, but also, in appropriate circumstances, permit the intended recipient to recover the money from the actual recipient.[21] Accordingly, there is no difficulty in finding a common-law remedy permitting Payee—the intended recipient—to recover the amount he was supposed to have received from Depositary Bank. Indeed, such an approach was commonly used—as an alternative or substitute for the conversion of the instrument rationale adopted by the U.C.C.—in the pre-Code decisions dealing with problems of payment of checks over forged indorsements.[22]

21. King County v. Odman, 111 P.2d 228 (Wash. 1941) (true owner of land permitted to recover rentals paid by tenant to one thought to have been owner); RESTATEMENT (THIRD) OF RESTITUTION AND UNJUST ENRICHMENT § 47 (Tentative Draft No. 5 2007); 4 GEORGE E. PALMER, THE LAW OF RESTITUTION § 21.4 (1978).

22. Allen v. M. Mendelsohn & Son, 93 So. 416 (Ala. 1922); Merch. & Mfrs. Ass'n v. First Nat'l Bank, 14 P.2d 717 (Ariz. 1932); *cf.* U.S. Portland Cement Co. v. U.S. Nat'l Bank, 157 P. 202 (Colo. 1916) (payee can recover from depositary bank that collected check over forged

The advantage of an approach focusing directly on the improper payment rather than on questions of title to the check is illustrated by problems concerning the proper plaintiff in actions against banks for payment of checks over forged indorsements. Consider first cases where a check was purloined by the scalawag before it was received by the intended payee. Under pre-Code law and under Article 3 prior to the 1990 revision, the case law was divided on whether a payee who did not receive delivery could sue the depositary bank that collected the check for the scalawag.[23] The fact that the check was not delivered to the intended payee presented no conceptual difficulties to courts that based a depositary bank's liability to the payee on a theory of assumpsit to recover money that ought to have been paid to payee. As one court put it, the argument against liability "sticks too closely to the check or draft; we consider the question of liability for the money that appellee got. . . ."[24] By contrast, courts that based the cause of action on a conversion theory had to go through complex gyrations concerning constructive delivery, the "mailbox rule," and the like, in order to establish that the payee did get title to the check and so could

indorsement in action for money had and received on theory that payee can "ratify" collection of check from payor and thus depositary bank holds funds due to payee); Henderson v. Lincoln Rochester Trust Co., 100 N.E.2d 117 (N.Y. 1951) (same). For discussion of the theories of recovery, see Friedrich Kessler, *Forged Indorsements*, 47 YALE L. J. 863, 874 (1938).

It is, though, sometimes a bit difficult to tell whether courts were applying a restitution based theory or a tort-property based theory, in part because even if the problem is viewed as a matter of conversion of the payee's property interest in the check, the payee could bring an action in assumpsit for money had and received by virtue of the "waive the tort and sue in assumpsit" device. Arnold v. The Cheque Bank, 1 C.P.D. 578 (1876); Nat'l Union Bank v. Miller Rubber Co., 129 A. 688 (Md. 1925); Indep. Oil Men's Ass'n v. Fort Dearborn Nat'l Bank, 142 N.E. 458 (Ill. 1924).

23. J. C. Vance, Annotation, *Right of Check Owner to Recover Against One Cashing It on Forged or Unauthorized Indorsement and Procuring Payment by Drawee*, 100 A.L.R.2d 670 (1965).

24. Allen v. M. Mendelsohn & Son, 93 So. 416, 417 (Ala. 1922).

bring a conversion action.[25] The 1990 revision, however, takes the view that actions against depositary banks must be based on a conversion theory. Accordingly, for purely formal reasons, the revision says if the check was never delivered to the intended payee, "the payee has no conversion action because . . . [u]ntil delivery, the payee does not have any interest in the check."[26]

A similar problem is presented if the drawer attempts to sue a depositary bank that takes a check over a forged indorsement. In this situation, most courts have not allowed a conversion action. The explanation generally given is that conversion is an action to vindicate rights of property. Thus, the only proper plaintiff in a conversion action is someone who had a property interest in the check. In the hands of the drawer, however, a check is not a valuable item of property. Since the drawer has no property interest in the check, it cannot have a conversion action. Teachers of commercial law are fond of reciting the clever remark in a leading case that in the hands of the drawer "the value of its rights was limited to the physical paper on which they were written."[27] The 1990 revision explicitly confirms the result of such cases, explaining that the drawer has no conversion action because "the check represents an obligation of the drawer rather than property of the drawer."[28]

In these situations, there is room for reasoned disagreement over the ultimate question whether the depositary bank should be liable. But, for that disagreement to be reasoned, it must be based on good reasons. In favor of allowing the actions, there is an argument for avoiding circularity of actions. For example, in the case of the payee

25. Lund's Inc. v. Chem. Bank, 870 F.2d 840, 851–52 (2d Cir. 1989); Ind. Nat'l Bank v. Holtsclaw, 98 Ind. 85 (1884); Crisp v. State Bank, 155 N.W. 78 (N.D. 1915).

26. U.C.C. § 3-420 cmt 1.

27. Stone & Webster Eng'g Corp. v. First Nat'l Bank & Trust Co., 184 N.E.2d 358, 362 (Mass. 1962).

28. U.C.C. § 3-420 cmt 1.

who never received delivery, suppose that one says that the payee cannot sue the depositary bank. The result is that the payee is entitled to recover from the drawer on the underlying obligation for which the check was drawn; the drawer can recover from the payor bank for wrongfully paying over a forged indorsement, and the payor bank can recover from the depositary bank for breach of warranty. A direct action by the intended payee against the depositary bank would be much simpler. Allowing the conversion action does, however, present some problems. The reason that the check never reached the intended payee may have been that it was negligently addressed by the drawer. If the payee is forced to look to the drawer, and the drawer proceeds against the payor bank, it is more likely that facts about the payor's possible negligence will be explored. The point is not that the result reached in the conversion cases, and confirmed by the 1990 revision, is necessarily wrong. Rather, the point is that to decide whether the result is right or wrong, we should consider arguments that actually make sense, rather than abstract questions about whether a drawer or an intended payee who did not receive delivery has a property interest in the check. The check, after all, is just a piece of paper on which an instruction about a funds transfer happens to have been written. It is hard to imagine any other context in which issues about who can sue for someone's failure to follow an instruction would be addressed by asking who owned the instruction.

V. IMPOSTORS AND FICTITIOUS PAYEES

Consider another highly complex area of the law of checks, the problem of impostors and fictitious payees. Suppose that Scalawag comes to Dupe and says "Hi, I'm Santa Claus, will you please give me $100 cash so that I can make Christmas toys for good girls and boys."

If Dupe does so, Dupe has just lost the $100 and has no right of recovery from anyone except Scalawag. Now suppose that Dupe gives Scalawag a check for $100, payable to Santa Claus, drawn on Dupe's account at Payor Bank. Scalawag indorses it in the name of Santa Claus, deposits it for collection at a bank, receives the money from the bank, and disappears. Does Dupe have any complaint against Payor Bank?

If we asked the question free from the distractions of negotiable instruments law, the answer would be obvious. Even though Payor Bank is absolutely liable for paying out money in a fashion not instructed by its customer, it is hard to see any way that Dupe could make out a case against Payor Bank. Payor Bank did exactly what Dupe instructed—it paid money to the person that Dupe foolishly thought was Santa Claus. If, however, we put on our negotiable instruments glasses—or blinders—the question becomes trickier. Dupe intended that Santa Claus be the owner of the check. Scalawag would be entitled to collect the check only if it bore the genuine indorsement of the payee. The payee was Santa Claus, and Scalawag is not Santa Claus. So, the indorsement must be a forgery. "Therefore," Dupe has an action against Payor Bank for paying the check over a forged indorsement.

There is a long-standing and complex body of law dealing with such cases and related matters, such as cases where a dishonest employee causes the employer to issue payroll checks to bogus employees and then collects the checks.[29] The basic technique is to preclude the trick argument by having a rule saying that the indorsement is not to be treated as a forged indorsement. If you like, one can state the result by saying that the words written by Dupe really were the indorsement of Santa Claus. The same result was reached

29. White & Summers, *supra* note 4, at 581–91.

through a slightly different doctrinal route under the N.I.L., which treated an instrument that had been made payable to a fictitious person as though it had been made payable to bearer.[30] There is nothing particularly surprising about the outcome. The only puzzling thing is why anyone would think that this is a problem that warrants explicit and extensive treatment in the statute.

Not surprisingly, the answer lies in history. Recall the accommodation bill dispute discussed in Chapter 8. The classic case, *Gibson v. Minet*,[31] arose out of the insolvency of the Livesey, Hargreaves firm of cotton manufacturers in Lancashire. The bill at issue in the case had been made payable to the order of one "John White." The bill appeared to have been indorsed by White and was thereafter transferred to another party. The bill was drawn to make it appear that it arose out of an actual cotton sale. In the case itself, however, there was no actual John White. Rather, that name had just been made up to make it appear that the bill arose out of some real transaction. In fact, it was just a way for Livesey to raise money by creating a false appearance that it had generated "real bills" from its mercantile operations. By the time the bill came due, Livesey had failed, and the holder of the bill sought to recover from the acceptor.

Under the rules governing procedure in actions on bills, one suing on a bill had to prove his title in order to establish a prima facie case. If the bill was payable to bearer, title was established merely by possession. On the other hand, if the bill was originally payable to the order of a specified person, the plaintiff had to prove the authenticity of the first indorser's signature.[32] Thus the plaintiff

30. N.I.L. § 9(3).

31. 126 Eng. Rep. 326 (H.L. 1791).

32. Instruments were typically indorsed in bank. Thus once the initial payee had indorsed in blank, the instrument was treated as payable to bearer. Subsequent indorsements, therefore, were not essential to the chain of title, though they added credit to the instrument.

found itself in the peculiar position that in order to establish its claim, it had to accomplish the impossible task of proving the authenticity of the signature of John White—a person who did not exist. The solution that the English court came up with was to permit the plaintiff to resort to the pleading fiction of declaring on the bill as if it had been made payable to bearer.

By the time that the N.I.L. was drafted in the late nineteenth century, the original fictitious payee cases, like the accommodation bills controversy of which they were a part, had passed into history. But, the idea that an instrument payable to a fictitious person could be treated as though it had been made payable to bearer remained part of the law and lore of negotiable instruments law. So, when courts were confronted with check fraud cases involving fictitious payees and padded payrolls, they drew upon the old technique of pleading fictions that had been used in the late eighteenth-century accommodation bill cases. Of course, that "solution" would have been entirely unnecessary if the law of checks had been treated on its own terms rather than as a part of the law of bills and notes.

It is hard to believe that all the complexity of the law of check fraud is really necessary. In the examples discussed above, the basic rule is pretty simple. For the forged indorsement cases, the loss rests with the depositary bank that took the check over the forged indorsement. The fictitious payee cases are even easier since, were it not for the added complexity of negotiable instruments law and history, the issue would not be much more complicated than saying that if you want to write a check to Santa Claus, don't complain to your bank. Of course, this is an oversimplification. There are some genuine issues here, as well as in other check fraud scenarios. But it seems abundantly clear that these problems could be handled far more simply if the rules were not written in the language of negotiable instruments law.

VI. CHECKS AS PAYMENT SYSTEMS LAW RATHER THAN NEGOTIABLE INSTRUMENTS LAW

Let us briefly consider how we might design a modern body of law for the check system. The basic concept would be rather simple. First, rather than regard checks as negotiable instruments that embody parties' obligations, we would regard them simply as instructions to the financial system directing a transfer of bank credit from one party to another. So viewed, all of the elaborate rules in Part 1 of Article 3 on the formal requirements for status as a negotiable instruments would be unnecessary. So too, the rules set out in Part 3 of Article 3 on the liabilities of parties on the instrument would be unnecessary. There would be nothing odd about such a view. The law of credit cards and debit cards works perfectly well without any notion that a person who makes payment by using a credit card or a debit card incurs any liability "on the instrument."

Second, we could dispense with the notion that checks are items of property that are transferred from party to party. In Chapter 7, we saw that checks are rarely if ever transferred from one party to another outside of the banking system. In any event, if we dispense with the idea that checks are reifications of parties' obligations, then there would be no reason to have rules about transfer of checks. Thus, none of the rules on transfer in Part 2 of Article 3 would be needed.

Third, we could dispense with the idea that it makes sense to talk about whether someone was or was not a holder in due course of a check. Throughout this book, we have seen that the holder in due course concept plays little if any useful role in any modern setting.[33]

33. With respect to checks, that point was made long ago. Albert J. Rosenthal, *Negotiability—Who Needs It*, 71 COLUM. L. REV. 375 (1971).

Thus, none of the rules on holders in due course in Part 3 of Article 3 would be needed.

Fourth—and this is an easy point—there would be no need for the elaborate rules on dishonor set out in Part 5 of Article 3. As was seen in Chapter 8, the only people who might be troubled by that deletion would be the loony tax protestors who would have to find some other purported legal justification for failing to pay their taxes. So too, there would be no need for the rules set out in Part 6 of Article 3. As was seen in Chapter 8, those rules are really just a version of general suretyship rules. They are unnecessary even for notes, and have no relevance to checks.

The only thing left in Article 3 that might have some application to the check system are the several rules set out in Part 4 of Article 3 that play some role in the allocation of losses from check fraud, such as the rules on negligence in 3-406 and the rules in 3-405 on employer's responsibility for some kinds of employee check fraud. Some of those are rules that deal with genuine issues, but there is no reason that they should be set out in an article of the U.C.C. on negotiable instruments. As was shown earlier in this chapter, the rules on check fraud are unnecessarily complex as a result of treating check fraud problems by asking questions about the theft of the check, rather than by writing rules that deal directly with responsibility for the misdirected payment. Again, the analogy to credit cards and debit cards is instructive. No one would think that it would make sense to write fraud rules by asking whether the parties who processed an unauthorized credit card or debit card transaction did or did not become the true owner of the credit card slip. Indeed, in modern practice, one would have to ask whether someone did or did not become the true owner of the electronic message containing the transaction information. Yet that is precisely how the law of checks deals with forgery and fraud problems.

We could, then, write a sensible modern law for checks that dispenses with virtually everything that is now found in Article 3. Instead, we might use Article 4 as a starting place. As we have seen, Article 4 could be greatly simplified by confining attention to matters that are of genuine modern significance, dispensing with all the dross that should be of interest only to historians. Just as virtually all of Article 3 would become superfluous if one dispensed with the idea that checks are embodiments of parties' obligations, so too much of Article 4 could be greatly simplified by treating checks simply as instructions to banks. Moreover, much of Article 4 could be greatly simplified by forgetting history. For example, as was seen earlier in this chapter, the rules on final payment could be made much simpler if they were written to deal with modern methods of check collection rather than with problems that might have arisen in the days before modern check processing. Consider as well the law governing the allocation of loss from check fraud. Those rules are unnecessarily complex because they are written in terms of "transfer" of checks. Moreover, there is the utterly bizarre phenomenon that essentially the same warranty rules are set out, using slightly different language in Article 4, Sections 4-206 and 4-207, and in Article 3, Sections 3-416 and 3-417. One doubts if there has ever been a student who could understand why we have the duplicated rules. The answer is probably that there is no reason, or at least no good reason.

To be sure, the discussion in this chapter does not fully show what a modern law of checks might look like. The only way to truly see what a modern law of checks might look like would be to try to write it.[34] It does, however, seem unlikely that any such process

34. For some efforts in the direction of a unified payments law, see L. Ali Khan, *A Theoretical Analysis of Payment Systems*, 60 S.C. L. Rev. 1 (2008); Anita Ramasastry, *Confusion and Convergence in Consumer Payments: Is Coherence in Error Resolution Appropriate?*, 83

could result in a body of law as poorly adapted to modern conditions as the current law of the check system found in Articles 3 and 4. Writing the law of the check system on the basis of negotiable instruments concepts makes about as much sense as writing the rules in Latin and the leaving it to law school classes and case law to provide a Latin-English dictionary.

CHI-KENT L. REV. 813 (2008); Linda J. Rusch, *Reimagining Payment Systems: Allocation of Risk for Unauthorized Payment Inception*, 83 CHI-KENT L. REV. 561 (2008).

10

Overcoming the Past

As we have seen, negotiable instruments law does not provide a sensible foundation for a modern law of the check-based payment system. Moreover, the law of promissory notes would be simpler and more coherent if it were treated simply as an aspect of the general law of contract. Thus, the law set out in Article 3 makes little sense either as the basis of a modern statutory law for the check-based payment system or as the basis of a statutory law of promissory notes. So, how are we to deal with a body of law that has become essentially obsolete?

I. REPEAL, REVISION, OR UNIFICATION

If the only concern were to create a sensible modern law for promissory notes and checks, the solution would be simple. U.C.C. Article 3 should be repealed, and Article 4 should undergo a major revision.[1] Better still, we would draft a new statute for the check

1. Repeal of Article 3 is, of course, is a radical proposal, but it is not without precedent. Consider U.C.C. Article 6. As promulgated in the original version of the U.C.C., Article 6 set out the law of bulk sales. The basic notion was that if a merchant or manufacturer is going to sell essentially all of its assets, then its creditors should be notified in advance so that they can take any action that they might deem appropriate to protect their claims. As a way of enforcing that notice requirement, Article 6 provided that if such notice was not given, then

collection system based on modern concepts about payment systems rather than attempting to squeeze modern transactions into the ill-fitting categories of negotiable instruments law.

One obstacle to implementing such a proposal is the sense of familiarity that lawyers have with Article 3. As the old saying goes, "if it ain't broke, don't fix it." But the assumption that the law on this subject works reasonably well is just wrong. This book has shown that all of Article 3, and much of Article 4, is seriously broken. The fact that this is not widely recognized may be partly a problem of viewpoint. The people discussing whether Article 3 should be repealed are going to be people who are already familiar with it. Lawyers are profoundly conservative. We readily see problems with any suggested change in the law, but tend to overlook problems with the existing law, simply because it is familiar. So repeal or radical reform of Article 3 is likely to seem troublesome. Yet, if there were no Article 3 and someone suggested enacting it, everyone would easily see that it would make no sense to write a statute for modern payment transactions on the basis of concepts drawn from eighteenth-century law.

Consider the matter from the standpoint of those who are not already familiar with Articles 3. Anyone who teaches the subject will realize how difficult it is for students to understand this body of law. Or, consider the ultimate consumers and users of any body of

creditors of the seller could pursue their claims against the assets even in the hands of the transferee. In 1984, the sponsors of the U.C.C. undertook a project to revise Article 6. Many members of the Drafting Committee came to the conclusion that the best revision would simply be repeal, because changes in the way that business is conducted and modern developments in credit information had rendered the basic concept of Article 6 an anachronism. The suggestion that Article 6 be repealed met with some opposition, largely from some debt collection entities that found the procedures of Article 6 useful. So the Code sponsors put forth, in the alternative, a proposed revised version and a recommendation for repeal. The overwhelming majority of states have opted for repeal. Steven L. Harris, *Article 6: The Process and the Product—An Introduction*, 41 ALA. L. REV. 549 (1990).

law—judges. It is fairly uncommon to encounter judges who are deeply familiar with payment systems law or negotiable instruments law. A judge confronted with a problem concerning promissory notes or checks is likely to find the statute extraordinarily complicated and confusing. That perception is not wrong. It is exactly right. The statute is confusing, and it is so because it is based on concepts drawn from a financial and legal system that passed into history more than a century ago.

Political reality, however, is probably the most significant obstacle to repeal. Even if the logical case for repeal is compelling, it seems unlikely that anything will happen unless someone is willing to spend the political capital to bring the issue to the attention of lawmakers. Law reform for the sake of intellectual coherence is unlikely to attract political attention. It is unlikely that the problems created by the fractionalization of payment systems law have yet reached the point that there is political will to work toward a thorough revision and unification of payment systems law. To the current generation of lawyers and law professors, the lesson of the ill-fated proposed Uniform New Payments Code of the late 1970s and early 1980s still speaks loud.[2]

There might be other ways of taking small but useful steps toward modernization of payments law. Perhaps it would be worth separating questions about the rights and duties of users against providers from questions about the rights and duties of providers among themselves. Issues about rights and duties of providers among themselves

2. Fred H. Miller, *U.C.C. Articles 3, 4 and 4A: A Study in Process and Scope*, 42 ALA. L. REV. 405 (1991). A symposium held at Cardozo Law School in April 2007 considered whether the time has come to reconsider the possibility of unification of payment systems law. *Symposium: Rethinking Payments Law*, 83 CHI-KENT L. REV. 475–972 (2008). There is, however, little reason to suppose that an ambitious payment systems law project is politically feasible anytime in the near future.

are currently covered by very different bodies of law, such as U.C.C. Articles 3 and 4 for checks, Article 4A for electronic funds transfers, Federal Reserve Board rules, and rules of private organizations such as NACHA and ECCHO.[3] It seems likely that each of those bodies of law has its own political constituency, so that unification may be politically difficult. Issues about rights and duties of users against providers are also covered by different bodies of law, such as U.C.C. Articles 3 and 4 for checks, Article 4A for electronic funds transfers, the federal Electronic Funds Transfer Act for consumer electronic payments, and portions of the Truth in Lending Act for credit cards. It seems far less clear that each of those bodies of law has its own political constituency. Given how unlikely it is that users of payment systems realize that their rights differ depending on which system they use, it seems fairly implausible to suppose that users of different payment systems actually want different bodies of law.[4]

In some other areas of payments law, we already have a fairly sharp division between issues about users' rights and issues about providers' rights. The U.C.C. approach, in Articles 3 and 4 for checks or Article 4A for wire transfers, is to set out a comprehensive body of law governing not only the rights of users against providers, but also the rights of providers among themselves. By contrast, both the Federal law for credit cards in the Truth in Lending Act and the Federal law for debit cards in the Electronic Funds Transfer Act deal only with the relationship between the consumer user and the financial institution with which the user deals. Issues about the relationships among the financial institutions involved in the credit card

3. NACHA is the National Automated Clearing House Association. Its activities are described on its website, http://www.nacha.org. ECCHO is the Electronic Check Clearing House Organization. Its activities are described on its website, http://www.eccho.org.

4. Others may disagree, *e.g.*, Clayton P. Gillette & Steven D. Walt, *Uniformity and Diversity in Payment Systems*, 83 Chi-Kent L. Rev. 499 (2008).

and debit card systems are left to private rules and agreements. That difference in approach might offer a route to some rationalization of payments law.

It is probably unrealistic to suppose that we will see, anytime in the foreseeable future, a project of the sort contemplated at the time of the proposed Uniform New Payments Code that would deal comprehensively with all legal aspects of all payment systems. It might, however, be worth considering an expansion of the approach that has already developed in EFTA and TILA. Those bodies of law deal only with the relationship between users of payment systems and providers of payment systems. Within that scope, the legal rules are mandatory and not subject to variation by agreement. We might work toward the articulation of a general body of law governing the relationship between users of payment systems and providers of payment systems. We might limit the law to consumer users, or we might extend it to all users. But we could try to make the user's rights and duties essentially the same no matter what payment system happens to be used.

Legal questions concerning rights and duties among the providers of the payment system pose very different questions. If the issue is only whether a loss is borne by one category of bank or another, we might well be willing to leave that to an agreement among the parties. After all, such matters probably do not pose undue risks of abuse of users by providers. By contrast, issues of rights and duties between providers and users raise problems that may well not be well addressed by private agreement. Under current conditions, it would be difficult to undertake a legislative drafting project even on matters involving only the relationship between users and providers. Nonetheless, there might be ways of working toward coherence. The American Law Institute has developed "Principles" projects on a variety of topics that are governed by other statutes, such as the

ALI Principles of Corporate Governance. It might be possible to find enough areas of similarity among the laws governing different payment systems that one could try to formulate at least some general principles of payment system law, at least on issues of the rights of users against providers.

But, let us suppose neither repeal of Article 3 nor any serious effort toward unification of payment system law is politically feasible, at least in the immediate future. What can be done to minimize the harm done by the pernicious persistence of history?

II. THE LESSONS FOR PRACTICING LAWYERS AND JUDGES

First let us consider the problem from the standpoint of practicing lawyers and judges. Suppose that we have a case involving a check or promissory note in which the lawyers and judges have an intuitive sense of the just outcome. A conscientious judge should base a decision on a certain rule only if the rule actually provides an intellectually honest basis for the decision. All too often, however, it seems that lawyers and judges seize upon some poorly understood rule drawn from negotiable instruments law merely because it happens to produce a result that seems just in the particular case. Unfortunately, that often only muddies the law for future cases. Let us examine two such cases.

In *McCarthy v. Sessions,*[5] Husband bought farm equipment from Seller on open account credit. The equipment was used by Husband and Wife on a farm that they jointly owned. Later, Husband and Wife signed a promissory note for the unpaid amount of the debt.

5. 572 N.Y.S.2d 749 (N.Y. App. Div. 1991).

After Husband died, Seller sued Wife on the note. Wife defended on grounds of lack of consideration, arguing that the note was given for an antecedent debt on which Husband alone was liable. If Wife had signed the note at the time of the original loan, it would have made no difference whether the loan proceeds were used by Husband alone or by Husband and Wife. She would have been liable either as a principal or a guarantor. But, in the case itself, she signed the note after the loan was made. Accordingly, she could seek to take advantage of the suretyship rule that a guaranty given after the loan is made is not supported by consideration.

The after-acquired surety argument, like the general problem of "past consideration" of which it is a subset, might well be thought more a quirk of contract theory than a response to a genuine concern.[6] So the *McCarthy* court might well have either declined to allow the defense on its merits, or it might have said that precedent compels the result even though it makes little sense.[7] The *McCarthy* court did reach the result that the debt should be enforced, but did so by a thoroughly confused frolic through Article 3. The court

6. On the suretyship problem, see Restatement (Third) of Suretyship and Guaranty § 8 (1996). On the general contract law problem of "past consideration," see E. Allan Farnsworth, Contracts 565–63 (4th ed. 2004). For no apparent reason, the *McCarthy* court thought that it mattered that Wife was not an accommodation party because she benefitted from the equipment that Seller provided on credit. 572 N.Y.S.2d at 750–51. The problem in the case was timing, not whether Wife was a guarantor or principal.

7. In New York, where the *McCarthy* case occurred, the contract analysis is slightly complicated because of a statute that rejects the "past consideration" argument provided that the subsequent promise is contained in a signed writing that recites the past consideration. N.Y. Genl. Oblig. Law § 5-1105. That provision did not help in the scenario in *McCarthy*, since there was no recital of consideration. That is just a problem of poor statutory drafting. The point of the statute is that the "past consideration" argument makes little sense. That is true whether or not the writing happens to contain a recital. *See* Robert Braucher, *Freedom of Contract and the Second Restatement*, 78 Yale L. J. 598, 605 (1969) (noting that the New York statute is "too restrictive in formal requirements"). It is not entirely clear how the New York courts should deal with the poorly drafted New York statute. Suppose that the legislature has adopted a statute saying that "invalid arguments shall not be accepted on Tuesdays." What is a court to do if the case is heard on Wednesday?

persuaded itself that the Seller was a holder in due course and, as such, took free from Wife's defense. That makes no sense. *McCarthy* was a simple dispute between the payee and maker of a note. The note had never been transferred. The holder in due course doctrine had no possible application. Even if one somehow thought that the holder in due course rules might matter, the Seller would not qualify as a holder in due course because the Seller was obviously aware of Wife's defense. After all, it was clear that Wife was signing a note for an obligation incurred by Husband.[8]

Next, consider *Bank One v. Myers*.[9] Bank lent money to Buyer, and Buyer used the money to purchase a mobile home from Seller. Buyer contended that the mobile home was defective and brought suit against Seller for breach of warranty. Buyer stopped making payments on the note to Bank, and Bank sued on the note. Buyer sought to defend the action on the note by raising the breach of warranty contentions. Aside from Article 3, the case would be simple. Buyer borrowed money from Bank and used the money to buy something from Seller. The thing turned out to be defective. Obviously Buyer has a breach of warranty action against Seller. Equally obvious is the fact that Buyer has no defense to liability on the loan made by Bank.[10] It is not a defense to an action on a debt to say "I'm unhappy with the thing I bought with the money that I borrowed."[11]

8. Curiously, the *McCarthy* court was so confused by the holder in due course concept that it missed the point that Article 3 happens to contain a rule rejecting the past consideration argument. U.C.C. § 3-303. In New York, which has not adopted the 1990 revision, the relevant provision is former U.C.C. § 3-408.

9. 470 N.E.2d 485 (Ohio Ct. App. 1984).

10. The case might be different if Seller and Bank were the same entity or were closely related. Nothing in the opinion, however, suggested any connection between Bank and Seller.

11. If the facts had been different, the holder in due course rules might have been relevant. Suppose that Buyer bought the mobile home from Seller and give Seller a note for the purchase price. If Seller had transferred the note to Bank, then Bank could qualify as a holder in due course who would take free from the defense that Buyer might have had against Seller.

The *Myers* case was another simple two-party scenario that has nothing to do with Article 3 holder in due course issues. The court, however, persuaded itself otherwise. As was noted in Chapter 8, the statement in the former version of Article 3 that "a payee may be a holder in due course"[12] was the occasion of much confusion. Given that statement, it was always hard for people to see that the holder in due course doctrine has nothing to do with a simple case in which the payee sues the maker of a note and the maker raises defenses arising out of the transaction between the payee and maker. Part of the solution to that confusion was the statement in former Article 3 that a holder in due course takes free of any "defenses of any party to the instrument with whom the holder has not dealt." That provision was often used as a textual basis for rejecting the argument that the payee of a note could prevent the maker from raising simple defenses by referring to the holder in due course doctrine. That argument never made any sense, but the "with whom he has not dealt" language provided a convenient way of disposing of the bogus argument.

In the *Myers* case, the confusion cut the other way. The court said that under Article 3, Bank could be a holder in due course, but that would mean only that Bank took the note free from defenses of any party with whom bank had not dealt. In the case itself, Bank had dealt with Buyer. "Therefore," according to the court, Bank was subject to defenses of Buyer, including the defense that the mobile home that Buyer bought from Seller was defective. In other words, the court persuaded itself that it was a valid defense to an action on a note to say that "I'm unhappy with the thing I bought with the money that I borrowed." Even judged by the standards of Article 3

That would be the routine scenario of the problem of the holder in due course doctrine in consumer sales. But that has nothing to do with the case itself, where Buyer borrowed from Bank and used the money to pay Seller.

12. Former U.C.C. § 3-302(2).

case law, that notion is astonishingly confused. One is reminded of the Sorcerer's Apprentice scene in the movie *Fantasia* where Mickey Mouse cannot stop the consequences of his invocation of a magic that he does not fully understand.

III. THE LESSONS FOR TEACHERS OF PAYMENT SYSTEMS LAW

Now let us consider the problem from the perspective of students attempting to learn this body of law. The solution for them largely rests with law professors. How should we teach the law of promissory notes and the check system if we realize that Articles 3 and 4 are anachronistic? The answer is actually quite simple. Be honest. It would be unimaginable for a teacher of property law to cover estates in land without explaining that the fundamental concepts come from feudal structures for allocation of political power. Yet that is essentially what we do if we teach the law of checks and promissory notes in an ahistoric fashion. There is no point in saying or implying that negotiable instruments law makes sense as applied to modern transactions. It only confuses the students to teach this body of law through hypotheticals in which checks or other negotiable instruments are transferred from person to person outside the banking system. If the law had developed in a different fashion, perhaps we could dispense with teaching negotiable instruments law altogether and just teach modern payment systems law. But, for the foreseeable future, the statute is likely to remain wedded to the ill-fitting negotiable instruments framework. Why not simply tell the students that this is the case?

One approach is to try to avoid discussion of the basic concepts of negotiable instruments law, or at least, to postpone that discussion until after one has worked through the law of various payment systems. That is the approach taken by Professor Mann is his excellent casebook on the topic.[13] But that approach is problematic. Once students leave the classroom, they are going to have to deal with legal materials, including both cases and secondary sources, in which the old negotiable instruments concepts play a far more prominent role. Without a good sense of history, they are likely to have difficulty figuring out how to handle those materials.

An alternative would be to be more honest about presenting negotiable instruments law as history. One can begin the payments course with a brief treatment of forms of payment systems that long pre-date the modern check system. A brief treatment of the private law of currency provides an easy way of introducing some of the basic concepts, such as the rule that a person who takes stolen currency can take free from the claim of the true owner. Then one can discuss how payments were made in the era that predated the modern banking system. Classic cases such as *Miller v. Race*[14] can be examined as vehicles for a brief study of the law governing instruments that in former times actually did circulate as a medium of exchange. After these preliminaries, one can cover the mid-twentieth-century disputes over the holder in due course doctrine as a problem of what to do about a legal doctrine that has long outlived its usefulness. Then, one can turn to modern payment systems, starting with the check system. One must simply acknowledge that, for better or worse, the law of the check system happens to have been built on a foundation of negotiable instruments concepts. One need not, and should not, make any effort to justify that by making up

13. Ronald J. Mann, Payments Systems and Other Financial Transactions (4th ed. 2008).
14. 97 Eng. Rep. 398 (K.B. 1758).

hypothetical examples in which checks get transferred from person to person outside the banking system. Rather, one can simply admit that the law makes no sense, but that's the way it is.

IV. CONCLUSION

The fundamental problem is that the entire structure of the current law of checks and notes is profoundly anachronistic. Time and again, we have seen in this book that if one steps back from the seeming familiarity of the rules of negotiable instruments law, one would be hard pressed to offer any coherent explanation for why there even is a rule on a certain issue in the statute, let alone for why the rule resolves the matter as it does. We have seen that in large part the rules still set out in the statute are products of disputes and issues that may once have been significant, but no longer are. Often the statutory rules are nothing more than the detritus of other long forgotten laws such as the Stamp Acts.

There are, of course, some areas where Articles 3 and 4 happen to be the repository of law on genuine issues, such as the allocation of loss from unauthorized checks. On such issues one can have a fair degree of confidence that rules found in Articles 3 and 4 are probably a response to genuine modern problems. But, as we have seen throughout this book, that is often not the case once one moves a bit outside of the core of the legal rules on the check system. Perhaps the only safe way to approach issues that might be governed by a rule in Article 3 or 4 is to consider how the dispute would be resolved if there were no special statutory rules on the issue. Having done that, one can consider whether the statute actually compels a different result, or whether the rule stated in the statute is merely a way of expressing a more general legal rule. In other words, one should be very careful about any argument of the form "this is a negotiable instrument and therefore . . . ." As we have seen, it is frequently the case that the statute contains a rule on a given subject purely as a result of historical quirk. But, that is very difficult for anyone to see, other than the few of us who have devoted an inordinate amount of time to the study of the history of negotiable instrument law.

As Maitland famously observed, "The forms of action we have buried, but they still rule us from their graves."[15] The situation is even worse with the law of bills and notes, for we have not yet given it the burial it so richly deserves. Even if burial is not feasible, we must realize that we are not dealing with a living law, but with a zombie. Only if we realize how anachronistic this body of law is can we find ways of dealing with it intelligently or working toward a truly modern law of payment systems.

15. F. W. Maitland, The Forms of Action at Common Law 2 (1909).

INDEX

ABA. *See* American Bankers Association
Accelerated depreciation, 78–79
Accommodation bills, 36, 184–85
Accommodations parties
guarantors, 187–92
provisions, 179–86
Agents, signatures by, 96–102
Airline tickets, 46–47
Allis-Chalmers Credit Corp. v. Herbolt, 80–82, 92–93
Alteration discharge rule, 102–10
A.L. Trade Finance, Inc. v. Laminaciones de Lasaca, S.A., 91–92
American Bankers Association, Bank Collection Code, 130–31, 143
American Express Travel Related Services Co., Getty Petroleum v., 159–60
American Fuji Seal, Inc. v. U.S., 153
American Law Institute
Principles of Corporate Governance, 234
"Principles" projects, 233–34
Restatement of Mortgages, 83–84
Restatement (Third) of Suretyship and Guaranty, 197–98
American Uniform Negotiable Instruments Law of 1896 (N.I.L.). *See* Uniform Negotiable Instruments Law of 1896 (N.I.L.)
Ames, James Barr, 2n. 4, 117, 193
Antedating, negotiable instruments law, 94–96
Apple Bank for Savings, Morrow v., 156
Articles of U.C.C. *See* Uniform Commercial Code (U.C.C.)
Atlantic Banking and Trust Co., 126
ATMs, 4
Automated Clearing House (ACH), 5
Automated teller machines (ATMs), 4

Bank Collection Code, 130–31, 143
Banknotes, transfer of in 18th and 19th centuries, 31–34
private bank notes, circulation of, 33–34
Bank One v. Myers, 236–38
Banks, disputes with customers, 111–45
check collection law, history of, 125–34
modern treatments, 133–34
and confusion, 134–45
loss allocation, 112–24
forged drawer's signature scenario, 115–20
fraud indorsement scenario, 112–15, 119–21
unauthorized charge in general, *123*

Beutel, Frederick K., 125, 131–32
Bills of exchange, 28–29
Bills of Exchange Act of 1882 (England)
  accommodations party, 185
  alteration, 109
  check transfers, 147n. 1
  and myth of negotiability, 41
  payment systems law, 2, 7
  postdating and antedating, 95–96
  suretyship defenses, 192
Bills of lading, negotiable, 48–49
Brentar v. Rupert, 160–61
Britton, William Everett, 125
Brown County Coop Ass'n v. Rasmussen-King Cattle Co., 105
Brown, Tindal v., 172
Buller, Judge, 173
Byles, John, 41

Calabresi, Guido, 13
Cardozo Law School, 231n. 2
Centerre Bank v. Campbell, 79, 83–84
Chalmers, Mackenzie D., 2n. 3
Channelview Bank, Community National Bank v., 162
"Charter Oak," 64–65
Chattels, 32
Check 21 Act, 61–63
Check collection law, history of, 125–34
  dishonored checks, 134
  modern treatments, 133–34
Check collection rules, complexity of, 209–15
Check fraud rules, complexity of, 216–21, 226
Checking accounts maintained by corporations, 135
Checks
  bogus, 136–37
  cow, story of check written on side of, 200–201
  dishonored, 3, 214
  "for deposit only," 205
  "illegal" copies of, 62n. 35
  MICR (magnetic ink character recognition), 59–61
    facsimile signatures, 141–42
  modern law of. *See* Modern law of checks
  phony, 8
  reification, 58–63
  system, 3–7
    common use of, 9
  transfers of. *See* Checks, transfers of
Checks, transfers of, 148–66
  cases, 152–63
  confusion about check transfer, consequences of, 163–66
  coursebooks, payment systems, 147–51
  "crossed check" device, 146n. 1
  fictitious payee rule, 160n. 36
  forged indorsements, cases, 152–63
  mortgages, 155–56
  Social Security checks, 157–58
Cheques Act of 1957, 114n. 4
Chut, Edgar v., 27
Citizens Bank, Maryland Industrial Finishing Co., Inc. v., 153
Cohen, Neil, 198n. 52
Collection. *See also* Check collection law, history of; Check collection rules
  payment versus, guarantees, 190–91
Commercial paper, 37–38
Community National Bank v. Channelview Bank, 162
Confusion
  banks, disputes with customers, 134–45
  check transfers, 163–66
Congress
  Check 21 Act, 61–63
  and dishonored checks, 3
  Electronic Funds Transfer Act, 75–76
Connecticut charter (1687), 64–65
Consumer sales and demise of holder in due course doctrine, 69–72
Contracts
  promissory notes as, 198–99
  for sale of goods, history, 95
Cook, SEC v., 159
Coursebooks, check transfer in, 147–51
Cow, story of check written on side of, 200–201
Credit card bill, 75
Credit cards

purchases, 74–75
system, development of, 4
"Crossed checks," 146n. 1, 205n. 11
Crossed Checks Act of 1876, 147n. 1
C.W. Haynes & Co., Midfirst Bank v., 86–87

Dean Witter Reynolds, Stella v., 157
Debit cards
origins of, 4
purchases, 75
reification, 58
wire transfers, 232
Deeming, technique of, 52
Defenses
notes, 167–70
"personal" defenses, 22
"real" defenses, 22
suretyship, 192–98
Depository Trust Company
electronic records, 38
paperless paper, 66
Depreciation, accelerated, 78–79
Diamond Mortgage Corp., 84–85, 87
Discount
mercantile notes, 35–36
use of term, 39n. 39
Dishonor
check collection law, 134
notice of, 170–76
Documents of title, reification and, 47–49
Drawee, law of bills and notes, 25
Drawer, law of bills and notes, 19–20, 25

ECCHO (Electronic Check Clearing House Organization), 232
Edgar v. Chut, 27
EFAA (Expedited Funds Availability Act), 3
EFTA. *See* Electronic Funds Transfer Act (EFTA)
Eggert, Kurt, 87–88
Electronic Check Clearing House Organization (ECCHO)_, 232
Electronic collection of checks, 6
Electronic Funds Transfer Act (EFTA), 4, 75–76, 232–33
Electronic payments, 1
Electronic records, 38

English Bills of Exchange Act. *See* Bills of Exchange Act of 1882 (England)
English Stamp Acts. *See* Stamp Acts
Erie Railroad Case, 15
Expedited Funds Availability Act (EFAA), 3

Facsimile signatures, 137–43
Fair dealing, facsimile signatures, 139
Fed. *See* Federal Reserve Board
Federal Reserve Bank, 73–74
Federal Reserve Bank of Richmond v. Malloy, 125–28
Federal Reserve Board, 3, 66
Federal Reserve System
check collection rules, 211–12, 215
creation of, 34
and real bills theory, 36n. 32
Federal Rules of Evidence, 168n. 3
Federal Trade Commission
consumer sales, 72
FTC rule, 74
Fictitious payee rule, 160n. 36
Fifth Amendment, 159
Fifth Third Bank, Olympic Title Ins. Co. v., 157
Financial crisis of 2007, 17
First Commerce Corp., Jefferson Parish School Board v, 135–39, 142–44
First National Bank of Boston Massachusetts, 34
First National Bank v. Robertson, 103
First National Bank, Wisner v., 214
Ford Motor Company, 162–63
Forged drawer's signature scenario, 115–20
Forged indorsements, cases, 152–63
Fraud
check fraud rules, complexity of, 216–21, 226
material alteration, 104n. 23, 110
outsider fraud cases, 138
Fraud indorsement scenario, 112–15, 119–21
FTC rule, 73–76, 79

Getty Petroleum Corp. v. American Express Travel Related Services Co., 159–60
Gibson v. Minet, 223–24

Gilmore, Grant, 43n. 43, 44, 45n. 13, 88
Gonzalez, United States v., 159
Good faith, facsimile signatures, 138–39
Gramatan, 101n. 19
Grocery stores, check transfers, 147–51
Guarantees, "collection" versus
"payment," 190–91
Guarantors, accommodations
parties, 187–92

Harris v. Resolution Trust Co., 161
Herbert, A. P., 200
Herbolt, Allis-Chalmers Credit Corp. v., 80–82, 92–93
Herbolt, Ross, 80–82
Hillsboro Farmers Exchange, 80
Hill, State v., 157–58
Holder in due course doctrine, 18
  continuing applications of, 77–82
  demise of, 68–93
    in consumer sales, 69–72
    FTC rule, 73–76, 79
    and mortgages, 82–89
    problems caused by holder, 89–93
    problems with, 73–77
  generally, 11–12
  indorsement of checks, 203
  and reification, 50n. 11
  relevance of, 236n. 11, 237
"Honesty in fact." facsimile signatures, 138–39

Impostors, 221–24
Indorsement of checks, modern law of checks, 202–5
Indorsers, law of bills and notes, 30
Intelogic Trace Texcom Group, Inc. v. Merchants National Bank, 161–62

Jackson, Andrew, 29–31
Jefferson Parish School Board v. First Commerce Corp., 135–39, 142–44
Jenks, Edward, 44
Judges, lessons for, 234–38

Kent, Chancellor, 96n. 9
Kirkpatrick, State v., 158–59

Laminaciones de Lasaca, S.A., A.L. Trade Finance, Inc. v., 91–92
Lancashire, early 19th century, 32–33
"Law merchant," 22
Law of bills and notes. *See also* Law of checks and notes
  classical area, 24–31
    bills of exchange, 28–29
    example, 24–25
    exchange transaction, 25
    indorsers, 30
    obligation, 28
    transferability, 29
  drawee, 25
  drawer, 19–20, 25
Law of checks and notes, 19–44
  myth of negotiability, origins of, 39–44
  negotiability, traditional account of, 21–23
    defenses, 22
  transfer of bills and notes, 18th and 19th century, 31–39
    accommodation bills, 36
    banknotes, 31–34
    commercial paper, 37–38
    discounting mercantile notes, 35–36
    private bank notes, circulation of, 33–34
    redemption, 33
Lawyers, lessons for, 234–38
Leary, Fairfax, 82, 214
Legal history, study of, 43
Letter of indemnity, 49n. 8
Letters of credit, history, 95
Livesey, Hargreaves firm, 223–24
Llewellyn, Karl, 2n. 5
Loss allocation
  banks, disputes with customers, 112–24
    forged drawer's signature scenario, 115–20
    fraud indorsement scenario, 112–15, 119–21
    unauthorized charge in general, *123*
"Lost note affidavit," 57
Lost or stolen bank checks, 205–9
Lumber Bridge Bank of North Carolina, 125–28

MacDonnell, John, 43
Maitland, E. W., 241
Malloy, Federal Reserve Bank of Richmond v., 125–28
Mann, Ronald J., 149, 164, 239
Mansfield, Lord, 116–17, 172–73
Maryland Industrial Finishing Co., Inc. v. Citizens Bank, 153
Massachusetts rule, banking disputes, 129–30, 133–34
McCarthy v. Sessions, 234–36
Mentschikoff, Soia, 50n. 11
Mercantile notes and bills, 71
Merchants National Bank, Intelogic Trace Texcom Group, Inc. v., 161–62
Merrill Lynch, Pierce, Penner and Smith, Inc., Sun Bank, N.A. v., 158
Metaphor and reality, paperless paper, 64–67
MICR (magnetic ink character recognition), 59–61
  facsimile signatures, 141–42
Microfilm, 55n. 21
Midfirst Bank v. C.W. Haynes & Co., 86–87
Miller v. Race, 42, 239
Minet, Gibson v., 223–24
Modern law of checks, 200–228
  check collection rules, complexity of, 209–15
  check fraud rules, complexity of, 216–21, 226
  fictitious payees, 221–24
  impostors, 221–24
  indorsement of checks, 202–5
    "crossed checks," 205n. 11
  lost or stolen bank checks, 205–9
  payments systems law, checks as, 225–28
Modern law of promissory notes, 167–99
  accommodations parties
    guarantors, 187–92
    provisions, 179–86
  actions on notes, 167–70
  contracts, promissory notes as, 198–99
  defenses, 167–70
  dishonor, notice of, 170–76
  presentment, 170–76
  protest, 170–76
  renewal notes, 176–79
  suretyship defenses, 192–98
Modern payment systems law
  anachronistic nature of payment systems law, 12–17
  current state of, 1–17
  electronic payments, 1
  negotiable instruments law, 7–12
    anachronism, 17–18
    holder in due course doctrine, 11–12, 18
  century, 2–7
Morrow v. Apple Bank for Savings, 156
Mortgage-backed securities, 86
Mortgage Electronic Registration System (MERS), 57–58n. 27
Mortgages
  checks, transfers of, 155–56
  holder in due course doctrine, demise of, 82–89
  and reification, 55–56
  securitized, 89n. 39
  "semi-organized secondary mortgage market," 84–85
Mox, George and Marjorie, 87–88
Myers, Bank One v., 236–38
Myth of negotiability, origins of, 39–44

National Automated Clearing House Association (NACHA), 232
National Bank Act, 33–34, 35n. 29
National Conference of Commissioners on Uniform State Laws (1896), 2n. 4
Neal, Price v., 116–19, 121–24
Negligence
  check transfers, 164
  and forgery, 119
Negotiability
  concept of, 7–8, 21
  myth of, origins, 39–44
  origins of, 72
  traditional account of, 21–23
Negotiable Instruments Law of 1896 (N.I.L.). *See* Uniform Negotiable Instruments Law of 1896 (N.I.L.)
New Jersey Supreme Court, 69

New York Rule, banking disputes, 129–30, 133–34
New York Stock Exchange, 51
N.I.L. *See* Uniform Negotiable Instruments Law of 1896 (N.I.L.)
Non-accommodation co-makers, 195–96
Non-negotiable instruments, history, 23
North Dakota Supreme Court, 103–4
Notes. *See specific topic*

Obie & Associates, 84–85, 87
Obligation, law of bills and notes, 28
October 1987 stock market crash, 52–53
Ogden, James Matlock, 41n. 41
Ohio Citizens Bank v. Venture Metal Products Co., 162–63
Ohio Court of Appeals, 81
Olympic Title Ins. Co. v. Fifth Third Bank, 157
Oswald Machine & Equipment, Inc. v. Yip, 154
Owens, Unico v., 69–72

Paperless paper, 45–67
- airline tickets, 46–47
- metaphor and reality, 64–67
- reification, 45
  - applicability of term, 48n. 7
  - and checks, 58–63
  - and documents of title, 47–49
  - and notes, 54–58
  - and securities, 49–53

Parsons, Theophilus, 173–74, 187–88
Past, overcoming, 229–41
- practicing lawyers and judges, lessons for, 234–38
- teachers of payment systems law, lessons for, 238–40
- U.C.C. Article 3: repeal, revision or unification, 229–34

Payment systems law. *See also* Modern payment systems law
- checks as, 225–28
- rights and duties between providers, 233
- teachers of, lessons for, 238–40

Peacock v. Rhodes, 29
"Personal" defenses, 22
Photocopies, 55n. 21
Pigot's Case, 107
Postdating, negotiable instruments law, 94–96
A Practical Compendium of the Law of Bills of Exchange, Promissory Notes, Bank-Notes, Bankers' Cash-Notes and Checks (Byles), 41
Practicing lawyers and judges, lessons for, 234–38
Presentment, modern law of promissory notes, 170–76
Price v. Neal, 116–19, 121–24
Promissory notes, 9
- modern law of. *See* Modern law of promissory notes

Protest, modern law of promissory notes, 170–76
Punch Magazine, 200

Race, Miller v., 42, 239
Rasmussen-King Cattle Co., Brown County Coop Ass'n v., 105
Real bills theory, 36n. 32, 183n. 25
"Real" defenses, 22
Receivables financing, 72
Redemption, transfer of bills and notes, 18th and 19th century, 33
Regulation CC, 3–4
Reification, 45
- applicability of term, 48n. 7
- and checks, 58–63
- and documents of title, 47–49
- and mortgage lending, 55–56
- and notes, 54–58
- and securities, 49–53

Renewal notes, 176–79
Repeal of U.C.C. Article 3, proposed, 229–34
Resemblance, facsimile signatures, 140–41
Resolution Trust Co., Harris v., 161
Restatement of Contracts, 192
Restatement of Mortgages, 83–84
Restatement (Third) of Suretyship and Guaranty, 197–98
Revision of U.C.C. Article 3, proposed, 229–34
Rhodes, Peacock v., 29
Richmond FRB, 125–28
Robertson, First National Bank v., 103

Roeder, Taylor v., 82–84
Rupert, Brentar v., 160–61

Scrutton, Thomas, 44
Securities and reification, 49–53
Securitized mortgages, 89n. 39
Security agreements, history, 95
"Security entitlement," 53
SEC v. Cook, 159
"Semi-organized secondary mortgage market," 84–85
Sessions, McCarthy v., 234–36
Signatures
  by agents, 96–102
  facsimile, 137–43
Social Security checks, transfers of, 157–58
Stamp Acts, 40, 95–96, 108–9
Stanfield v. White, 104
State v. Hill, 157–58
State v. Kirkpatrick, 158–59
Statute of Frauds, 13–14
Stella v. Dean Witter Reynolds, 157
Stock market crash, October 1987, 52–53
Sun Bank, N.A. v. Merrill Lynch, Pierce, Penner and Smith, Inc., 158
Supreme Court, late nineteenth century, 15–16
Suretyship defenses, 192–98
Swift v. Tyson, 15

Taxes
  accelerated depreciation, 78
  evasion of, 95
Taylor v. Roeder, 82–84
Teachers of payment systems law, lessons for, 238–40
Teaching materials, check transfer in, 147–51
Tickets, 46–47
TILA. *See* Truth in Lending Act (TILA)
Tindal v. Brown, 172
Transferability, law of bills and notes, 29
Transfer of bills and notes, 18th and 19th century, 31–39
  accommodation bills, 36
  banknotes, 31–34
  commercial paper, 37–38
  discounting mercantile notes, 35–36
  private bank notes, circulation of, 33–34
  redemption, 33
Tribe, Larry, 19n. 1
"Trombone party," 186n. 28
Truth in Lending Act (TILA), 86, 232–33
Tulane Law Review, 131
Tyson, Swift v., 15

U.C.C. *See* Uniform Commercial Code (U.C.C.)
Unauthorized charge in general, *123*
Unico v. Owens, 69–72
Unification of U.C.C. Article 3, proposed, 229–34
Uniform Commercial Code (U.C.C.)
  Article 2, 10–11, 95
  Article 3
    accommodation party provisions, 179–86
    check fraud rules, 219
    checks, transfers of, 148, 151
    check system, 7
    and commercial paper, 37
    concepts of, 8–9
    forged drawer's signature, 117
    generally, 2
    and history, 94, 96
    holder in due course doctrine, 11–12, 18, 82, 84, 87, 89, 237
    introductory passages of books, 10
    lack of modern significance, 15
    lost or stolen bank checks, 206–7
    mortgages, 84
    and myth of negotiability, 39
    payments systems law, checks as, 225–27
    promissory notes, 167–99
    reification, 45, 55
    repeal, revision, or unification of, 229–34
    as response to modern problems, 240
    scope of, 10–11
    Section 3-113, 94, 96
    Section 3-202(4), 191
    Section 3-301, 113n. 3
    Section 3-305, 170n. 5

Section 3-305(a)(2), 178
Section 3-308, 168
Section 3-405, 160n. 36
Uniform Commercial Code (U.C.C.) (*Cont'd*)
Section 3-406(a), 119n. 15
Section 3-407, 102, 103n. 20, 105–6, 110
Section 3-407(1), 105, 106n. 27
Section 3-412, 167–68
Section 3-416, 227
Section 3-417, 227
Section 3-417(a), 121n. 16
Section 3-419, 185–86, 191
Section 3-419(b), 191
Section 3-419(f), 181n. 23
Section 3-501, 175
Section 3-604, 176
Section 6-605(f), 196–97
signatures by agents, 96–97
suretyship defenses, 192–98
viability of, 18
Article 3 (revised)
check fraud rules, 220
generally, 6
holder in due course doctrine, 79, 83–84, 90
mortgages, 83–84
Section 3-302(g), 90, 92–93
Section 3-312, 207–9
Section 3-402, 97, 100–101
Section 3-402(b)(1), 98
Section 3-403, 99, 101
Section 3-403(2)(b), 99
signatures by agents, 97–102
Article 4
check collection law, 125
checks, transfers of, 148, 151
check system, 2–3, 7, 59
electronic collection of checks, 6
payments systems law, checks as, 227
as response to modern problems, 240
Section 4-103, 138, 142–44
Section 4-103(a), 136, 141
Section 4-201, 134
Section 4-206, 227
Section 4-207, 227
Section 4-208(a)(1), 121n. 16
Section 4-214, 202–3
Section 4-215, 210n. 14, 211
Section 4-215(1), 210
Section 4-215(a), 211
Section 4-215(a)(3), 211
Section 4-215(b), 211
Section 4-301, 212, 215
Section 4-302, 211–2
Section 4-401, 142
Article 4A
check fraud rules, 217–18
wire funds transfers, 5
wire transfers, 232
Article 5, 95
Article 6, 230n. 1
Article 8, 50n. 11
Article 8 (revised), 51–53
Article 9, 38, 95
and Regulation CC, 3–4
Section 1-103, 197n. 49
Section 3-104, 9
Section 3-104(b), 9
Section 3-106, 10
Uniform Negotiable Instruments Law of 1896 (N.I.L.)
anachronism, 17–18
on bills, 96
check collection law, 125
check collection rules, 213–15
equity securities, 50n. 11
fictitious payee cases, 224
history, 94–110
alteration, 102–10
antedating, 94–96
postdating, 94–96
signatures by agents, 96–102
holder in due course doctrine, 11–12, 18
and myth of negotiability, 41
overview, 7–12
payment systems law, 2
renewal notes, 178
Section 136, 213
Section 137, 214
Section 150, 213–14
suretyship defenses, 192–93
Uniform New Payments Code, 231, 233

Uniform Stock Transfer Act of 1910, 50n. 11
United States v. Gonzalez, 159
Universal, 69, 73
U.S., American Fuji Seal, Inc. v., 153
U.S. Savings Bonds, 8

Venture Metal Products Co., Ohio Citizens Bank v., 162–63

Weimar Germany, 66
White, Stanfield v., 104
Whitman, Dale, 57
Williamsburg, Virginia
conference (1978), 5–6
Wire funds transfers, 5, 6, 232
Wisner v. First National Bank, 214
Written agreements, 13–14

Yale Law Journal, 131
Yip, Oswald Machine & Equipment, Inc. v., 154

www.ingramcontent.com/pod-product-compliance
Ingram Content Group UK Ltd.
Pitfield, Milton Keynes, MK11 3LW, UK
UKHW020846150926
475595UK00003B/28

9 780199 856220